The Tyndale New Testament Commentaries

General Editor: PROFESSOR R. V. G. TASKER, M.A., B.D.

THE FIRST EPISTLE OF PAUL
TO THE CORINTHIANS

KEVIN TAYLOR

THE FIRST EPISTLE OF PAUL
TO THE
CORINTHIANS

AN INTRODUCTION AND COMMENTARY

by

THE REV. LEON MORRIS,
B.Sc., M.Th., Ph.D.

Vice-Principal, Ridley College, Melbourne

Wm. B. Eerdmans Publishing Company
Grand Rapids, Michigan

Library of Congress Catalog Card Number: 58-10233

First Edition, July 1958
Eleventh printing, March 1979

ISBN 0-8028-2257-6

PHOTOLITHOPRINTED BY EERDMANS PRINTING COMPANY
GRAND RAPIDS, MICHIGAN, UNITED STATES OF AMERICA

GENERAL PREFACE

ALL who are interested in the teaching and study of the New Testament today cannot fail to be concerned with the lack of commentaries which avoid the extremes of being unduly technical or unhelpfully brief. It is the hope of the editor and publishers that this present series will do something towards the supply of this deficiency. Their aim is to place in the hands of students and serious readers of the New Testament, at a moderate cost, commentaries by a number of scholars who, while they are free to make their own individual contributions, are united in a common desire to promote a truly biblical theology.

The commentaries will be primarily exegetical and only secondarily homiletic, though it is hoped that both student and preacher will find them informative and suggestive. Critical questions will be fully considered in introductory sections, and also, at the author's discretion, in additional notes.

The commentaries are based on the Authorized (King James) Version, partly because this is the version which most Bible readers possess, and partly because it is easier for commentators, working on this foundation, to show why, on textual and linguistic grounds, the later versions are so often to be preferred. No one translation is regarded as infallible, and no single Greek manuscript or group of manuscripts is regarded as always right! Greek words are transliterated to help those unfamiliar with the language, and to save those who do know Greek the trouble of discovering what word is being discussed.

There are many signs today of a renewed interest in what the Bible has to say and of a more general desire to understand its meaning as fully and clearly as possible. It is the hope of all those concerned with this series that God will graciously use what they have written to further this end.

R. V. G. TASKER.

CONTENTS

7

AUTHOR'S PREFACE

IT is no new observation that the letters of St. Paul are not easy reading (2 Pet. iii. 15f.), but for him who is prepared to take time and trouble their study is immensely rewarding. Not least is this the case with 1 Corinthians, a letter arising out of the practical difficulties besetting a far-from-ideal first-century Greek church. Here we have a typical Pauline letter. The apostle praises his correspondents for their Christian virtues, and rebukes them roundly for their many failings. He adds to their knowledge with some great passages, notably his discussion of love in chapter xiii and of the resurrection in chapter xv. Whatever he touches he deals with in the light of great Christian principles. He sees things temporal always in the light of things eternal. What he writes has relevance to our own, in many ways very different, needs. He shows us how to take our problems back to the light shed upon them by the great Christian verities. We cannot fail to profit as we ponder his words.

In writing this commentary I have been greatly indebted to very many. Notably is this the case with regard to the commentaries to which I have referred in the notes. I have endeavoured to indicate my many indebtednesses in specific matters, but I have learned more from my predecessors than I can sufficiently acknowledge. I have also found some of the modern translations very helpful, for what are translations but compressed commentaries?

Finally I would like to express my gratitude to Miss G. Mahar and Miss M. McGregor who very kindly typed the manuscript for me.

LEON MORRIS.

CHIEF ABBREVIATIONS

AG	*A Greek-English Lexicon of the New Testament and other Early Christian Literature* by W. F. Arndt and F. W. Gingrich (Cambridge, 1957).
AV	English Authorized Version (King James).
Barclay	Commentary on 1 Corinthians by William Barclay in *The Daily Study Bible* (The Saint Andrew Press, 1956).
Beet	Commentary on 1 Corinthians by J. Agar Beet (Hodder & Stoughton, 1889).
Bull. Ryl. Lib.	The Bulletin of the John Rylands Library.
Calvin	Commentary on 1 Corinthians by John Calvin, translated by J. Pringle (Calvin Translation Society, 1848).
Edwards	Commentary on 1 Corinthians by T. C. Edwards (Hodder & Stoughton, 1885).
Ellicott	Commentary on 1 Corinthians by C. J. Ellicott (Longmans, Green & Co., 1887).
EVV	English versions, the Authorized Version and the Revised Version.
Godet	Commentary on 1 Corinthians by F. Godet, translated by A. Cusin (T. & T. Clark, 1887).
Grosheide	Commentary on 1 Corinthians by F. W. Grosheide in *The New London Commentary on the New Testament* (Marshall, Morgan & Scott, 1954).

HDB	*A Dictionary of the Bible*, ed. J. Hastings, 5 vols. (Edinburgh, 1904).
Hodge	Commentary on 1 Corinthians by Charles Hodge (Nisbet, 1873).
Idiom Book	*An Idiom Book of New Testament Greek* by C. F. D. Moule (Cambridge, 1953).
ISBE	*The International Standard Bible Encyclopaedia*, 5 vols. (Chicago, 1937).
JTS	*The Journal of Theological Studies.*
Kay	Commentary on 1 Corinthians by W. Kay (Macmillan, 1887).
LAE	*Light from the Ancient East* by A. Deissmann, translated by L. R. M. Strachan (London, 1927).
Lightfoot	*Notes on the Epistles of St. Paul* by J. B. Lightfoot (Macmillan, 1904).
LS	*A Greek-English Lexicon* compiled by H. G. Liddell and R. Scott, revised and augmented by H. S. Jones and R. McKenzie (Oxford, 1940).
LXX	Septuagint Version.
MM	*The Vocabulary of the Greek Testament* by J. H. Moulton and G. Milligan (Hodder & Stoughton, 1914–29).
Moffatt	Commentary on 1 Corinthians by James Moffatt in *The Moffatt New Testament Commentary* (Hodder & Stoughton, 1943).
Parry	Commentary on 1 Corinthians by R. St. J. Parry in *The Cambridge Greek Testament*, 1926.

Proctor	Commentary on 1 Corinthians by W. C. G. Proctor in *The New Bible Commentary* (Inter-Varsity Fellowship, 1953).
Prolegomena	*A Grammar of New Testament Greek* by J. H. Moulton, vol. i, Prolegomena (Edinburgh, 1906).
Robertson and Plummer	Commentary on 1 Corinthians by A. Robertson and A. Plummer in *The International Critical Commentary* (T. & T. Clark, 1929).
RSV	American Revised Standard Version, 1946.
RV	English Revised Version, 1881.

The translations by E. J. Goodspeed, R. Knox, J. B. Phillips, H. J. Schonfield and R. F. Weymouth are cited by the translator's surname.

ACKNOWLEDGEMENTS

Scripture quotations from the Revised Standard Version of the Bible (copyrighted 1946 and 1952 by the Division of Christian Education, National Council of Churches, U.S.A.) are used by permission. Quotations from the Rev. J. B. Phillips' translations of New Testament books are by courtesy of the publishers, Geoffrey Bles Ltd.

INTRODUCTION

I. BACKGROUND

THE geographical position of Corinth, on the narrow neck of land between the Corinthian Gulf and the Saronic Gulf, was its guarantee of commercial prosperity. Merchants and sailors preferred sending goods across the isthmus to risking the long voyage round the rocky, storm-tossed capes at the south of the Peloponnese.[1] It was a natural stopping-place on the route from Rome to the East, and the place where a number of trade routes met. Old Corinth was totally destroyed by the Roman, L. Mummius Achaicus, in 146 B.C. But when, a century later, the city was re-founded as a Roman colony it speedily regained much of its former greatness.

As the new city was a Roman colony its inhabitants were at first, of course, Romans. Greeks seem to have been reluctant to settle there for a time, but eventually they came back in numbers. The city also attracted men from many Eastern races. Included among them was a Jewish population large enough to have a synagogue (Acts xviii. 4). The Roman element[2] in the population is illustrated by the number of Latin

[1]See G. E. Wright and F. V. Filson, *The Westminster Historical Atlas to the Bible*, London, 1946, pp. 80, 88f. In the case of large ships this must have meant transhipping the cargoes. Smaller vessels were hauled across the isthmus 'by means of a ship tramway with wooden rails' (ISBE, vol. II, p. 710). Nero attempted to cut a canal, but without success. The modern canal follows the course planned by Nero.

[2]Parry sees evidence of the Roman character of the city in that it was the first city of Greece to admit the gladiatorial games (p. ix). Robertson and Plummer on the contrary maintain that by New Testament times the original Italian colonists 'had become to a large extent Hellenized' (p. xi). There is truth in both views. Corinth's population comprised a medley of races which had retained most of the worst features of the original stocks.

names which are associated with Corinth in the New Testament, such as Lucius, Gaius, Tertius, Erastus, Quartus (Rom. xvi. 21–23), Crispus, Titus Justus (Acts xviii. 7, 8), Fortunatus and Achaicus (1 Cor. xvi. 17). But the way in which Greek habits of thought became dominant is revealed by the questtions raised in Paul's Corinthian correspondence, and the manner in which they are treated. Edwards says of Corinth: 'Of Greek cities the least Greek, it was at this time the least Roman of Roman colonies.'[1] It was a city where 'Greeks, Latins, Syrians, Asiatics, Egyptians, and Jews, bought and sold, laboured and revelled, quarrelled and hob-nobbed, in the city and its ports, as nowhere else in Greece'.[2]

Old Corinth had been a by-word for licentiousness,[3] and this hotch-potch of races would have hastened the process by which the new Corinth also acquired an unsavoury reputation. A. M. Hunter says that in the New Testament period Corinth in the popular mind suggested 'culture and courtesans. . . . "Corinthian words" implied pretensions to philosophy and letters, and "to Corinthianize" was polite Greek for "go to the devil" '.[4]

Yet for all that the city had great prestige. It was populous.[5] Trade flowed through it, and the city prospered materially. It was the capital of the Roman province of Achaia. The Isthmian Games were celebrated nearby, and under the city's aegis. The finest athletes were attracted.

The city to which Paul came preaching the gospel was, therefore, a very cosmopolitan place. It was an important city.

[1]P. xii.

[2]Moffatt, p. xvii. He goes on to say that in Paul's time 'the majority were sharp, clever Levantines' (*ibid.*).

[3] This may be illustrated from the fact that in connection with the worship of Aphrodite there were 1,000 sacred prostitutes in Old Corinth.

[4]*Introducing the New Testament*, London, 1945, p. 76.

[5]A. M. Hunter speaks of 'its half million inhabitants' (*ibid.*), while Godet (p. 5) and ISBE (vol. II, p. 713) put the number between 600,000 and 700,000. Ellicott, however, thinks of 'a busy city of 100,000 souls' (p. xv). While there is no doubt that Corinth had a large population there does not seem to be evidence available on which to form an accurate estimate of its number.

It was intellectually alert. It was materially prosperous. It was morally corrupt. There was a pronounced tendency for its inhabitants to indulge their desires of whatever sort. In the words of von Dobschütz: 'The ideal of the Corinthian was the reckless development of the individual. The merchant who made his gain by all and every means, the man of pleasure surrendering himself to every lust, the athlete steeled to every bodily exercise and proud in his physical strength, are the true Corinthian types: in a word the man who recognized no superior and no law but his own desires.'[1]

Some have felt that it was the evil side of Corinth that induced Paul to preach there. A city so corrupt needed the purifying influence of the gospel. While this would not have been out of the apostle's mind, the probability is that the overriding consideration was the city's geographical situation. It was a centre from which the gospel could radiate out to the surrounding districts. There was a large floating population. Merchants and travellers would stay a few days and be on their way. Anything preached in Corinth could be sure of a wide dissemination.[2]

II. PAUL AT CORINTH

When Paul first reached Corinth he was experiencing a great deal of discouragement. At Philippi he had had a promising beginning smashed by the opposition of fanatical Jews. The same thing had happened at Thessalonica and at Beroea. In Athens he had had little success. Small wonder that when he came to busy, proud, intellectual Corinth he came 'in weakness, and in fear, and in much trembling' (1 Cor. ii. 3). His companions on this missionary journey, Silas and Timothy, were occupied in Macedonia, so that Paul was probably alone, which would not have made things any easier.

[1] Cited in Parry, p. x.
[2] 'As was his custom, the apostle sought to spread the gospel in a centre in which he could touch men from various lands' (*The New Bible Handbook*, ed. G. T. Manley, London, 1947, p. 359).

I CORINTHIANS

Arrived at Corinth, he lodged with Aquila and Priscilla, Jews who had been expelled from Rome by a decree of the Emperor Claudius, and, like Paul, tentmakers by trade. When Silas and Timothy rejoined him they brought news that, despite all opposition, Paul's converts at Thessalonica were standing firm. Paul saw that, despite the difficulties and discouragements he had met, the blessing of God was upon the work that he had done. The news put new heart into him, and he gave himself over to the proclamation of the gospel with renewed energy. He 'was pressed in the spirit, and testified to the Jews that Jesus was Christ' (Acts xviii. 5).

However, his preaching did not prove acceptable to the Jews, and he was constrained to leave the synagogue. Not very tactfully he went to the house of Justus, next door to the synagogue,[1] and this apparently became his new preaching base.[2] The 'chief ruler of the synagogue', one Crispus, believed, together with his household (Acts xviii. 8). But these are the only Jewish converts at Corinth of whom we read in Acts (unless Aquila and Priscilla were converted there), and it is in harmony with this that Jewish names do not figure in the Corinthian Epistles.[3] But many of the Corinthians believed and were baptized. Paul was encouraged by a vision (perhaps at the time of his expulsion from the synagogue) assuring him that God had 'much people in this city' (Acts xviii. 10). He remained in Corinth for a matter of eighteen months, and evidently made many converts. We are not told expressly, but it seems likely that here, as elsewhere, the bulk of the believers came from the class of the devout pagans who had attached themselves loosely to the synagogue. They were dissatisfied

[1] Cf. Lake, 'It must be admitted that he chose a position which was not likely to avoid trouble, though it had the advantage of being easily found by the God-fearer who had previously frequented the synagogue' (*The Earlier Epistles of St. Paul*, London, 1919, p. 104).

[2] This appears to be the meaning of Acts xviii. 7, rather than that he ceased living with Aquila and Priscilla, and came to live with Justus.

[3] It is possible that there is another Jew. The Sosthenes who is joined with Paul and Timothy in the salutation (1 Cor. i. 1) may be the ruler of the synagogue of Acts xviii. 17. But this is far from certain.

with pagan life and pagan morality. They found themselves attracted by the lofty morals and the pure monotheism of the Jews, but repelled by their narrow nationalism, and by some of their ritual practices, such as circumcision. These people generally gave Christianity a warm welcome. They found in it a faith that satisfied, and one that was free from those things they found objectionable in Judaism. Some of the converts were people of substance. Gaius is spoken of in Rom. xvi. 23 (almost certainly written from Corinth) as 'mine host, and of the whole church'. The same verse refers to Erastus as 'the chamberlain of the city'. If we are right in thinking of Chloe (1 Cor. i, 11) as a Corinthian convert, she would have been a wealthy woman, owning slaves, and with interests in both Corinth and Ephesus (but she is perhaps more likely to have been an Ephesian with interests in Corinth). She is not likely to have been from the upper classes. The name 'Chloe' was an epithet of the goddess Demeter. Those who bore the names of deities were usually slaves or freed persons, consequently most commentators think of Chloe as a freedwoman, albeit a wealthy one. Paul's references to some of the believers engaging in litigation and attending private banquets point to free men, and men of means. But despite these examples, the bulk of the believers came from the lower social strata, as is emphasized in 1 Cor. i. 26ff.

Throughout Greece Paul found that as soon as his mission looked like being successful the Jews stirred up opposition.[1] Corinth was no exception. The Thessalonian Epistles, almost certainly written from Corinth, show us something of the determined opposition he was experiencing (1 Thes. ii. 15; 2 Thes. iii. 1f.). He was compelled to cease preaching in the synagogue. Later his enemies brought him before the proconsul, Gallio, accusing him of persuading men to worship God 'contrary to the law' (Acts xviii. 13). Gallio speedily saw

---

[1]'He was not merely a renegade Pharisee who believed in messiah, but a successful one' (Moffatt, p. xiii). That was what they found impossible to forgive.

that Paul was not a lawbreaker, but that the dispute was purely religious. He accordingly dismissed the case, and Paul was free to continue his work unhindered. From the length of his stay we gather that he regarded his mission at Corinth as possibly the most important he had undertaken up till this point.

III. PAUL'S SUBSEQUENT RELATIONS WITH THE CHURCH AT CORINTH

After Paul left Corinth the work of extending and consolidating the church was carried on by Apollos, a learned man from Alexandria. This man had previously been in Ephesus, where, although baptized only with the baptism of John the Baptist, he had preached Christ. His preaching was heard by Aquila and Priscilla, who 'took him unto them, and expounded unto him the way of God more perfectly' (Acts xviii. 26). Armed with this new knowledge Apollos went to Achaia, of which province Corinth was the capital. Here his eloquence was employed to show 'by the scriptures that the Messiah was Jesus' (Acts xviii. 28). This seems to be the meaning of the Greek (though RV has 'Jesus was the Christ'). The expression implies that preacher and hearers alike looked for the coming of the Messiah. But Apollos was able to say 'The Messiah you expect is Jesus'.[1]

It is often said that Apollos used the allegorical method of interpreting Scripture. He may well have done so, but the only evidence is that he came from Alexandria, the home of allegorical interpretation. But whatever his method it almost certainly differed from that of Paul. Paul's preaching had a studied simplicity (1 Cor. ii. 2–4): that of Apollos was probably highly rhetorical (Acts xviii. 24, 27f.). There was no fundamental difference in the message preached, for Paul speaks of Apollos as continuing the work that he had begun (1 Cor. iii. 6, 8). But the difference in presentation was enough

[1] Cf. K. Lake, *op. cit.*, p. 110; J. H. A. Hart in JTS, vol. VII, p. 32.

to cause a certain partisanship on the part of some of the Corinthians.[1]

Some time after this Paul wrote a letter to the Corinthian church, a letter that has perished. The evidence for its existence is found in 1 Cor. v. 9, where Paul says that he had previously written a letter telling the believers 'not to company with fornicators'. We know nothing more about this letter or how Paul came to write it. Some scholars think that part of it is preserved in 2 Cor. vi. 14–vii. 1. If, as is probable, this hypothesis is to be rejected, the letter has entirely disappeared.[2] This need cause no surprise. Paul's reference to it in 1 Cor. v. 9 shows that it had been misunderstood. He mentioned it only to clear up a misconception as to what it meant. Thus the newer letter superseded the older, and accordingly there was no point in preserving it.

Next came contacts made by Paul with certain Corinthians. The household of Chloe brought him news of cliques in the church (1 Cor. i. 11). A letter was sent to him from the church (1 Cor. vii. 1), presumably brought by Stephanas, Fortunatus and Achaicus (1 Cor. xvi. 17). Paul accordingly set himself to write to the church. The letter we know as 1 Corinthians is the result. From this letter we learn that all was not well in the Corinthian church. There is some very plain speaking.

Paul evidently felt that the situation was beginning to grow serious, for he determined to send Timothy, and indeed sent him before he despatched 1 Corinthians (see 1 Cor. iv. 17, xvi. 10f.). That Timothy paid only a short visit is indicated by

[1]Cf. Robertson and Plummer, 'In these cities, with their mobile, eager, and excitable populations, crazes of some kind are not only a common feature, but almost a social necessity. . . . As Renan says . . . let there be two preachers, or two doctors, in one of the small towns in Southern Europe, and at once the inhabitants take sides as to which is the better of the two. The two preachers, or the two doctors, may be on the best of terms: that in no way hinders their names from being made a party-cry and the signal for vehement dissensions' (p. xx). Proctor remarks that the process would have been helped by the multiplicity of races at Corinth (p. 969).

[2]See R. V. G. Tasker's Introduction to the Commentary on 2 Corinthians in this series.

the fact that he is joined with Paul in the salutation in 2 Corinthians. By the time that letter was written he was away from the city again (unless, as is possible, he never reached it). But Timothy was not able to effect very much.

The situation worsened rather than grew better. It is curious that we do not have information as to the exact cause of the trouble. It may have been one or other of the matters mentioned in 1 Corinthians. We do not know. But clearly it involved a denial of Paul's authority. Paul felt it necessary to leave his work in Ephesus and to pay a hurried visit in the attempt to set things right. Some have doubted whether this is a fair reconstruction of events, but certain passages in 2 Corinthians make it fairly certain. Thus Paul says, 'This is the third time I am coming to you' (2 Cor. xiii. 1), and, 'Behold, the third time I am ready to come to you' (2 Cor. xii. 14), while in 2 Cor. xiii. 2 he looks back to 'when I was present the second time' (RV). When these words were written a visit additional to that when the church was founded had clearly been made. The words will not refer, as some have maintained, to Paul's intentions, rather than to an actual visit. As Moffatt cogently argues, 'Against people who suspected his consistency and good will, it would have been of little use to plead that he had honestly intended to come, that he had been quite ready to visit them.'[1] He must be referring to a visit paid. His references to coming again in sorrow or heaviness (e.g. 2 Cor. ii. 1) indicate the unpleasant nature of that visit.

Some scholars place this visit before the writing of 1 Corinthians,[2] but no good reason has been shown for this. That Epistle seems to imply one previous visit only, the one during which the church was founded (e.g. ii. 1, iii. 2, xi. 2). Another visit is foreshadowed (1 Cor. iv. 19), but it is not yet an accomplished fact. Paul's knowledge of affairs at Corinth is not personal, but derived from Chloe's household (1 Cor. i. 11; cf.

[1]*An Introduction to the Literature of the New Testament*, Edinburgh, 1927, p. 117.
[2]See the list in Robertson and Plummer, p. xxiv.

v. 1, xi. 18), and from a letter from the Corinthian church
(1 Cor. vii. 1). The second visit was clearly a very painful
affair. The general tone of 1 Corinthians is inexplicable after
such a visit. It seems much more in accordance with the evidence to think of the situation implied in 1 Corinthians as
deteriorating after the receipt of that letter. Thus the painful
visit became necessary.

Though this visit evidently produced some plain speaking,
it failed to clear up the situation. Paul went away from
Corinth profoundly disturbed. T. W. Manson[1] thinks he went
to Macedonia. He denies that a hurried visit was paid from
Ephesus, and suggests that Paul finished his work in that city
and then proceeded with his plan outlined in 2 Cor. i. 15ff.
The advantage of this is that it does away with the necessity
for postulating a visit from Ephesus. The disadvantage is that
to get Paul to Troas (2 Cor. ii. 12) he has to postulate a special
missionary expedition in the region of Troas. Also that in
2 Cor. i. 15ff. Paul speaks of the plan as though it had been
abandoned, not as though he had begun to carry it out. It
seems better to think of the painful visit as an interruption of
the Ephesian ministry, so that he now returned to Ephesus.

Paul determined on another letter. This obviously had a
very severe tone, and cost him much to write (2 Cor. ii. 4,
vii. 8).[2] Had it not been successful it might conceivably have
meant a final rupture between Paul and this church that he
had founded. Like the first letter he wrote to the Corinthians,
this severe letter has been lost, unless, as some scholars think,
part of it is preserved in 2 Cor. x–xiii.[3] The letter was appar-

---

[1] *Bull. Ryl. Lib.*, vol. xxvi, pp. 327ff.

[2] F. B. Clogg refers to this whole episode as 'what must have proved one
of the most distressing experiences of his life' (*An Introduction to the New
Testament*, London, 1940, p. 39).

[3] K. and S. Lake maintain that 'there is overwhelming reason for believing that II Cor. x–xiii is part of the severe letter and that II Cor. i–ix is a
later letter' (*An Introduction to the New Testament*, London, 1938, p. 122).
M. Dibelius, on the other hand, says, 'ancient letters had a fairly certain
protection against such accidental interweavings, in the fact that the address of the letter stood on the reverse of the papyrus. This would make it

ently taken by Titus, who was to return via Macedonia and Troas. Paul was impatient to know how it had been received. He went to Troas, but, not finding Titus, could not rest there. He crossed to Macedonia (2 Cor. ii. 12f.). Here Titus met him with the good news that all was well (2 Cor. ii. 14ff., vii. 6ff.). Out of his great joy Paul wrote the letter we call 2 Corinthians. Almost certainly he visited the church soon afterwards.

Thus we have knowledge of three visits Paul paid to Corinth:

1. When the church was founded.
2. The painful visit.
3. A visit after 2 Corinthians had been sent.

There were four Epistles:

1. The 'Previous' Letter.
2. 1 Corinthians.
3. The Severe Letter.
4. 2 Corinthians.

A more detailed discussion of this framework more properly belongs to the Introduction to 2 Corinthians. Here it is sufficient to notice enough of the evidence for us to place 1 Corinthians in its proper position in the sequence of Paul's dealings with the church at Corinth.

IV. THE OCCASION AND PURPOSE OF I CORINTHIANS

The immediate occasion of the Epistle was the letter which Paul had received from the Corinthian church, and to which a reply was necessary. Accordingly he wrote, answering the questions that had been put to him, questions about marriage

difficult accidentally to take part of one letter for another letter, and an editor who without visible grounds made two letters out of four would be a strange figure, especially if he deleted from the intermediate letter the essential matter referred to in 2 Cor. ii and vii, and yet used a fragment of that letter in 2 Cor. x–xiii. Hence we shall have to content ourselves with the loss of these two letters, viz. the original first and the intermediate third' (*A Fresh Approach to the New Testament and Early Christian Literature*, London, 1936, p. 154).

and celibacy, about food offered to idols, probably also about public worship and spiritual gifts. There were difficulties in the minds of the Corinthian Christians. Paul wrote to resolve those difficulties.

But what mattered much more to Paul was clearly the news that had come to him independently of the letter. There were disquieting irregularities in the conduct of the believers at Corinth. Paul was troubled by the 'tendency on the part of some members to make the break with pagan society as indefinite as possible. . . . The Church was in the world, as it had to be, but the world was in the Church, as it ought not to be.'[1] So much did this matter to Paul that he spent six chapters dealing with it before he so much as touched on the matters about which they had written to him.

He was troubled about the divisions within the church. Parties had been formed attaching to themselves the names of Paul or Apollos or Peter, or even of Christ. Paul spends a lot of time dealing with this, and clearly he deemed it very serious. Then there was a case of incest. Yet the church had not censured the offender. Probably, as L. Pullan puts it, 'They found it hard to hate the sensuality which in their earlier days they had regarded as divine.'[2] There was also a quarrelsome spirit. Some members of the church had actually gone to law with others, and Paul felt that this had to be put right. Next his attention turns to sexual impurity. Gross sins of this kind could not be permitted to continue. First and foremost 1 Corinthians is a letter directed at the reformation of conduct.

Having dealt with these grave evils, Paul turns to the matters mentioned in the letter written to him. Then he includes a magnificent passage on the resurrection, elicited, it would seem, by the fact that some of the Corinthians denied that the dead will rise (1 Cor. xv. 12). The result of all this is ' "an inexhaustible mine of Christian thought and life." ' Nowhere else in the NT is there a more many-sided embodiment

---

[1]Moffatt, p. xv.
[2]*The Books of the New Testament*, London, 1926, p. 135.

of the imperishable principles and instincts which should inspire each member of the body of Christ for all time.'[1]

Paul's purpose, then, in writing this Epistle, is principally to set right disorders which the Corinthians took lightly, but which he regarded as grave sins. Secondly, he wrote to answer some questions put to him. Thirdly, he wrote to give some doctrinal teaching, particularly on the resurrection.[2]

It is very much an occasional letter, directed to the immediate local needs of Paul's converts.[3] But it would be a mistake on that account to regard it as irrelevant to our needs. The heart of man does not change, and the principles on which Paul works are just as important to us as to the Corinthians of the first century. As Godet puts it, 'the tendency to make religious truths the subject of intellectual study rather than a work of conscience and of heart-acceptance, the disposition resulting therefrom, not always to place the moral conduct under the influence of religious conviction, and to give scope to the latter rather in oratorical discourse than in vigour of holiness,—these are defects which more than one modern nation shares in common with the Greek people.'[4] Not only does Paul deal with problems which have a way of recurring in other ages and regions; he gives us the principle on which to act. He deals with everyday problems 'from a central point of view, and places everyday troubles in the light of eternity'.[5]

V. THE AUTHENTICITY OF THE EPISTLE

Very few scholars have seriously doubted the authenticity of I Corinthians. Robertson and Plummer can say, 'Both the

---

[1]A. Robertson in HDB, vol. I, pp. 489f.

[2]T. W. Manson sees the Epistle as probably written against the background of Paul's 'struggle with agents of Palestinian Jewish Christianity either under the direct leadership or acting in the name of Peter' (*op. cit.*, p. 118). However, although Manson's article is very stimulating, he does not seem to have established this point.

[3]Cf. A. H. McNeile; this is 'the most intensely practical of all St. Paul's letters. The whole of it was written to meet immediate needs of his converts' (*An Introduction to the Study of the New Testament*, Oxford, 1927, p. 122).

[4]P. 2.   [5]M. Dibelius, *op. cit.*, p. 155.

external and the internal evidence for the Pauline authorship
are so strong that those who attempt to show that the Apostle
was not the writer succeed chiefly in proving their own in-
competence as critics.'[1] There is accordingly no need for us to
do more than indicate briefly where the strength of this
evidence lies.

The external attestation is all that we could wish. It is
cited in 1 Clement, a first-century letter, being the first
example of a New Testament document to be cited with the
name of its author. It is freely quoted by Ignatius and Poly-
carp. From then on it is often referred to, and no one expresses
doubt as to its authorship. None of Paul's other letters appears
to have been quoted as widely and as early as this. In the
Muratorian Fragment (a list of books accepted as canonical,
probably at Rome, and dating from some time after the
middle of the second century) and in some other lists it is the
first of Paul's letters. No satisfactory reason has been given
for this, but clearly it indicates something of the importance
attached to 1 Corinthians.

The internal evidence likewise points us to Paul. The style
and language are those of the universally accepted Pauline
writings. The letter fits in with what we know of the situation
in Corinth. It reads naturally as Paul's attempt to deal with a
difficult situation. It contains forthright condemnations of the
Corinthians. This is important in view of the fact that the
Corinthian church accepted the letter as authentic, and indeed
treasured it up so that it has been preserved and not lost as
have others of Paul's letters. The very preservation of such a
letter by the Corinthian church is strong evidence of
authenticity.[2]

There is likewise little that need be said about the integrity
of the Epistle. Occasionally critics have suspected interpola-
tions but not often. And then the reasons they have put for-

[1]P. xvi.

[2]J. Agar Beet points out that no church would accept, 'without careful
scrutiny, so public a monument of its degradation' (p. 5).

ward have not commended themselves. J. Weiss, for example, suggested that a number of writings have been combined to form our Epistle, but he has found few followers. We must not expect the same orderly classification of topics in a letter as in a theological treatise. I Corinthians reads very much like an original letter. As Moffatt says, 'if some editor really put together fragments from two or three letters, he has done his work so well that it is beyond our powers to recover their original shape and sequence.'[1] There is, then, no reason for doubting that this is a genuine writing of St. Paul, and that it is free from any substantial interpolation.[2]

VI. THE DATE AND PLACE OF ORIGIN

The place of origin of the Epistle is indicated clearly enough by Paul's statement, 'I will tarry at Ephesus until Pentecost' (i Cor. xvi. 8). But at just what point during his stay at Ephesus he wrote it is not immediately obvious.

Acts xviii. 18–21 records a brief visit to Ephesus immediately after the mission which had established the church at Corinth. But it seems impossible to think that our Epistle was written during this period. There is no indication that anything was seriously amiss in the church when Paul left it, but by the time I Corinthians was penned much had happened. We must allow time for this. Again, there is the 'previous' letter. Even when the position began to develop it was this letter and not I Corinthians which was sent off. We conclude then that our Epistle dates from Paul's longer sojourn at Ephesus, which is described in Acts xix. Paul is recorded as having gone to Macedonia and then to Greece in Acts xx. if., so that we must find a place for our letter before that. The

---

[1]P. xxvi.

[2]Robertson and Plummer say there may occasionally be doubt about a word, 'but there is probably no verse or whole clause that is an interpolation' (p. xviii). Moffatt is of opinion that 'The evenness of style and the genuine epistolary stamp of the letter are so well marked that, in spite of Kabisch's hesitation . . . its unity hardly requires detailed proof' (*An Introduction to the Literature of the New Testament*, Edinburgh, 1927, p. 113).

stay at Ephesus was prolonged. Paul speaks of giving warnings 'by the space of three years' (Acts xx. 31). If the apostle's determination to stay till Pentecost means that he planned to depart then, and if this plan was carried out, then we must place 1 Corinthians during the last of the three years at Ephesus. If so, it will be towards the beginning, rather than the end, of that year, for we must allow time for the events leading up to the writing of 2 Corinthians before the year was up.

One of the important points for the chronology of the New Testament is afforded by the statement in Acts xviii. 12 that Gallio was proconsul of Achaia while Paul was in Corinth. This verse seems to mean that Gallio came to Corinth during Paul's time there.

An inscription at Delphi gives the decision of the Emperor on a question referred to him by Gallio, and from the date of the inscription it seems that Gallio entered on his office during the early summer of A.D. 51.[1] The impression left by the narrative of Acts is that Paul left Corinth not so very long after Gallio's arrival (though not immediately after; cf. the 'yet a good while' of Acts xviii. 18).

There does not seem to be anything which enables us to date the Epistle with precision. The Gallio date is the last fixed point before its composition. But when we allow time for the events narrated in Acts xviii. 18–xix. 1, between Paul's departure from Corinth and his arrival at Ephesus on his third missionary journey, we see that our Epistle would have been written somewhere about the mid-fifties.

[1] I have referred to this inscription in my Tyndale Commentary on 1, 2 Thessalonians, London, 1956, p. 15. The inscription is quoted and discussed by Kirsopp Lake, *The Beginnings of Christianity,* vol. v, London, 1933, pp. 460ff.

ANALYSIS

I. INTRODUCTION (i. 1–9).
a. Salutation (i. 1–3).
b. Thanksgiving (i. 4–9).

II. DIVISION IN THE CHURCH (i. 10–iv. 21).
a. The fact of division (i. 10–17).
   i The parties (i. 10–12).
   ii. Not due to Paul (i. 13–17).
b. The 'foolishness' of the gospel (i. 18–ii. 5).
   i. The message was 'foolish' (i. 18–25).
   ii. The believers are insignificant (i. 26–31).
   iii. Paul's preaching was not in human wisdom, but divine power (ii. 1–5).
c. A revealed message (ii. 6–16).
   i. The gospel is not human wisdom (ii. 6–9).
   ii. Words 'which the Spirit teacheth' (ii. 10–13).
   iii. Spiritual discernment (ii. 14–16).
d. A carnal misunderstanding (iii. 1–9).
   i. Carnal Christians (iii. 1–4).
   ii. The true relation between Paul and Apollos (iii. 5–9).
e. The foundation and the building (iii. 10–17).
   i. The test of good building (iii. 10–15).
   ii. The temple of God (iii. 16, 17).
f. The preachers' lowly place (iii. 18–iv. 13).
   i. Worldly wisdom is foolishness (iii. 18–23).
   ii. God's commendation is what matters (iv. 1–5).
   iii. Learn from Paul and Apollos (iv. 6, 7).
   iv. The trials endured by the apostles (iv. 8–13).
g. A personal appeal (iv. 14–21).

III. MORAL LAXITY IN THE CHURCH (v. 1–vi. 20).
a. A case of incest (v. 1–13).
   i. The fact (v. 1, 2).
   ii. The punishment of the offender (v. 3–5).

COMMENTARY

I. INTRODUCTION (i. 1-9)

a. Salutation (i. 1-3)

1. Paul's opening is the usual one in a first-century letter: first the name of the writer(s), then that of the addressee(s), and a prayer. But to each part Paul gives a characteristically Christian twist. For example, his name is followed by his designation as *an apostle* (which is very appropriate in this letter where his apostolic authority is to be invoked so freely to put wrong matters right). Paul stresses the divine origin of his apostolate (cf. Gal. i. 1). This is the thought in *called* (cf. Rom. i. 1), and in the insistence that it is *through the will of God*. The three expressions place impressive emphasis on the reality of the divine commission. With him Paul associates Sosthenes. This may be the man mentioned as 'the chief ruler of the synagogue' in Acts xviii. 17, in which case he was subsequently converted. But the name is not so uncommon as to make this by any means certain.

2. The Epistle is addressed to *the church of God which is at Corinth. Ekklēsia, church*, is a word which in ordinary Greek could apply to any secular assembly (it is used of the rioting Ephesians in Acts xix. 32, 41; cf. verse 39). The Christians by-passed the regular Greek words in use for religious brother-hoods, and made this their characteristic name for the be-lievers. They were probably influenced also by the fact that it is used in the LXX of the assembly of the Israelites. It points to the fact that the Church is not merely one religious group among many. It is unique. Ordinary words will not do. But it is not any 'assembly': it is the *ekklēsia of God*. Here the Church is further defined as *them that are sanctified in Christ Jesus*

34

and as *called to be saints*. Both expressions bring out the thought that Christians are set apart for the service of Christ. *Saints* is from the same root as *sanctified*. With us the idea conveyed by both words is that of high moral character. The Greek rather suggests a being set apart for God (though, of course, the character implied in such separation is not out of mind).

Some have suggested that *with all that in every place* etc. is meant to widen the salutation to include all Christians. This is the most natural interpretation of the Greek. T. W. Manson suggests that the word *topos, place*, should be taken in the sense 'place of worship', as in certain Jewish synagogue inscriptions.[1] But a strong objection to both is that the Epistle gives no sign of being intended as a circular or a general manifesto. It sticks stubbornly to local issues. It is accordingly better to take the phrase closely with *saints*. The Corinthians are called to be saints together with other people. The calling upon the name of Jesus Christ is an unusual way of describing Christians (albeit a readily intelligible one). Its importance is that in the Old Testament it is the name of Jehovah upon which men call (see especially Joel ii. 32). The highest place is being assigned to Christ.

3. *Grace* is one of the great Christian words. It resembles the usual Greek salutation, but there is the world of difference between 'greeting' (*chairein*) and 'grace' (*charis*). Grace reminds us of God's free gift to men, and more especially of His free gift in Christ. *Peace* is the usual Hebrew greeting. But the Hebrew, *shalōm*, means more than does 'peace' in English. It is not simply the absence of strife, but the presence of positive blessings. It is the prosperity of the whole man, especially his spiritual prosperity.

This became the typical Christian greeting. It is found in practically every letter in the New Testament (sometimes with the addition of 'mercy'). It is typical not only that these qualities should be mentioned, but that God the Father and

[1]*Bull. Ryl. Lib.*, vol. xxvi, p. 103.

the Lord Jesus Christ should be linked as joint-Authors. No higher place could be given to Christ.

b. Thanksgiving (i. 4–9)

4, 5. Paul usually has a thanksgiving at the beginning of his letters. In view of his subsequent trenchant criticisms of the Corinthians it has been felt by some that this thanksgiving is ironical. There seems no real basis for this. It is Paul's habit to encourage and praise his converts where he can. Although much was amiss in the lives of the Corinthian believers, there is no reason for doubting that 'the Christian community at Corinth must have presented as a whole a marvellous contrast to their heathen fellow-citizens' (Lightfoot). Paul gives sincere thanks for this.

Merely human achievement means little to Paul. He knows so well that in the flesh 'dwelleth no good thing' (Rom. vii. 18). His thanks are not for anything that the Corinthians have done by their own efforts, but for what *the grace of God* given *by Jesus Christ* (better, '*in* Jesus Christ') has accomplished in them. Two points are singled out, *utterance*, the telling forth of the truth, and *knowledge*, the grasp of the truth. 'He selects the gifts of which the Corinthians were especially proud '(Parry). Cf. the combination of these two in 'the word of knowledge' (xii. 8).

6. *The testimony of Christ* is the witness to Christ borne by Paul and his companions. The gospel is good news. Its proclamation is often described as either the activity of the herald (who simply passes on the words given to him), or, as here, the bearing witness to what God had wrought. In either case the derivative nature of the gospel is stressed. It comes from God. The preacher simply passes it on, bears witness to it. This witness *was confirmed* in the Corinthians. The verb is often used in the papyri in a legal sense of guaranteeing.[1] Paul is saying that the changed lives of the Corinthians demonstrated

[1] See Deissmann, *Bible Studies*, Edinburgh, 1901, pp. 104ff.

conclusively the validity of the message that had been preached to them. The effects of the preaching were the guarantee of its truth.

7. The result of all this is that the Corinthians lack no *gift*. This word is used (1) of salvation (Rom. v. 15), (2) of God's good gifts in general (Rom. xi. 29), and (3) of special equipments of the Spirit, for example, speaking with tongues (1 Cor. xii. 4ff.). Here the thought is the wide one (2). God had enriched their lives and they lacked no spiritual gift. The reference to the second coming of the Lord is unexpected. The connection of thought may be that the present foretaste of the Spirit turns our thoughts to the fuller experience of the last great day (cf. Rom. viii. 23; Eph. i. 13f.). *Apokalupsin*, rendered *coming*, means 'unfolding', 'revelation'. There are different ways of looking at the second advent. This way sees it as a revealing of Christ. We shall see Him as He is (cf. 1 Jn. iii. 2).

8. The verb *confirm* is that used in verse 6. Christ, who has enriched them, given them grace and every good gift, will see to it that right through until the last time nothing is lacking to them. The enriching with the Spirit's gifts is itself an assurance, a foretaste of things to come. Just as the end time may be referred to as the revelation of Christ, so it may be spoken of as *the day of our Lord Jesus Christ*. The characteristic thing about it is that our Lord is in it. Because it is His day, and because it is He who will *confirm* them, they may be assured that they will be *blameless* in that day. *Blameless* signifies 'unimpeachable'; no charge can be laid against those whom Christ guarantees (cf. Rom. viii. 33).

9. This is not a vain boast. It is a sure confidence grounded on the fact that *God is faithful*. The continuance of the favours mentioned in the preceding verses may be confidently looked for. The character of God is at stake.

Paul goes back to beginnings. This faithful God had *called* the Corinthian Christians *unto the fellowship of his Son Jesus Christ our Lord*. The opening words of this Epistle reminded us that Paul's position as an apostle was due to the divine call. Now we see that there is a call to every believer. It is because God has called him and not because of his own initiative that he has become a Christian. A genitive after *koinōnia, fellowship*, can be subjective ('fellowship with'), or objective ('fellowship in'). An example of the former is Phil. i. 5, where 'your fellowship' (lit. 'fellowship of you') means 'fellowship with you'. Objective genitives are like 'the fellowship of his sufferings' (Phil. iii. 10), which points to fellowship 'in' suffering. Here it is possible that Paul means that the fellowship is a common partaking of Christ. But the genitive of a person is more likely to be subjective, with the meaning 'fellowship with Christ' (Ellicott thinks it is both, *viz.*, fellowship 'in Him and with Him'). The word is the direct antithesis to *divisions* in verse 10.

It is worth stopping to notice the way Paul dwells lovingly on the name of his Saviour. Nine times in these nine verses he makes use of this name, and he will do it again in the next verse. Christ is absolutely central. Paul lingers over the name.

II. DIVISION IN THE CHURCH (i. 10–iv. 21)

a. The fact of division (i. 10–17)

i. The parties (i. 10–12). *Now, de,* is adversative. It sets what follows over against the preceding as a contrast to it. So far from 'fellowship' being realized, there is division. Paul leads into the subject with a tender appeal. He uses the verb *beseech*, the affectionate address, *brethren*, and implores them *by the name of our Lord Jesus Christ*. The full title heightens the solemnity of his appeal. This one name stands over against all party names.

That ye all speak the same thing is an appeal for agreement. This 'strictly classical' expression 'is used of political communities which are free from factions, or of different states which entertain friendly relations with each other' (Lightfoot). The use of party cries always tends to deepen and perpetuate division, and Paul calls for their abandonment. *Divisions*, *schismata*, does not signify 'schisms', but 'dissensions'. The divisions were internal. Paul asks that the situation be remedied and that they *be perfectly joined together*. This is the rendering of a Greek verb which has to do with restoring anything to its rightful condition. It is used of mending nets (Mt. iv. 21). It is used of supplying what was lacking to the faith of the Thessalonians (1 Thes. iii. 10). The condition of the Corinthian church was far from what it should have been. Restorative action was demanded. Paul looks to them to come to a united *mind* (= 'frame of mind') and *judgment* (= 'opinion').

11. The source of Paul's information is disclosed. Chloe is not otherwise known. As her name is mentioned it is perhaps more likely that she was an Ephesian than a Corinthian. But we do not know. Nor do we know whether she was a Christian, though this may be judged probable. At any rate, members of her household had *declared* the situation to Paul. The word means 'made clear'. Paul was not left in any doubt. It may also be that the word 'implies that the Apostle was reluctant to believe the reports which had come to his ears' (Edwards). *Contentions* points us to quarrels. There was a spirit of factiousness. Feelings were aroused. In Gal. v. 20 this is castigated as one of the 'works of the flesh' (the translation there being 'variance').

12. Paul's charge becomes precise. *Every one of you* need not be pressed to indicate that there were no exceptions at all, but it shows that the trouble was widespread. *I am of Paul* means 'I am a disciple of Paul', 'I follow Paul's way', and so with the other designations. Considerable ingenuity has been expended in the attempt to give an outline of the teachings of the various factions, but certainty is unattainable. From the general tone of Paul's references to Apollos, and from all that we know of this disciple from other passages, it is clear that there was no difference in their teaching. The party choice would have been made on the basis of their methods of preaching. Probably Apollos was more elaborate and rhetorical than Paul.

The *Cephas* party (Cephas is the Aramaic form of the name 'Peter') raises difficulties of another sort. We do not know whether Peter had ever been in Corinth or not. If he had been, the basis of attachment may have been personal. But there were other considerations. Peter was an older Christian than Paul. He had been the leader of the original Twelve. He seems to have been somewhat more ready to conform to the Jewish Law than was Paul (cf. Gal. ii. 11ff.). There may possibly have been some different emphasis in his preaching from that of Paul, though if so it must have been slight. But a section of the Corinthians felt that there was something about Peter that made him the man to appeal to.

Some have thought that there was no *Christ* party. They understand *and I of Christ* as Paul's own interjection at the end. The construction of the sentence makes this most unlikely. The Greek seems to point to a fourth party. Whether these people were simply tired of the other three, and so said 'We belong to Christ, not to any teacher', or whether they had some distinctive tenets we have no means of knowing. If the former, they had yet absorbed the spirit of partisanship and themselves become a party. What is clear is that there were definite groups. Paul condemns the spirit which led to their formation. He does not except those who clung to his own name. The whole thing was wrong. He would have none of it.

ii. Not due to Paul (i. 13–17). The apostle's indignation explodes in a series of questions. *Is Christ divided?* has been understood in more ways than one. Some take it not as a question, but as an indignant exclamation, 'Then Christ is divided!' The balance of the passage makes this unlikely. Others take the verb as middle (as it is in Lk. xii. 13). This would yield a good sense, 'Has Christ shared (you) with others?' It would indicate that only part of them had been devoted to Christ. But the verb seems more likely to be passive. This could mean, 'Has Christ been apportioned?' (i.e. to one of the conflicting groups; cf. Moffatt, 'Has Christ been parcelled out?'), or, 'Has Christ been divided up?' This last is the most likely meaning. But whichever interpretation be adopted Paul is envisaging an utter impossibility. Christ is one, and the Church, which is His body, must be one.

The second question, *was Paul crucified for you?*, also refers to something unthinkable. It directs attention to the centrality of the cross. The Corinthians, with their emphasis on wisdom, seem to have overlooked this. None other than Christ could accomplish the crucial work of redemption. The third question reminds them that they had not realized the significance of their baptism. They had been baptized into Christ, not into any man. Their allegiance accordingly was to Christ alone.

14–16. This leads Paul to a reminiscence of his practice when among them. He had baptized very few converts, and he now regards this as providential. He thanks God for it. It is of interest that Christ Himself delegated baptism to His followers (Jn. iv. 1f.). It may well be that Peter followed the same practice (Acts x. 48). Paul had made exceptions in the cases of Crispus, Gaius, and the household of Stephanas (the mention of the latter after a little interval is a natural touch in a dictated letter). Many think that this was done on account of the importance of these men. This seems unlikely, for, as Godet says, 'this idea would contradict the very drift of the whole passage'. Paul had his reasons, but he does not disclose them. Verse 16 leaves open the possibility that there may have been a few others, but clearly it was well known that it had not been Paul's practice to baptize.

He gives us the importance of this in verse 15. It ruled out any attempt to bind converts to him personally. The 'name' in antiquity meant far more than it does with us. It stood for the whole personality. It summed up the whole man. The preposition used here is *eis*, 'into', which is somewhat stronger than *en* or *epi* which are also used in connection with baptism. 'Into the name', as Robertson and Plummer point out, 'implies entrance into fellowship and allegiance, such as exists between the Redeemer and the redeemed.' There could be no suggestion that Paul had said or done anything to bring his converts into such a relation to him personally. He had pointed men to Christ.

17. The essence of Paul's commission was not to administer rites, even important rites like baptism, but *to preach the gospel*. Preaching is the primary function in the original commission given by Christ to the Twelve (Mk. iii. 14). Throughout the New Testament this function remains primary. The apostles had a unique place as the witnesses to the saving act of God in Christ. Their main business was to proclaim it. Thus they spent their time in ceaseless labours as they made this gospel known.

Some at least of the Corinthians were setting too high a value on human wisdom and human eloquence in line with the typical Greek admiration for rhetoric and philosophical studies. In the face of this Paul insists that preaching *with wisdom of words* was no part of his commission. That kind of preaching would draw men to the preacher. It would nullify the cross of Christ. The faithful preaching of the cross results in men ceasing to put their trust in any human device, and relying rather on God's work in Christ. A reliance on rhetoric would cause men to trust in men, the very antithesis of what the preaching of the cross is meant to effect.

b. The 'foolishness' of the gospel (i. 18–ii. 5)

i. The message was 'foolish' (i. 18–25). Paul proceeds to develop the contrast between worldly wisdom and the wisdom of God. From the way he uses the term *wisdom* we deduce that some of the Corinthians had put great emphasis on this quality. In bold and forceful language Paul contrasts the way of God, which seems folly to the sophisticated Christians, with the ineffectiveness of that which the world counts as wisdom.

18. *The preaching* is literally 'the word'. There is a contrast with 'wisdom of words' ('words' is really singular) in the previous verse. The term is one which is a little unusual in such a passage. It directs attention to both the manner and the matter of the apostolic preaching. The message does not please the perishing, any more than the stark simplicity with which it was presented. In their worldly wisdom they see nothing in it but *foolishness* ('nonsense', as Phillips renders). *Them that perish* and *which are saved* represent a pair of present participles. The present gives the thought of a process which is going on. We could render: 'them who are perishing', and 'us who are being saved'. There is a sharp contrast. Ultimately all must fall into either the class of the saved or that of the lost. There is no other. Those who are being saved have not yet all the wisdom of heaven, but they have been brought into a newness of life which enables them to weigh spiritual things. As a result they penetrate to the true greatness of the gospel, whereas those who perish are blind to anything but the superficial. 'Wisdom' is the opposite of 'foolishness', and we accordingly would expect Paul to speak of the gospel as 'the wisdom of God'. Instead, as in Rom. i. 16, he characterizes it as *power*. It is not simply good advice to men, telling them what they should do. Nor is it a message about God's power. It *is* God's power.

19. Characteristically Paul clinches his argument with a citation from sacred Scripture. His quotation is from Is. xxix. 14, with a slight variation from the LXX. The principle Paul is expounding is thus nothing new. From of old God's way had stood in marked contrast with that suggested by the wisdom of men. Men have always felt that their own way must be the right one (cf. Pr. xiv. 12, xvi. 25). But God confutes their 'wisdom'. He reduces their systems to nothingness. He destroys their wisdom. In this context there is not much difference between *wisdom* and *understanding*. Properly the former denotes mental excellence in general, the latter the intelligent critical discerning of 'the bearings of things' (see Lightfoot on Col. i. 9). Neither can stand before God.

20. In the manner of Is. xxxiii. 18 a series of rhetorical questions hammers home the point. Some have thought that *the wise* points us to the Greek sophist, and *the scribe* to the Jewish exponent of the Law, with *the disputer of this world* a general term to include both. Others reverse the significance of the first and the last. But it is unlikely that Paul had such distinctions in mind. His concern is to demonstrate that no human wisdom can avail before God. *Wise, scribe,* and *disputer of this world* are three typical terms to describe those who are learned and acute as the world counts wisdom. There is a glance at the transitory nature of human wisdom in the use of *aiōn* for *world* rather than *kosmos* (which occurs in the latter part of the verse). This world is but a passing show, and its wisdom passes with it. God has not simply disregarded this wisdom. He has *made* it *foolish.* Paul wants there to be not the slightest doubt as to the divine rejection of all that rests on a basis of merely human wisdom.

21. It is unlikely that *the wisdom of God* here denotes the revelation of God's wisdom in nature. Some commentators take it to mean that men have failed to heed the voice of God in one way, so He speaks to them in another. But the thrust of the passage is against such views. Paul surely means that God in His wisdom was pleased to save men by the way of the cross and in no other way. *Pleased* fixes attention on God's free and sovereign choice. It was not in His plan at all that men by their exercise of wisdom should attain to the knowledge of Him. He pleased to reveal Himself in quite a different way.

Paul does not hesitate to bring out the total unexpectedness of this way by his bold assertion that it is *foolishness*. Men never have acclaimed the gospel as a masterpiece of wisdom. To the natural man it does not make sense. Paul was not unaware of what he was up against as he preached the gospel. The word rendered *preaching, kērugmatos,* does not mean, as the English might suggest, the act of preaching. It directs attention rather to the content of the message. It is not merely the fact that men preach the gospel that is 'foolish'; it is the gospel itself, the message that God saves men through a crucified Saviour. Men do not receive salvation by exercising wisdom. It comes to *them that believe* (the tense is present continuous, indicating a habitual faith).

22. In setting the Jews' demand for a *sign* (lit., 'signs') over against the Greeks' quest for *wisdom* Paul brings out the characteristics of the two nations. The Jews throughout their history were very matter-of-fact. They showed little interest in speculative thought. Their demand was for evidence, and their interest was in the practical. They thought of God as manifesting Himself in history in signs and mighty wonders. In the light of this they demanded a sign from the Lord (Mt. xii. 38, xvi. 1, 4; Mk. viii. 11 f.; Jn. vi. 30). They thought of the Messiah as One attested by striking manifestations of power and majesty. A crucified Messiah was a contradiction in terms.

The Greeks were absorbed in speculative philosophy. No names were more honoured among them than the names of their outstanding thinkers. From the lofty heights of their culture they looked down on and despised as barbarians all who failed to appreciate their *wisdom*. That this *wisdom* often degenerated into meaningless sophistries or the kind of pursuits mentioned in Acts xvii. 21 meant little to them. They still remained proud of their intellectual acuteness and found no place for the gospel. Proctor refers to 'the high intellectual perception of the Greek philosophers' and to 'the nobility of

45

much of their writing'. But he adds, 'Yet all this has no saving power for mankind.'

23. In contrast with this (*but*, *de*, is adversative, and *we*, *hēmeis*, is emphatic) Paul sets the preaching of *Christ crucified*. The verb *preach* is that appropriate to the action of a herald. The message came from God, not the preacher. In this sense it is a peculiarly Christian term. It is used little, if at all, in this way in the classics, in the LXX, or in current religious systems such as the mystery religions. *Crucified* is a perfect participle. Not only was Christ once crucified, but He continues in the character of the crucified One. The crucifixion is permanent in its efficacy and its effects.

But the Jews will have none of it. To them a crucified Messiah is a complete impossibility, *a stumblingblock*, an occasion of offence. Nor is it any better with the Greeks. To them it is *foolishness*, sheer unmitigated folly. God would never act like that! The crucifixion is the heart of the Christian faith, but it is acceptable to neither Jew nor Greek. *Greeks* in this verse is not the same word as that in the verses immediately before and after. It is usually rendered 'Gentiles', and is the ordinary word for all non-Jewish peoples. Paul includes all mankind in the rejection of the crucified Messiah.

24. But that is not the whole story. If the natural man, be he Jew or Greek, instinctively rejects the message of the cross, the man who is called of God, Jew or Greek, welcomes it. There is an emphasis on the thought of calling, and we could translate, 'the called themselves' (as RV mg.). The relevant fact is that they have been called by God. All else is unimportant. Here, as is usual in Paul's writings, *called* has the thought of effectual calling. It is implied that the call has been heeded and obeyed. Men called like this know that the crucified Christ means power. Before they were called they could not overcome the power of sin. Now they can. Christ is *the power of God*.

He is also *the wisdom of God*. This whole passage is concerned
with wisdom. The Corinthians had evidently emphasized it.
The Greeks habitually sought it out. The cross seems nothing
else than arrant folly. Yet that cross whereon the Son of God
hung for men proved to be God's power. In it sin was defeated.
And it proved to be also God's wisdom. The wisdom of the
world could not find God, nor had it power over evil. The
cross revealed God and it gave men the power they needed.
On the level of the search for wisdom that 'foolishness' of God
proved itself to be the true wisdom.

25. So Paul rounds off the section with the conclusion that
what in God proud man is wont to dub *foolishness* is *wiser than
men* and anything that is in man. The suffering Messiah hang-
ing from the cross appears to be weak. But it is *the weakness of
God* that He displays, and this is *stronger than men* and anything
that men can produce.

The sign-seeking Jews were blind to the significance of the
greatest sign of all when it was before them. The wisdom-
loving Greeks could not discern the most profound wisdom of
all when they were confronted with it.

ii. The believers are insignificant (i. 26–31). The thought
of the contradiction God's method offers to the wisdom of men
is illustrated by the kind of people He has called to be His own.
He might have chosen to put the gospel in a form which would
have appealed primarily to the intelligentsia. Human wisdom
would concentrate on outstanding men. But God has no
need of human wisdom. Rather He chooses those who have
little to commend them from the worldly standpoint. These He
transforms, and uses as His instruments for the effecting of His
purpose. His power works miracles in the most hopeless
material. Thus the wisdom of God is shown to excel the best
that men can produce.

26. *Ye see* is probably better taken as imperative, as RV,
'Behold your calling' (cf. Moffatt, 'look at your own ranks,

my brothers'). Paul is inviting his readers to reflect on the type of person whom God has, in fact, chosen. *Calling* refers to the divine call, and not to 'vocation' in our sense of the term. Paul emphasizes once more the divine initiative. The state of affairs he is describing did not come about because the only people who would interest themselves in Christianity were the depressed classes. It came about because God chose to work His marvels through people who were, from the human point of view, the most unpromising. It is probably for the same reason that *not many wise men after the flesh* heads Paul's list. Wisdom has been much in mind throughout this discussion. The Corinthians had the typical Greek reverence for wisdom. But Paul decisively rejects this as the criterion whereby God chooses His own. That is not to say that there are none from the classes mentioned. On the contrary, *not many* implies that there were some, though not a large number. *Mighty* is a general term for principal people. *Noble* applies to family, and indicates those of noble rank. But 'the things which elevate man in the world, knowledge, influence, rank, are not the things which lead to God and salvation' (Hodge).

27. The repetition of *hath chosen* underlines the purpose of God. There is a change of gender from *the foolish things* (neuter) to *the wise* (masculine, *sc.* 'men'). The neuter concentrates attention on the quality of foolishness possessed by these people, rather than on themselves as individuals. *Confound, kataischunē*, means 'put to shame', i.e. by the contrast between the estimate the wise form of themselves and that which God's choice reveals. It is preceded by the conjunction *hina* indicating purpose. Paul makes sure we do not overlook God's plan in all this. *Mighty* translates a different Greek word from that used in the previous verse. The difference in meaning is not great, this word having something of an emphasis on physical strength. Some commentators take *of the world* to mean 'in the world's judgment'. But this is to miss the sting of Paul's words. God has not chosen only those whom the world counts *foolish* and *weak*: He has chosen those who really are the *foolish* and the *weak* in this world.

28. *Base* means 'low-born' (often with the added notion of morally worthless). It is the direct antithesis to 'noble' in verse 26. It has the article, as has the following expression, so that we should read 'the base things . . . the things which are despised'. This last is a strong word, signifying 'to treat as of no account' (Knox, 'contemptible'). But the following expression, 'the things which are not', is even stronger. God's activity in men is creative. He takes that which is nothing at all and makes of it what He pleases. *Katargeō, bring to nought,* is not easy to translate. It occurs twenty-seven times in the New Testament and is translated in seventeen different ways in AV. RV does away with seven of these, but brings in another three. Obviously it is not easy to get its significance. Basically it means something like 'to render idle' or 'inoperative', and all its usages derive from this. Here the meaning is that the *things which are not* render completely ineffective the *things that are.*

29. God does all this with the purpose of taking away from all men every occasion of boasting. Whatever men may do before one another there is no room for boasting 'before God' (this is the true reading, not *in his presence*).

30. From the negative Paul turns to the positive. The saved are *of him, of, ex,* giving the idea of source. Their new life derives from God (cf. Rom. ix. 11; 2 Cor. v. 18; Eph. ii. 8). They are *in Christ Jesus.* Whole books have been written about this enigmatic phrase which Paul habitually uses to describe the relationship of believers to Christ. Briefly we may say that it indicates that the believer stands in the closest possible relationship to his Lord. Christ is the very atmosphere in which he lives. Yet we must not interpret this mechanically. Christ is a Person. The phrase describes personal attachment to a personal Saviour. E.Best has shown that the expression also has a corporate aspect. To be 'in Christ' is to be closely related to those others who are also 'in Christ'.[1] It is to be part of the body of Christ. The adversative conjunction *de*, *but*, and the emphatic *ye* set believers in strong contrast to the worldly wise of the preceding verses. The contrast with worldly wisdom comes out in another way when Christ is said to be *made unto us wisdom*. Paul has already argued forcibly that the apparent 'foolishness' of the gospel is the true wisdom, and this is his thought here, too. The wisdom of God is embodied in Christ, who offered Himself that men might be saved. Here is the real wisdom, let the philosophers argue as they will.

In AV the qualities which follow are linked with *wisdom* as co-ordinate with it. The Greek seems rather to mean that these three are subordinate to *wisdom*, and explanatory of it. The *wisdom* of which Paul writes includes these other three. *Righteousness* in this context will stand for that righteousness which Christ makes available for men, 'the state of having been justified', in Edwards' phrase. Christ is our righteousness (cf. 2 Cor. v. 21). We know no other. Again, He is our *sanctification*, for we could never attain holiness in our own strength. Sanctification is accomplished only in the divine power. Christ is our *redemption* (last with a certain emphasis, and perhaps as pointing to the last great day, the consummation of redemption), because He has paid the ransom price in His own body on Calvary.

31. Verse 29 has excluded all glorying in human achievement. Here we find the true basis of glorying. There is room for a real expression of our delight in what Christ has done for us. But all glorying must be in what He has done, and not in the puny things that we, at best, can achieve. Characteristically Paul proves his point from Scripture. We should not overlook the significance of the application to Christ of words

---

[1] *One Body in Christ*, London, 1955, chapter 1. This chapter gives an excellent summary of several views of the meaning of the phrase.

which in Je. ix. 23f. refer to Jehovah. No higher view could be taken of the Person of Christ.

iii. Paul's preaching was not in human wisdom, but divine power (ii. 1–5).

Paul reminds his hearers that his own preaching when in their city had conformed to what he has been saying about the 'foolishness' of the gospel. There was nothing attractive about it. It was an unvarnished setting forth of the simple gospel. But precisely because his preaching was so simple and unpretentious its results convincingly demonstrated the power of God.

1. The emphatic *kagō*, *und I*, stresses that Paul was not making an exception of himself. He, too, was a living example of the truth he was expounding. *Excellency* is a word with a comparative force. It means 'superiority', 'pre-eminence'. Paul claims no such thing either for his *speech*, the way in which he presented his facts, or for his *wisdom*, the way in which his mind marshalled his facts. He characterizes his' message as *the testimony of God*. The preaching of the gospel is frequently regarded in the New Testament as an activity like that of a herald. Viewed in this way it is the passing on of a message given (see note on i. 23). But it is also frequently regarded as the bearing witness to given facts. Preaching the gospel is not delivering edifying discourses, beautifully put together. It is bearing witness to what God has done in Christ for man's salvation.

2. Accordingly Paul deliberately excluded not only from his preaching, but also from his knowledge, everything but that one great central truth. He made it his resolve to know among them only Jesus Christ, who, as we have already seen, is both the power of God and the wisdom of God (i. 24, and cf. i. 30). The particular point about Christ that is singled out is the crucifixion. That is the heart of the gospel (for the force of the perfect participle *crucified* see on i. 23). On that Paul concentrated.

3. From the message Paul switches attention to the manner of the preaching. The account given in Acts makes it clear that Paul had had much to discourage him just before he came to Corinth (see Introduction, pp. 17 ff.). He must have been rather downhearted, and this was reflected in his general manner. In any case the Corinthians were not very impressed by his personal presence as we see from 2 Cor. x. 10. So Paul tells us that he had been without strength, and afraid, even to the point of trembling (Phillips, 'I was feeling far from strong, I was nervous and rather shaky'). At the same time his fear was primarily of God rather than of men. It was fear in the light of the task committed to him—what Kay calls 'anxious desire to fulfil his duty'.

4. It is not easy to see the difference between *my speech* and *my preaching*. *Speech* is literally 'word'. We saw it used in i. 18 (where it is rendered 'preaching') to include both the manner and the matter of the preaching. The word rendered *preaching* is that denoting the message proclaimed in i. 21. Probably Paul is not differentiating between the two with any exactness. He employs both terms to stress both the message he preached and the way he preached it. *Enticing* translates a very unusual word (found only here, in fact) meaning 'persuasive'. Thus Paul roundly eschews the methods of human wisdom. Then positively he says that his preaching had been a clear demonstration of the power of the Spirit. The word translated *demonstration, apodeixis,* signifies the most rigorous proof. Some proofs indicate no more than that the conclusion follows from the premises. But with *apodeixis* 'the premises are known to be true, and therefore the conclusion is not only logical, but certainly true' (Robertson and Plummer). Paul's claim is that his very defects had meant the most convincing demonstration of the power of the Spirit. It is possible for arguments to be logically irrefutable, yet totally unconvincing. Paul's preaching had carried conviction because of the power of the Spirit.

5. *That*, *hina*, means 'in order that', and indicates purpose. Right from the beginning Paul had wished to ground his converts in the divine power, and to make them independent of human wisdom. That was why he had made no attempt to employ rhetorical arts, but had contented himself with the simplest approach. That was the reason for his concentration on that message which was so unpalatable to natural men, the message of the cross.

c. A revealed message (ii. 6-16)

i. The gospel is not human wisdom (ii. 6-9). Up to this point Paul has been insisting that the gospel owes nothing to human wisdom. Both the message and the messengers were despised by the wise and the great of this world. But he does not mean that Christianity is contemptible, and he now proceeds to show something of its profundity and dignity. It embodies *the wisdom of God*. In the light of this all petty human wisdom fades away.

6. *Howbeit* is the adversative *de*. Paul is not excluding all wisdom from the Christian purview, but only worldly wisdom. *Wisdom* actually comes first in the Greek with emphasis. 'We *do* speak wisdom' is the thought, 'even though the world does not recognize it.' The plural *we* links Paul's teaching with that of other Christian teachers. There was no division among them.

The true *wisdom* is spoken among the *perfect*. Paul is possibly, as a number of commentators think, indulging in a little gentle irony at the expense of the Corinthians' estimate of their own spiritual state. More probably, he is perfectly serious. *Teleioi* does not denote those who are without flaw, but those who are mature, who have reached their end or aim (*telos*). Paul recognizes that not all Christians have full understanding. There are 'babes' among them (iii. 1), but the wisdom of which he speaks is appreciated by those who are mature in the faith. To them he can impart 'all the counsel of God' (Acts xx. 27). Yet it should be remembered that the New Testament does not envisage 'grades' of Christians. All should go on to maturity (Heb. vi. 1). Some of the Gnostics classified men into permanent groups according to their spiritual potential. They held that some were 'perfect', while others could never attain that standing. Paul is not dividing men into religious castes like this. He simply recognizes the facts. When men first believe they do not all at once grasp the full implications of the faith. At first all are 'babes'. But the way to advance is open to everyone. There is no spiritual truth that is not available for even the humblest believer to appropriate. By *wisdom* Paul accordingly does not mean some secret teaching withheld of set purpose from the rank and file. He means the 'meat' to which he refers in iii. 2. And if there are some who, as yet, can take only the 'milk', that is not to be regarded as permanent. All must go on to maturity, when they can enter into the *wisdom* of which Paul speaks.

With unwearied persistence the apostle points out that the *wisdom* of which he speaks is not *the wisdom of this world*. For some time he has been stressing this. Now he adds another point, *nor of the princes of this world* (lit. 'this age'). There have been commentators in both ancient and modern times who have taken this expression to refer to demons. Paul, it is said, saw Christ as engaged in a gigantic struggle not primarily with earthly powers, but with the forces of the unseen world. There are undoubtedly passages in Paul's writings which refer to such forces (e.g. Rom. viii. 38f.; Col. ii. 15). But it may be questioned whether this is his meaning here. Two points are especially important. The one is that throughout this whole passage Paul's contrast is between the wisdom and power of God as shown in the gospel, and the wisdom and power of men. To introduce now the thought of the wisdom of demonic powers is to bring in an extraneous concept. The other is that in verse 8 it is *the princes of this world* who crucified Christ in ignorance. The most probable understanding of this is of the Jewish and Roman leaders, all the more so since in Acts iii. 17 the same word *princes, archontes* (there translated 'rulers'), is used of them. It is also there said that they carried out the crucifixion in ignorance. By contrast the demons are explicitly said to have known who Jesus was (Mk. i. 24, 34, etc.). We conclude, therefore, that it is the temporal rulers that Paul has in mind. Probably his use of *aiōn* is not without a glance at the transitory nature of their office. The truth of the gospel is permanent. This transitoriness is in mind also in the concluding *that come to nought*. Here we have once more the verb *katargeō* (see on i. 28). The meaning is that these *princes* are being rendered completely ineffective. Their vaunted power and wisdom are made null and void.

7. *But* is the strong adversative *alla*. The *wisdom* we speak is utterly opposed to the *wisdom* mentioned in the previous verse. It is God's wisdom, and the word *God* is in an emphatic position. *Mustēriŏn*, translated *mystery*, has about it nothing of the mysterious in our sense of the word. It does not signify a puzzle which man finds difficult to solve. It signifies a secret which man is wholly unable to penetrate. But it is a secret which God has now revealed. At one and the same time the word points to the impossibility of man's knowing God's secret, and to the love of God which makes that secret known to man. Paul describes the secret as *the hidden wisdom*, emphasizing the fact that men outside Christ are still in the dark about it. It is revealed to believers, but it is not a matter of common knowledge among the sons of men. It remains hidden from unbelievers.

Paul stresses that the gospel is no afterthought. It is something planned in the mind of God from *before the world* (lit. 'before the ages'). His verb is *proorizō*, which means 'to foreordain'. It stresses the plan of God and the sovereignty of God. The addition *unto our glory* adds the thought of the tenderness of God. From before all time He was concerned for our well-being, and planned the gospel that we should enter into *our glory*.

8. God's secret was not known by any way other than revelation. For all their eminence *the princes of this world* did not know it. This is shown by the fact that they crucified Jesus. He Himself said of His executioners, 'they know not what they do' (Lk. xxiii. 34). Paul reasons that had they really understood who Jesus was and the consequent enormity of rejecting Him, they would never have done the deed they did. *The Lord of glory* (' the Lord whose essential attribute is glory', Ellicott) is an outstanding and unusual title. This is the only place where it is applied to Christ, though Jas. ii. 1 is similar. The epithet *of glory* is applied to the Father in Acts vii. 2; Eph. i. 17. In the apocryphal *Book of Enoch* the whole expression *the Lord of glory* is used of God. More than one scholar has thought that this is the loftiest title Paul ever applies to Christ. Whether this be so or not, it certainly is an exalted title. It fitly stands alongside the application to Christ of a scripture originally referring to Jehovah in i. 31. Both show that Paul habitually assigned to Christ the highest place of all.

9. The difficulty about this verse is the source of Paul's quotation. The formula *kathōs gegraptai* is one he uses when citing Holy Writ. But there is no passage in the Old Testament which runs exactly like this. Perhaps the nearest is Is. lxiv. 4, though Is. lxv. 17 (note that 'mind' here is 'heart' in the LXX) and Is. lii. 15 have been suggested. From the time of Origen some have thought that Paul was quoting from *The Apocalypse of Elias*, an apocryphal book now lost, or from *The Ascension of Isaiah*. It is far from certain, however, that either of these books was in existence at the time. Another view is that this is a saying of our Lord which has not been recorded in the Gospels. That there were such sayings is indisputable (cf. Acts xx. 35), but whether Paul would cite them in this way is another matter. Where was this one written? On the whole it seems best to think of this verse as a rather free citation of Is. lxiv. 4 with reminiscences of other scriptural passages.

Heart in the New Testament does not stand for the emotions, as with us. Among the Greeks the seat of the emotions was rather the intestines (cf. our 'bowels of compassion'), while thought was located in the midriff, the diaphragm. *Heart* stood rather for the whole of a man's inner life, including thought and will as well as the emotions, though sometimes it inclines to one or the other. Here the mind is perhaps most in view. Paul's thought is that there is no method of apprehension open to man (eyes, ears, or understanding) which can give him any idea of the wonderful things that God has made ready for *them that love him* (cf. Rom. viii. 28). The verb *hath prepared* reinforces the thought of verse 7, that God is working out His plan. The glories that come to believers are not haphazard, but are in accordance with God's plan from of old.

ii. Words 'which the Spirit teacheth' (ii. 10–13). *Unto us* comes first in the Greek with emphasis. Paul is in no doubt as to who has the truth, the learned philosophers or the humble Christians. *Unto us*, believers, great things have been revealed. But the emphatic *unto us* is immediately followed by *hath revealed*, as though to remove any suggestion of superiority. There can be no feelings of pride where it is recognized that all is of God. Believers know what they know, not because of any skill or wisdom of their own, but because it has pleased God to reveal it to them.

Paul speaks of the revelation as having been accomplished by the Holy Spirit. This is a kind of turning point, for while he has previously mentioned the Spirit occasionally in his argument, he now begins to dwell upon His activities. *Searcheth* does not mean that the Spirit searches with a view to obtaining information. Rather it is a way of saying that He penetrates into *all things*. There is nothing which is beyond His knowledge. In particular Paul specifies *the deep things of God*. *Deep* is often used of the mighty deeps of the sea, and thus comes to signify 'unfathomable'. It points us to the impossibility of any creature knowing the innermost recesses of the divine counsel, 'the depths of God'. But they are known to the Spirit, and it is this Spirit who has revealed the truths of which Paul speaks.

11. The place of the Spirit is brought out by the analogy of man's nature. Nobody can really know what is going on inside a man, nobody except the man's own spirit. From outside other men can but guess. But the spirit of the man does not guess. He knows. In the same way, reasons Paul, no one outside God can know what takes place within God. Nobody can know but the Spirit of God Himself. That is to say, the Spirit knows God from the inside. There can be no question but that this passage ascribes full deity to the Spirit. And it also implies that the revelation of which Paul has been speaking is authentic. Because the Spirit who reveals is truly God, what He reveals is the truth of God.

12. Once again Paul sets Christians over against the wise heathen with an emphatic *we*. Whatever be the case with others, *we* take up our position as those who are led by God's Spirit. *The spirit of the world* is not an easy expression. Some understand it to mean Satan. This would give an excellent sense. One difficulty, however, is that Satan does not seem elsewhere to be referred to in just this way (though 'the prince of this world', Jn. xii. 31, comes near to it). Another is that it goes beyond what is required by the context. The wisdom of the world which Paul is opposing throughout this passage is not something satanic, but something human. For such reasons it seems a little more probable that we should accept the meaning 'the spirit of human wisdom', 'the temper of this world'. Believers have not received the spirit of worldly wisdom. In passing we might note that the word used for *world* here is *kosmos*, 'the ordered universe', and not *aiōn*, which was used in verses 7f., and which means 'the age', the world in its temporal aspect.

We who are Christ's have received *the spirit which is of God; that we might know the things that are freely given to us of God.* The small 's' for *spirit* in modern editions of AV seems to be an error. The original rightly had a capital. It is the Spirit of God that is meant. The Spirit brings assurance. The Christian has real knowledge. He does not simply act on the basis of general probabilities. That his certainty is a certainty of faith does not make it any the less a certainty.

13. What the Christian receives he passes on. So Paul says that these revealed truths are spoken by believers to others. This is done *not in the words which man's wisdom teacheth*. The worldly-wise way is not the way to commend the truth of God. Christian teaching is done in words *which the Holy Ghost teacheth*. The Spirit's activity extends to providing the actual words used, and is not confined to the supplying of general ideas. As Moule says, the expression 'is a very bold but quite unambiguous use of the Subjective Genitive'.[1]

This probably gives us the clue to the difficult expression which follows. It is fairly clear that the participle *sunkrinontes* should be rendered 'combining'. Although *comparing* is the meaning of this verb in 2 Cor. x. 12, this is far from being the usual meaning and should be adopted only if the context plainly indicates it. In this case it does nothing of the sort. A surprising number prefer 'interpreting' or the like (e.g. RSV, Phillips); again, it seems to me, without much reason. This meaning of the word is found only in the LXX, and there it is never used of interpreting anything other than dreams. In each case the context makes this meaning plain. It cannot be held to be a widely used meaning of the verb. It seems, then, that we should retain the usual meaning, 'combining'.

Another problem is the gender of *pneumatikois* (the second occurrence of *spiritual*). The form could be either masculine or neuter. In the former case the meaning would be 'combining spiritual things with spiritual men', i.e. teaching spiritual truths to spiritually-minded men. If it is neuter the significance will be, 'combining spiritual things (the words spoken) with spiritual things (the truths expressed)'. The solution is not easy, and a final decision perhaps impossible. But in the light of the context (Paul is explaining that Christian

[1] *Idiom Book*, p. 40.

preachers use words taught by the Spirit) I incline to the latter view.

iii. Spiritual discernment (ii. 14–16). Though what is taught is a revelation from God, and though it is taught in words given by the Holy Spirit, it is not received by all. Paul gives as the reason that *the natural man* has his limitations. *Psuchikos, natural,* has reference to the animal life. There is nothing evil about its associations. It does not mean anything like 'sinful'. But it does point to an absence of spiritual discernment. It refers to the man whose horizon is bounded by the things of this life. It is the worldly-wise man again, the man who has been so much in Paul's thoughts throughout this passage. Such a man *receiveth not* the things of the Spirit. The verb has an air of welcoming about it, being the usual word for receiving a guest. Thus the point is that *the natural man* does not welcome the things of the Spirit; he refuses them, he rejects them. Such a man is not equipped to discern the activities of God's Spirit. To him they are no more than *foolishness.* Paul goes so far as to say that it is quite impossible for him to *know* them (*know* is aorist infinitive, with the meaning 'get to know'). He gives as the reason that they are *discerned* in a spiritual manner. The verb, *anakrinetai,* is that used in a legal sense of the preliminary examination prior to the main hearing (the corresponding noun is used of such a preliminary examination in Acts xxv. 26). It comes to mean 'to scrutinize', 'to examine', and so 'to judge of', 'to estimate'. It may be that the use of a verb proper to such a preliminary examination is by way of reminding us that all human verdicts are no more than preliminary. It is God who gives the final verdict. Be that as it may, Paul is insisting that the man whose equipment is only of this world, the man who has not received the Holy Spirit of God, has not the ability to make an estimate of things spiritual.

15. By contrast, *he that is spiritual* can form a judgment on *all things.* By spiritual, *pneumatikos,* Paul does not, of course, mean a man who has a different natural endowment from that of the man he has just been considering, 'the natural man'. It is not a question of natural endowment at all, but of the working of the Spirit of God within him. When the Spirit enters a man's life everything is changed. One new thing that appears is the ability to make a right judgment. This is not because the man is now somehow greater than he was before, but because the Spirit of God equips him. *Judgeth* in this verse is the same verb as that rendered 'discerned' in the previous verse, and *judged* later on in this one. The *spiritual* man has the point of reference within himself. He is thus able to judge *all things*. The force of *all* should not be overlooked. The spiritual principle is the basis of his judgment on what men call the secular, as well as the sacred.

The second part of the verse, *yet he himself is judged of no man*, is to be taken in the sense 'of no natural man'. It is clear enough from the whole tenor of Paul's writings that he did not believe that men in whom was the Spirit of God could not be called upon to account for their actions (cf. xiv. 29). Much of this Epistle is nothing else than a criticism (even though a loving and a spiritual criticism) of *spiritual* men. His point is that the *spiritual* man cannot be judged by the natural man, for precisely the same reason that he himself can judge all things. He has the Spirit of God within him and the natural man has not. This makes him an enigma to the natural man. Because the natural man cannot know spiritual things (verse 14), he cannot judge the spiritual man.

16. This impossibility is shown by the question (taken from Is. xl. 13) *who hath known the mind of the Lord, that he may instruct him?* Paul has already spoken of the impossibility of knowing 'the things of God' (verse 11). Then his concern was to show that the Spirit does indeed have complete knowledge of 'the depths of God', and that is relevant here also. As none but the Spirit has knowledge of these depths it is manifestly impossible for the natural man to have knowledge of the man in whom the Spirit is, and who therefore, in a sense, shares in the divine (cf. 2 Pet. i. 4). It is because of this that Paul can make the bold assertion that *we* (the pronoun is emphatic) *have the mind of Christ*. He does not mean that the Christian is able to understand all the thoughts of the Christ. But he does mean that the indwelling Spirit reveals Christ. The spiritual man accordingly does not see things from the viewpoint of the worldly. He sees them from the viewpoint of Christ.

This is another passage significant for Paul's view of Christ. The question in Is. xl. 13 refers to the mind of Jehovah. But Paul moves easily to *the mind of Christ*, so closely does he associate the two.

d. A carnal misunderstanding (iii. 1-9)

i. Carnal Christians (iii. 1-4). Once again as Paul introduces a rebuke he softens it with the affectionate *brethren*. His *could not speak unto you* evidently refers to the days of the mission in Corinth. In those early days he was not able to address them as *spiritual*, i.e. as the kind of men he has just been speaking about. They were then *carnal*, which he explains as *babes in Christ*. It does not seem that Paul is finding anything amiss in the Corinthians at that stage of their Christian career. It is inevitable that those who have just been won for Christ should be *babes in Christ*. They cannot as yet be mature. They must be *carnal*.

2. In accordance with this was the teaching Paul gave them. In ii. 6 he has referred to speaking 'wisdom among them that are perfect'. In the first days of the mission that had been impossible. Then he had *fed* (lit. 'gave to drink') them *with milk, and not with meat* (cf. Heb. v. 12). The wise teacher always suits his instruction to the capacity of his pupils. Paul had not pushed the infant believers beyond their capacity, but had given them the milk that was suited to them. *Hitherto* means 'not yet'. He gave them *milk* for they were 'not yet' able to take *meat*. So far Paul is recounting what had happened, and there is no blame.

It is otherwise when he says *neither yet now are ye able. Neither yet now* is an emphatic expression. They ought to have made progress by this time. It was all very well for the Corinthians to have been in the position of *babes* when they actually were *babes*. But they should have outgrown that stage long ago.

3. Paul reaches the root of the matter with his accusation that they are *yet carnal*. He has changed his word for *carnal* from the *sarkinos* of verse 1 to *sarkikos*. The *-inos* termination signifies 'made of . . .'; thus in 2 Cor. iii. 3 tablets 'made of stone', *lithinos*, are contrasted with those 'made of flesh', *sarkinos*. The *-ikos* ending rather means 'characterized by . . .'; we see it in *psuchikos* of the 'natural' man and *pneumatikos* of the 'spiritual' man in ii. 14f. The difference between *sarkinos* and *sarkikos* is like that between 'fleshy' and 'fleshly'. *Sarkinos* is the more thoroughgoing word, but there is no blame attaching to it as applied to those who are young in the faith. But *sarkikos*, 'characterized by flesh', when used of those who have been Christians for years, is blameworthy. The mature believer is *pneumatikos*, 'characterized by spirit'. To be characterized instead by flesh, as the Corinthians were, is the very opposite of what a Christian should be. 'Flesh', of course, as often in Paul, is used in an ethical and moral sense. It indicates the lower aspects of man's nature, as in Rom. xiii. 14; Gal. v. 13; Eph. ii. 3, etc.

The accusation is made specific with the naming of *envying* and *strife* (*divisions* is absent from the better MSS). The former word basically means something like 'zeal', 'ardour'. It is usually ranked as a virtue by classical writers, and sometimes also by New Testament writers. However, this temper all too easily leads to jealousy and the like, and the characteristic New Testament view is that it is one of the 'works of the flesh' (Gal. v. 20, where it is rendered 'emulations'). *Strife* (Phillips, 'squabbling') is a word we have already met in i. 11, where it is rendered 'contentions'. Both *envying* and *strife* point to self-assertion and unhealthy rivalries. Whereas Christians should

be considerate of others, the Corinthians were asserting themselves. Paul asks whether this is not to be *carnal* (*sarkikos*), and
to *walk as men*. This latter will mean 'like natural men' (cf.
ii. 14).

4. *For* gives the reason for the previous statements. *While*
is the indefinite *hotan*, 'whenever'. Each time such an affirmation is made Paul's point is demonstrated over again. Paul
repeats the catch-cries of two of the parties. Why it should be
only two is not clear. But it may be significant that the two
he selects are the one going by his own name, and that attaching itself to Apollos, who might be thought to be close to Paul.
Again he asks 'are ye not men?' (RV; so the better MSS, rather
than *carnal* as AV), or, as Moffatt puts it, 'what are you but
men of the world?' Their outlook is that of worldly wisdom,
not that of Spirit-filled men.

We are now able to see the drift of Paul's argument. He has
introduced the matter of the dissensions in i. 10–12. After
disclaiming responsibility he has gone on to show that the
gospel is not a matter of worldly wisdom. To the wise of this
world it is folly. Believers are despised. Yet in it is divine
power. Those who accept it are indwelt by the Spirit of God.
The methods of worldly wisdom do not lead to this result.
Thus while the Corinthians might perhaps be able to justify
what they were doing by the arguments of the world, it was
utterly alien to the spirit of the gospel. Their divisions were a
standing witness to their worldly mentality, not to their
spiritual perception. Where they should have been 'spiritual'
(ii. 15), or 'perfect' (ii. 6), they were but 'carnal' Christians.

**ii. The true relation between Paul and Apollos (iii.
5–9).** According to the better MSS we should read, 'What then
is Apollos? and what is Paul?' The neuter 'what' rather than
who helps to take attention away from the persons of the
preachers, and concentrate it on their functions. *But* should be
omitted, so that what follows is the answer to the question.

Ministers translates *diakonoi*, a word applied originally to the service of a table waiter. Then it came to be used of service generally, and in the New Testament it is often used of the service that Christians should render God. In time it was applied to one of the regular orders of the ministry, the deacons, but this is not an example of that use. It is a word which stresses the lowly character of the service rendered. It accordingly ridicules the tendency to make much of preachers. Who would set servants on pedestals? The real work was done by God, as *by whom*, which is really 'through whom', shows. Paul and Apollos are nothing more than instruments 'through whom' He does His work. These ministers could work only *as the Lord gave* to them.

6–8. The process is likened to agriculture. Paul *planted* and Apollos *watered* (the same verb as that rendered 'fed' in verse 2), but neither could make the plants grow. The comparative unimportance of their work is stressed. Only God *gave the increase*. This verb is in the imperfect, a continuous tense, whereas the verbs of planting and watering are in the aorist. Paul and Apollos did their work, which is viewed as completed. But God's activity in giving the increase was continuous.

This important point being established, Paul goes on to draw conclusions. One of them is that neither the planter nor the waterer is important. The attention of the Corinthians should have been fastened on God, who alone effects all spiritual work, and not on His unimportant instruments. A second is that there is an essential unity between planter and waterer. Obviously the work of neither can be successful without that of the other. So far from himself and Apollos being rivals, Paul maintains that they are *one*. This does not mean that they have not made distinctive contributions. Paul goes on to point out that each has his own responsibility, and will receive his own 'wage' (rather than *reward*) *according to his own labour*. But this is a distinction before God, and not before men. Note that the criterion is not 'his success', but 'his labour'.

9. Three times in this verse the word *God* comes first: 'God's fellow-workers are we; God's husbandry, God's building are you.' The effect is to emphasize strongly the fact that the human instruments do not matter. All is of God, and all belong to God. It is not quite certain that *we are labourers together with God* is the right translation of *Theou gar esmen sunergoi*. It could mean 'fellow-workers with one another in God's service' and this would suit the context very well. Despite the attractiveness of this rendering, however, the translation of AV is probably to be preferred, for it is the more natural way to understand the Greek (cf. Mk. xvi. 20). It is a startling expression, which sets forth in striking fashion the dignity of Christian service. The word *geōrgion*, translated *husbandry*, occurs only here in the New Testament. The word can mean 'field', or the process of cultivation. There is a similar ambiguity about *oikodomē*, *building*, which may signify the edifice or the process of erection. Thus Paul may mean that the Corinthians are the field, the building, in which God is at work. Or he may mean that they are God's work in cultivation and building. Incidentally the metaphor of building is a favourite one with Paul, but it is not found often in the New Testament outside his writings.

e. The foundation and the building (iii. 10–17)

i. The test of good building (iii. 10–15). Paul develops the thought of building. He likens himself to a *wise masterbuilder*, though not without carefully inserting *according to the grace of God which is given unto me*. Grace, *charin*, means more than 'commission' (Moffatt, RSV). It includes the thought of God's enabling power. Paul will say nothing which will obscure the primacy of God and the insignificance of God's ministers. The *masterbuilder*, *architektōn*, was the man who superintended the work of building. Plato differentiates him from the *ergasti-*

kos as one who contributes knowledge rather than labour (see Robertson and Plummer). *Wise* in this context denotes 'skilful'. Paul's work was concerned with *the foundation*; that of . others with building on that foundation. Paul cautions every builder to *take heed how he buildeth*. *Hekastos, every man,* brings out the thought of individual responsibility. Some restrict the application of this passage to the work of teachers. But the words seem capable of more general application. While it is especially true of teachers, it is also true in a measure of every believer that he is engaged in building on the one foundation. Let him take heed how he builds!

The commentators vary as to exactly what is being built. Some, impressed by the emphasis on right teaching, refer the passage to doctrine. Others feel that it applies strictly to the body of believers. Probably neither is completely out of view. It is best, with Lightfoot, to see a reference to 'the Church as the witness of the truth'.

11. There must be no misconception as to the *foundation*. Paul does not wish to give the impression that a man can lay any foundation he chooses, and that it just happens that he had laid the foundation he did. There is only one foundation on which this spiritual edifice may be erected, one *that is laid*. That foundation *is Jesus Christ*. That is basic. No man may begin anywhere else. This is still worthy of emphasis in a day when so many build their 'Christianity' without Christ, on a foundation of good works, or humanism, or science.

12. But if there can be only one foundation it is otherwise with the superstructure. It is all too possible for astonishing varieties to make their appearance here. Paul singles out various materials which may be incorporated into the structure, and sometimes ingenuity has been exercised in trying to find edifying meanings for them all. Such labour is probably vain, for it seems that Paul is concerned simply with two classes, the valuable, typified by *gold, silver,* and *precious stones,* and the worthless, the *wood*, *hay*, and *stubble*. The workman may choose to make the building as worthy of the foundation as is possible. Or he may be content to put into it in slovenly fashion that which costs him nothing. *Precious stones* may be precious stones in our sense of the term, used for ornamentation, or they may be costly building materials, like marble. *Stubble* is what we would call 'straw'.

13. There will come a time of testing for all building. *The day* is not further defined, but clearly it is the day when Christ returns, the day of judgment (cf. 1 Thes. v. 4; Heb. x. 25). That day is often referred to in terms of the believer's joy at being united to his Lord. But the New Testament does not overlook the fact that it will also be a time of judging the work the believer has done. Here the thought is of a searching test, for it can be likened to *fire*. Fire purges out the dross, and leaves behind the pure metal. Here the picture is that of fire sweeping through a building. It consumes the combustible, and leaves what has been well built. *Declare*, *dēlōsei*, signifies 'to show in its true character', 'to reveal for what it is'. The subject of the verb *shall be revealed* is sometimes taken as *work*. It is more likely to be *the day*. The verb is present (giving a greater sense of certainty), and the meaning is 'the day reveals itself (or, 'is revealed') in fire' (cf. Mal. iv. 1). *Of what sort it is* points us to the important truth that it is the quality of the work, not the quantity that counts.

14, 15. The result of the fire of testing is to determine whether or not a man will receive a 'wage' (not so much *a reward* as the wage of the building worker whose work is approved). Cf. Lk. xix. 16–19; Rev. xxii. 12. All those who are here considered are saved. They have built on the one foundation, Jesus Christ. Even of the man whose work is burned up it is said *he himself shall be saved*. The distinction is not between the lost and the saved, but among the saved between those who have built well and those who have built poorly. *He shall suffer loss* means he will lose his *reward*, like a workman fined of his wages for poor workmanship. Being saved *so as by fire* may have been something of a proverbial expression to indicate one who was saved and no more (cf. the brand plucked from the burning of Am. iv. 11; Zc. iii. 2). *By fire* is really 'through fire'. The imagery is that of a man who has to dash through the flames to escape to safety. For a refutation of the view that this passage teaches a doctrine of purgatory see Godet *in loc.* The passage, of course, gives no countenance to such views. It is the fire of judgment of which it speaks, not a fire of purgation.

ii. The temple of God (iii. 16, 17). *Know ye not* is a mild rebuke. It introduces a question on a matter which ought to be common knowledge. Paul uses the device fairly often in this letter. Believers are *the temple of God*, which makes it clear that Paul is addressing the whole church, and not the teachers only. There is no article before *temple* in the Greek, but this does not imply that there are various temples. It simply puts a certain emphasis on their character as God's temple (though Godet renders 'a temple of God' on the grounds that the local church and not the Church universal is in view). There are two Greek words for 'temple', *hieron*, which includes all the temple precincts, and *naos* (used here) which denotes the shrine proper, the sanctuary. The word points us to the very presence of God. This is brought out explicitly with the assertion that the Spirit dwells in the Corinthian believers. *The Spirit of God* is not a common expression. It emphasizes the connection of the Spirit with the Father, and underlines the deity of the Spirit. The Spirit is God as He dwells in the Church. The words of this verse are sometimes applied to the individual believer, but it is vi. 19 which speaks of the individual as God's temple. Here the thought is that of the whole community of believers as God's shrine. *Temple* is singular, but *ye* is plural. The reference is to the Church.

17. The seriousness of the divisions at Corinth is seen in the light of this character of the Church as God's temple. Because it is God's temple the man who fails to react rightly towards it is guilty of no light sin. *Defile* and *destroy* are different translations of the same Greek verb, *phtheirō*. It is important to notice that the verb is repeated, for it shows that the punishment of the offender is not arbitrary; it is according to the manner of the offence. The verb has the twofold meaning of 'corrupt' and 'destroy'. It is the latter meaning which is required here. To engage in divisions is to 'destroy' the divine society, and consequently to invite God to 'destroy' the sinner. The word does not indicate either annihilation or eternal torment. It is not specific. It simply makes it clear that he who commits a grave sin lays himself open to a grave penalty. In verse 15 the bad workman is yet saved. Here a greater crime than inferior workmanship is in mind, and salvation is excluded. *Holy* means something like 'consecrated', 'set apart for God'. In the plural it is the usual New Testament word for the 'saints', those who are God's people. The word emphasizes the character of the Church as God's own possession, so that its 'destruction' is a very serious matter. The final *ye* is emphatic and brings home the character, and hence the responsibility of Paul's readers.

f. The preachers' lowly place (iii. 18–iv. 13)

i. Worldly wisdom is foolishness (iii. 18–23). Paul further rebukes the divisions of the Corinthians by showing the lowly place that the preachers, whom they have set up so high, really occupy. But first he deals with the foolishness of worldly wisdom, a subject which has occupied him already, and which obviously is very important. The things of God are not to be estimated in accordance with the rules of the philosophers.

18. First he calls for realism. It is easy enough to have a wrong view of ourselves, and Paul calls on the Corinthians to beware lest they fall into that error. *Dokei, seemeth,* is better translated 'thinketh'. It is not how a man appears to others that is in question, but what he appears to be to himself. There is an obvious reference to those who thought themselves *wise* in attaching themselves to this or that teacher. In the Greek *among you* immediately precedes *in this world*. The two expressions are in sharp contrast. The believer is both in the Church and in the world. But his relationships to the two are different. *World* is *aiōn*, 'age', with a hint at changing fashions. Paul counsels the man who is *wise in this world* to *become a fool, that he may be wise*. The values of the Christian are simply 'foolishness' to the man of the world (ii. 14). If anyone is to have real spiritual insight he must become what the world calls 'a fool'. The true wisdom is found in renouncing 'the wisdom of this world'.

19. In i. 20 Paul had asked, 'hath not God made foolish the wisdom of this world?' He returns to the thought with the assertion that such wisdom is *foolishness with God*. Throughout the whole of this opening part of the Epistle this is the thought to which he comes back again and again. The worldly wise, whom the Corinthians held in such high esteem, are totally unable to penetrate the divine mysteries. These are open to the humblest man of faith, but are for ever hid from the wise of this world. Their wisdom is nothing but *foolishness* in spiritual matters. Is this Paul's private opinion? Not at all. He quotes Scripture to drive home his point. His first citation is from Jb. v. 13, in a version differing from the LXX. It may be Paul's own translation from the Hebrew. *Panourgia, craftiness,* originally meant a 'readiness to do anything'. From this it developed a meaning rather like our 'cunning'. It could be used in a good sense, or in a bad sense, but the bad sense came to predominate. Paul does not minimize the capacity of the worldly wise within their own field. But he stoutly denies that their *craftiness* is of any avail against the might and the wisdom of God.

20. The second quotation is from Ps. xciv. 11. Whether Paul has substituted *the wise* for 'men' in this passage to bring out the best that the world can do, or whether he is quoting from a manuscript which had this reading we have no means of knowing. His point is that God knows the thoughts of every man. Nothing can be hid from Him. Moreover He knows the emptiness of such thoughts. The word rendered *vain, mataioi*, signifies 'without result', 'fruitless', 'empty'. The wise are unable to effect anything lasting. All their vaunted wisdom is concerned with things which pass away. Their thoughts are vain (Moffatt, 'futile').

21, 22. Paul turns the thoughts of the Corinthians away from the wisdom of men which had meant so much to them, to the far greater treasures that they really possessed in Christ. *Let no man glory* might be rendered 'let no man make his boast'. The Corinthians were ready to pride themselves on their wisdom, and on the teachers to whom they attached themselves. Paul is quite ready to find a place for glorying (cf. i. 31), but he does not find it in *men*. To elevate *men* in the way the Corinthians were doing is to make the biggest of all mistakes, that of elevating the creature. The Christian, by contrast, glories only in the Creator.

However, Paul is not developing his argument in that direction. Rather he is saying, 'Why do you limit yourselves by claiming that you belong to a particular teacher? Do you not realize that all teachers, yea all things that are, belong to you in Christ?' So far from enriching themselves by staking their claim to exclusive rights in one teacher, the Corinthians were impoverishing themselves. They were cutting themselves off from the treasures that were really theirs. Notice that Paul says *all things are your's*, and not simply 'all Christian teachers'. He puts no limit to their possessions in Christ. (Cf. Rom. viii. 32.)

Then he particularizes by referring first of all to the three teachers whose names were bandied about. So far from the teachers being outstanding people at the head of large and influential parties, they belonged to those whose ministers they were ('minister' = 'servant'). Then in a lyrical passage Paul goes on to ascribe to his friends the possession of all things present or to come. *The world, kosmos,* is the physical universe in which we live. It has not the ethical sense which is often associated with the word. Paul's saying, 'to me to live is Christ, and to die is gain' (Phil. i. 21) gives us the clue to his reference to *life* and *death.* Life in Christ is the only life, and the Christian possesses this. To the unbeliever *death* is the end of all things. But Christ has overcome death and for the Christian it is not disaster, but 'gain'. Cf. xv. 55-57 for the believer's song of triumph over death. *Things present* and *things to come* add up to an impressive total. Paul does not mention the past, probably because we were not responsible for it, and we can do nothing about it. But it is otherwise with the present and the future. There the man in Christ looks only for triumph. Paul sums up with *all are your's.*

23. But it does not end there. It is true that the Christian has great possessions in Christ. But these are his only because he is Christ's. It is also true that he has great responsibilities in Christ. *Ye are Christ's,* says Paul, by way of reminding them of these obligations. It is a thought to which he returns (vi. 19f.). Men who belong to Christ ought not to live in carnal fashion. They should let their lives tell forth whose they are. The self-assertiveness of the Corinthians was out of character. They acted as though they were their own masters. They really belonged to Christ.

The passage reaches its climax with *Christ is God's.* We have noted more than once how Paul sets Christ on a position of equality with the Father. He regards the Son as fully divine. This passage does not contradict such teaching, for Paul is not speaking of Christ as He is in His essential nature, but with reference to what He has done for men. Paul does not lose sight of the deity of the Son. But he does not lose sight either of the truth that the Son became man, and took a lowly place that He might bring about man's salvation. The extreme statement of this subordination is found in xv. 28. There, as here, the thought is that the Son did indeed take a place among men when He took upon Him to deliver man. He, too, is God's.

ii. God's commendation is what matters (iv. 1-5). From the glories of the Corinthians Paul turns his attention to the preachers. He is concerned to demonstrate that the judgment of men on ministers (and 'men' will include the partisan Corinthians) is of no importance whatever. To God they stand or fall, and only God is able to give a true judgment on them.

1. Men are to estimate them as *the ministers of Christ*. *Ministers* is not *diakonos* as in iii. 5, but *hupēretēs*, a word which Paul uses here only. It applied originally to an 'under-rower', i.e. one who rowed in the lower bank of oars on a large ship. From this it came to signify service in general, though generally of a lowly kind, often service with the hands. The preachers are also *stewards of the mysteries of God*. A 'steward' (*oikonomos*) was the overseer of an estate. Unless a rich landowner was to be a slave to his slaves he had to depute the routine work of administration. His deputy was called an *oikonomos*. This man had a responsible position. He was set over others and had a big task to discharge. But he was also subject to a master, and must render account of himself. In relation to the master, he was a slave; in relation to the slaves he was an overseer. For *mysteries* see on ii. 7. The sphere of the preachers' responsibility is God's revelation.

2. The Greek opens this verse with 'here', which AV omits. Paul is appealing to well-known contemporary practice with regard to *stewards*. The prime requisite is that they be *faithful*. In the nature of the case the work of an *oikonomos* was not closely supervised. The first essential then was that the steward be trustworthy. This is a principle of importance for all Christians, for, as we see from 1 Pet. iv. 10, all are stewards.

3. Paul thinks of himself not simply as a steward, but as God's steward. His responsibility is to his divine Lord alone (cf. Rom. xiv. 4). He lays it down accordingly that it is a very small matter to him what the Corinthians think of him. Or, for that matter, what anyone else thinks of him. *Be judged* is the verb *anakrinō*, which we saw used in ii. 14f. (where see notes). It does not denote the passing of final judgment, but the process of critical examination with a view to such judgment. Moffatt renders 'cross-question'. Paul is not interested in any preliminary human sifting. He is content to await the Judge. *Man's judgment* is a curious expression meaning literally 'human day'. It is found on an amulet of the second or third century (cited in AG), but as far as I know nowhere else. 'Day' would seem to be used in a way similar to its occurrence in iii. 13, i.e. with respect to a day of judgment. Paul is saying, then, that it matters little to him whether men pass a judgment on him or not.

He takes this to its logical conclusion. He himself is included among mankind, and so he goes on that he does not *judge* himself. It is tremendously difficult to come to an accurate assessment of one's own achievement, and Paul points out that in any case it does not matter. The Christian is to be judged by his Master. His own views on himself are as irrelevant as those of anyone else. This needs emphasis in a day when many are tempted to be introspective. Often they think that they themselves know just what their spiritual state is and just what their service for God has effected. The result may depress unduly or exalt above measure. But it is not our task to pass such judgments. We should get on with the job of serving the Lord. This does not mean that there is no place for times of heart-searching and rigid self-scrutiny with a view to more whole-hearted and more efficient service. It is an attempt to anticipate the judgment of the Lord that Paul is condemning.

4. *By* is used in the old English sense of 'against' (examples are quoted in Robertson and Plummer). Paul is saying that he is not aware of any great matter in which he has failed in his stewardship. But he does not rest his confidence in that. It is not that which brings about his acquittal. *Dedikaiōmai*, translated *justified*, is a legal word which means 'acquitted of a charge', 'declared "not guilty" '. Paul delights to use this word of the believer's standing in the sight of God. Thus 'justification' passes into the technical language of the Christian. However, in this verse it is probably not used in this technical sense, but has its regular legal meaning. Paul's acquittal does not stem from his own estimate of his work. The assessment is made by *the Lord. Judgeth* is *anakrinō* once more. While there is here no emphasis on the preliminary character of the judgment, yet it is in accordance with the meaning of *anakrinō* that the final judgment does not appear until the next verse. *The Lord*, as commonly in Paul, denotes the Lord Jesus.

5. Arising from all this is an exhortation not to *judge* (the usual verb, *krinō*) prematurely. The use of *mē* with the present imperative may imply that the Corinthians had been engaging in this activity. 'Stop judging' would then be the force of it. *Until* is *heōs an* with the subjunctive. This construction indicates that the fact of the coming of the Lord is certain, but the time is unknown. The Lord's judgment will be perfect, for He will uncover *the hidden things of darkness. Darkness* commonly has an ethical significance in the New Testament, and this may accordingly refer to evil deeds. But in this context it seems better to take it of all those deeds which in this present darkness are kept hidden. *The counsels of the hearts* refers rather to men's secret desires and motives, good and evil alike. It is only the Lord's judgment that can take account of secret deeds and motives (cf. Rom. ii. 16). This is the judgment that really counts. The man who is praised then has praise of God, i.e. he has the only praise that matters. *Of, apo*, indicates the finality of the judgment. It comes from God. There can be no appeal from it.

iii. Learn from Paul and Apollos (iv. 6, 7).

This use of the verb translated *transferred, meteschēmatisa*, is unique. The word means 'to change the form of', 'to transform'. It is used of such things as disguising oneself (cf. 2 Cor. xi. 15). Here the meaning is that Paul has done something like using a figure of speech (the corresponding noun, *schēma*, is often used of a rhetorical figure). He has been speaking about the function of ministers, more particularly of himself and Apollos. It might be thought that he was addressing his remarks primarily to such preachers, laying down how they should think of themselves and their work. But this is not so. He has not been concerned to teach Apollos and himself, but the Corinthians. His references to Apollos and himself are simply a literary device. As Phillips renders it, 'I have used myself and Apollos above as an illustration.' Paul's concern for the Corinthians comes out in the affectionate address, *brethren*, and the affirmation that what he has done he has done *for your sakes*.

Paul amplifies this with a statement of his purpose. AV reads smoothly, but it includes a verb (*to think*) which is absent from the better MSS. Paul's expression is something like 'that you might learn in us the "not beyond what is written" '. The words I have placed in inner quotes may themselves be a quotation or a catchword. The use of the article in front of them points to a well-known saying. The 'what is written' employs the formula usually used by Paul in quoting from holy Scripture. But our difficulty is that there is no passage in the Old Testament which runs exactly like this. Accordingly some have suggested a reference to other writings. Parry, on the basis of the papyri, argues for the sense, ' "not to go beyond the terms," i.e. of the commission as teacher'. This is possible. But, in the light of Paul's habit, it is more likely that there is a reference to Scripture, even though no passage is explicitly cited. Paul will be referring to the general sense of the Old Testament, as the rendering of RSV brings out, 'that you may learn by us to live according to scripture'. We may fairly conjecture that 'not beyond what is written' was a catch-cry familiar to Paul and his readers, directing attention to the need for conformity to Scripture. He is saying, then, that by considering what he has had to say about Apollos and himself, they will learn the scriptural idea of the subordination of man. Uniformly the Bible elevates God. The Corinthian emphasis on the persons of teachers meant that they were thinking too highly of men. Paul wants none of them to be *puffed up for one*, i.e. he desires that they have no feelings of pride as they contemplate the particular teacher to whom they have attached themselves. Being *puffed up* in this way in favour of one of them meant that they were *against another*. This is the evil of partisanship. There is a sense in which Christians may rejoice in the leadership given by their eminent men. But when they find themselves so much in favour of one leader that they are against another they have overstepped the bounds. *Puffed up* is a verb which Paul uses frequently in this Epistle (iv. 18, 19, v. 2, viii. 1, xiii. 4), but elsewhere once only. Evidently he regarded it as particularly appropriate to the case of the Corinthians. They, more than others, were addicted to the sin of pride. What is party spirit other than oneself writ large?

7. With the change to the singular, *thee* (incidentally, in an emphatic position), Paul addresses an imaginary Corinthian who has become puffed up. The verb *maketh to differ, diakrinei*, means first, 'to put a difference between', and then, 'to regard as superior'. It is probably the latter use here, 'Who regards you as superior?' The rhetorical question is followed by another which reminds them that man has no native endowment which he did not receive from God, and this by a third which emphasizes the incongruity of a man's boasting about what is, after all, nothing more than a gift that God has given him. It is the point made in the rejection of worldly wisdom all over again. By the standards of the world the Corinthians may have had something of which to boast. But Christians do not accept the standards of the world. They realize that in themselves they are nothing. They owe everything to the grace of God. There is no place at all for worldly activities like boasting.

iv. The trials endured by the apostles (iv. 8–13). Paul turns from his explanation of principles to a setting forth of the lowliness of the apostles as shown by the manifold trials they had to endure. He does this in the form of a contrast between their wretched lot and the comparative ease of the Corinthians. The result is an impassioned and incisive piece of prose. So biting is the irony that some have felt that Paul can hardly be addressing the church as a whole. There is nothing like it elsewhere in this Epistle. He must have in mind the leaders only. This, however, is a precarious inference. There is no indication that Paul is addressing different people in this section. The whole church would hear the letter read, and, in the absence of some mark of a change of addressees, would take it as meant for them all.

8. *Ye are full, kekoresmenoi este,* is a verb used properly of food (e.g. Acts xxvii. 38). It denotes satiation, a feeling of satisfaction. In contrast to Mt. v. 6, 'Blessed are they which do hunger and thirst after righteousness', the Corinthians felt no lack. The next two verbs are probably ingressive aorists: 'you have become rich' and 'you have begun to reign'. Both indicate that the Corinthians felt themselves secure and in want of nothing (a dangerous state; cf. Rev. iii. 17). Moffatt appositely cites the Stoic catch-cry (taught by Diogenes), 'I alone am rich, I alone reign as king.' Far from the Corinthians having progressed in the Christian faith, they were approximating to the Stoic idea of self-sufficiency. Some take *without us* to mean 'without our help'. But, as the second part of the verse makes clear, the thought is 'without our company'. The Corinthians held that they had attained a position to which neither Paul nor the other apostles laid claim. Paul goes so far as to express the wish that they really were in the royal position they imagined. Then perhaps he and the others might be associated with them in this splendour, and thus be benefited by their progress in the faith. *Would to God* is too strong a rendering for *ophelon*. In late Greek this simply expresses a wish. With the construction employed here it is implied that the wish has not been fulfilled. 'Would that you did reign (though in fact you do not)' is the sense of it.

9. This brings us to the actual plight of the apostles. Paul thinks of God as having set them in their position. He is not railing at some cross fate, but quietly accepting what God has done. The repeated reference to the present (down to verse 13) sheds light on the hardships Paul had to endure at Ephesus (cf. xvi. 9 and Acts xix. 23ff.). The verb *set forth, apedeixen*, means a little more than 'showed to be', 'exhibited'. There is the thought that God has made them to be last. He has appointed them to the last place. The imagery is derived from the arena, as Moffatt's rendering brings out, 'God means us apostles to come in at the very end, like doomed gladiators in the arena!' *Epithanatious, appointed to death*, is a rare word, and apparently refers to condemned criminals. Such were often paraded before the public gaze to be objects of derision. Thus Paul speaks of being made *a spectacle* (the word means 'theatre', and so, 'what one sees at a theatre'). The apostles are exhibited on a vast stage, for they are a spectacle *unto the world, and to angels, and to men*. The word *kosmos, world*, is used in its wide sense of 'the universe', here 'the universe of intelligent beings'. The following expressions (without the article in Greek) are then explanatory of this one, 'the world, both angels and men'. The New Testament often thinks of angels as spectators of human happenings. The combination *angels* and *men* embraces the totality of personal existence.

10. What is involved in being made a public spectacle is steadily brought out. The first point is that the apostles are *fools for Christ's sake.* Once again the incompatibility between what the world counts as wisdom and what Christians esteem is in mind. Paul has already more than once referred to this kind of thing. But this time he introduces a rather startling contrast by asserting that the Corinthians are *wise in Christ.* Paul's word for *wise* is different from that used hitherto in this Epistle. The word he now employs may be a means of putting some difference between the Corinthians and the worldly wise whom he has castigated earlier. Paul does not mean, though, that his friends are actually wise, but that they thought they had treasures of wisdom (which Paul could not claim for himself). Similarly, they held themselves to be *strong* and *honourable* (*endoxoi*, 'eminent', 'glorious'), whereas Paul knew himself to be *weak* (cf. ii. 3), and *despised* (*atimoi*, 'without honour'; the word was used of those deprived of citizenship).

11. Dropping comparisons, Paul now concentrates on the hardships suffered by the apostles. He is not thinking of the distant past, but brings things right up to date with *even unto this present hour.* The apostles lacked food and drink and clothing. The reference to hunger is in sharp contrast with the earlier 'ye are full' (verse 8). The apostles were roughly treated. *Buffeted* ('to strike with the fist') is the word used of the ill-treatment accorded Christ (Mt. xxvi. 67). They had no settled abode, but were as vagabonds.

12. Paul several times refers to the fact that he earned his living with his own hands (e.g. 1 Thes. ii. 9; 2 Thes. iii. 8). This is all the more significant in that the Greeks despised all manual labour, thinking of it as fit only for slaves. The word for *labour* is *kopiōmen*, which signifies really hard work, labour to the point of weariness. In the middle of this verse Paul again varies his construction, introducing the thought of the reaction of the apostles to the hardships that came upon them. They were *reviled* (another word used of Christ Himself, 1. Pet. ii. 23), but their response was to *bless*: they were *perse-*

cuted, but simply endured it. We are reminded of our Lord's injunction to His followers (see Lk. vi. 28).

13. The apostles are slandered, but they simply beseech. Such conduct did not commend itself to the Greeks. To them it was evidence of pusillanimity. Throughout this whole passage Paul is concerned to emphasize the contradiction between the values of the Christian, and those of the worldly-wise Greek. He reaches his climax with two points of comparison. He and his fellows are made as *the filth of the world*. Filth, *perikatharmata*, means 'that which is removed as the result of cleansing all round'. It is the refuse after a thorough cleaning. It does not differ greatly from the second epithet, *offscouring, peripsēma*, which is simply a little more precise. It is 'that which is wiped off as the result of rubbing all round'. Because such removal of refuse has the effect of cleansing, both words came to have the derived meaning of 'propitiatory offering', that offering which cleanses men from their sins. It was not applied to sacrifices in general, but to human sacrifices, which had been offered in some places. Yet even so the words did not come to acquire a noble tinge, for the people chosen to be sacrificed were those who could most easily be spared, the meanest and most worthless in the community. Paul's point, then, is that the apostles were regarded as being the vilest of men. His final *unto this day* (lit. 'until now') again brings out the point that his sufferings were no matter of past history. He was detailing the present condition of the apostles. The Corinthians might claim to occupy a splendid place, but Paul was under no illusion as to the place reserved for such as him in this world.

g. A personal appeal (iv. 14-21)

14. Paul's letters are real letters, not systematic theological treatises. They not infrequently contain those abrupt changes of tone and mood (as here) which are characteristic of letters. The apostle's sternness gives way to tenderness. What Paul has said might be understood as being meant to make the Corinthians feel shame. On occasion Paul might have just that intention (vi. 5, xv. 34), but it is not the case here. He has the warmest of feelings towards those he calls *my beloved sons*. His purpose is simply that of warning them. The verb here translated *warn, noutheteō*, conveys the thought of blame for wrongdoing (it is often rendered 'admonish'). But it is criticism in love that is meant, as this verse shows plainly. The cognate noun is used in Eph. vi. 4 of the duty of a father to his children.

15. Paul's affection is brought out in a reference to his unique relationship to the Corinthians. *Paidagōgous*, translated *instructers*, were not teachers, but slaves, who, under the direction of the fathers, superintended the welfare of the children. There is often something of a derogatory air about the term. The *paidagōgos* took the child to school, and generally looked after him. But at best he was a subordinate. He did not belong to the family. Though he might love the child dearly, he was not bound to him by ties of natural affection. The father stood in a different relation altogether. He had begotten the child, and he had the chief care for the child's welfare. By virtue of his activity in founding the church at Corinth Paul stood in the relation of a father in Christ to the believers. This makes two things clear. The one is that his affection for them was, in the nature of things, great. The other is that, no matter how much they had profited from the ministry of others, they owed most of all to Paul, and should therefore heed his injunctions.

16. Thus he can appeal to them to be *followers* (the word means 'imitators') of him. Appeals of this kind are made by Paul more often than we would expect. But he does not wish to attach his followers to himself personally. That would be in contradiction to the whole tenor of this passage. If he wants them to imitate him it is in order that they may learn thus to imitate Christ (cf. xi. 1; 1 Thes. i. 6). While in the different circumstances of today preachers may well hesitate to call others to imitate them, it still remains that if we are to commend our gospel it must be because our lives reveal its power.

17. Not much is known about Timothy's visit to Corinth (see Introduction, pp. 21f.). Clearly Paul felt that trouble was beginning and he sent Timothy to clear it up. This he was to do by reminding them of Paul's *ways which be in Christ*. Once more appeal is made to Paul's example. Nor was Paul counselling something different at Corinth from the practice *every where in every church* (cf. vii. 17, xi. 16, xiv. 33, 36). He made no exceptional demands on the Corinthians. He had said and done the same kind of thing at Corinth as elsewhere. He longed to see the same kind of behaviour there as elsewhere.

18. There were some who set themselves in opposition to Paul, and he accuses them of pride (for *puffed up* see on verse 6). They had evidently tried to bolster up their position with the confident assertion that Paul would not again visit the city. This would have been reinforced by the foregoing statement that Timothy (not Paul) was to visit them. They would say that Paul dared not face them. The Corinthians had nothing to gain from adherence to Paul, and nothing to fear from him either.

19. Paul assures them that such assumptions are groundless. He will come speedily *if the Lord will*. He does not regard himself as a free agent. He is at the Lord's direction, and the Lord might not open up the way for him to go to Corinth at this juncture. But his point is that it is only divine restraint of this kind that would stop him.

There is a characteristic Pauline differentiation between words and deeds at the end of the verse. His opponents at Corinth might produce fair speech, but could they show *power*? Paul often dwells on the fact that the gospel does not simply tell men what they ought to do. In it God gives them power to do it. It is not a question of whether Paul's Corinthian opponents could speak well, but of whether the power of God was manifest in them, 'that spiritual efficacy, with which those are endowed who dispense the word of the Lord with earnestness' (Calvin).

20. *The kingdom of God* is the most frequent topic in the teaching of Jesus. It is not so prominent in the rest of the New Testament, though Paul does mention it from time to time, and most of all in this Epistle (vi. 9, 10, xv. 24, 50). One feature of the Gospel view of the kingdom is that in it is God's power (seen, for example, in the casting out of devils, Lk. xi. 20). It is this aspect which is emphasized here. God's kingdom is not simply good advice. It is not *in word*, 'for how small an affair is it for any one to have skill to prate eloquently, while he has nothing but empty tinkling' (Calvin). Men know what they ought to do. The trouble is that, knowing the good, they do the evil. They need God's power to enable them to live as befits His kingdom. There is probably an intentional contrast with the claims of the Corinthians in verse 8. Here is the true royalty.

21. The question is not whether Paul will come, but how he will come. He puts the issue squarely to them. He could come *with a rod*, i.e. in sternness, ready to chastise and rebuke. Or, he could come *in love, and in the spirit of meekness*. But this assumes that they are ready to receive him as such. The choice rests with the men of Corinth.

III. MORAL LAXITY IN THE CHURCH
(v. 1–vi. 20)

Paul has been speaking of one manifestation of the pride of the Corinthians, and he turns to another. Sexual laxity was rife among first-century Greeks, but from the beginning the

Christian attitude to the prevailing practice and thought was one of uncompromising opposition. However, the Corinthians seem to have thought so much of their emancipation in Christ that they felt they could take a line altogether different from that of other Christians, and one which countenanced even worse evils than did the Greeks in general. It brings forth Paul's stern rebuke.

a. A case of incest (v. 1–13)

i. The fact (v. 1, 2). The beginning is rather abrupt. Paul does not waste time on niceties. His first word, *holōs*, is not well rendered *commonly*. The adverb means 'altogether'. With the negative it is the 'at all' in 'not at all'. Here we have the positive, and probably our nearest equivalent is 'actually'. *Porneia, fornication*, properly denotes the use of a harlot, but it comes to signify any form of sexual evil. *Named* is absent from the better MSS. Paul's point is not that the Gentiles do not talk about this sort of thing, but that they do not do it. Such cases were not unknown among the Gentiles, but they were not common and they were not countenanced. Even those who were notoriously lax in sexual matters reprobated such a union as this. The exact sin meant is not clear. The Corinthians knew the details, so that there was no necessity for Paul to be more explicit. *Have* might mean 'have to wife', or it might mean 'have as concubine'. *His father's wife* probably does not mean 'his mother', else Paul would have said so. But whether it means that the offender had seduced his step-mother, or that she was divorced from his father, or that the father had died, leaving her a widow, is not clear. What is quite clear is that an illicit union of a particularly unsavoury kind had been contracted.

2. In the face of this the attitude of the church has been all wrong. *Puffed up* (see on iv. 6) shows that the Corinthians' view of their own superior standing had governed their behaviour, rather than a due Christian humility. *Epenthēsate,* *mourned,* is often (though not by any means exclusively) used of mourning for the dead. It may accordingly be a way of hinting that the church has been bereaved of a member (cf. Moffatt, 'You ought much rather to be mourning the loss of a member!'). The conjunction *that, hina,* in this context may indicate contemplated result, i.e. what the result of mourning would have been, or it may be equivalent to an imperative, 'Let him . . . be taken away' (so Moffatt, RSV).

ii. The punishment of the offender (v. 3–5). *For* links this with the foregoing, while *I verily* is emphatic. The Corinthians had failed in their duty. But Paul's attitude is in sharp contrast. Those who were present and might have been expected to have taken action had done nothing. He who was absent, and might have pleaded distance as an excuse for inaction, was not to be deterred from taking strong measures. In striking fashion Paul depicts the kind of disciplinary assembly that should have been held. Though *absent in body,* he thought of himself as *present in spirit* (cf. Col. ii. 5). As president of the assembly he has already passed sentence. His verb is in the perfect, which gives an air of finality to the sentence. He does not name the man, but characterizes him from the nature of his deed.

4. Verses 3–5 are one long and difficult sentence in the Greek. We can notice only a few of the difficulties. 'In the name of (i.e. on the authority of) the Lord Jesus' (as the better MSS read) could be taken either with *ye are gathered together,* or with *to deliver such an one.* This solemn formula is more likely to go with the main verb *to deliver,* than with the subordinate verb. We would then have an opening which prepares us for a solemn judicial sentence, but the sentence itself is held back until the end for emphasis. There is a similar ambiguity about the verb with which we should take *with the power of our Lord Jesus.* It might be that the offender is to be delivered *with the power,* but, on the whole, it is more likely that Paul is affirming that they *are gathered together . . . with the power*. He is bringing out the solemn nature of the assembly. It is not only a gathering of a few obscure Corinthians. The apostle is there in spirit, and the Lord Jesus is there in power.

5. *To deliver such an one unto Satan* is an unusual expression. It occurs elsewhere only in 1 Tim. i. 20. It apparently signifies excommunication (see verses 2, 7, 13). The idea underlying this is that outside the Church is the sphere of Satan (Eph. ii. 12; Col. i. 13; 1 Jn. v. 19). To be expelled from the Church of Christ is to be delivered over into that region where Satan holds sway. It is a very forcible expression for the loss of all Christian privileges. It may include also the exercise of some such power as we see at work in Acts v. 1–10, xiii. 8–11. Deissmann argues, on the basis of certain heathen texts, that the words point to 'a solemn act of execration' (LAE, p. 303). More difficult is *for the destruction of the flesh*. It is hard to see how expulsion from the Church could have this effect. Two solutions have won support. The one sees in *the flesh* the lower part of man's nature, and takes the passage to mean the destruction of the sinful lusts. But it is difficult to see how handing a man over to Satan would have such a purifying effect. Rather we would expect the reverse, the stimulation of those lusts. Yet the possibility remains that Paul has in mind the effect on the offender of being severed from all that fellowship in the Church means. The contrast between a present experience of the things of Satan and the nostalgic recollection of the things of God might cause a revulsion of feeling and conduct, the fleshly lusts being destroyed. The other view is that *the flesh* is to be understood as physical, the reference being to sickness and even death. The difficulty is in seeing how this could be effected by excommunication. But in xi. 30 Paul speaks of physical consequences of spiritual failings. In the case of Ananias and Sapphira in Acts v we see the extreme example of this. Paul's own 'thorn in the flesh' was a 'messenger of Satan' (2 Cor. xii. 7). It may well be that Paul envisages the solemn expulsion of this offender as resulting in physical consequences. It is the effect of being withdrawn from the secure realm of the Church of God. On the whole, this second view seems the more likely. Paul conceives of this punishment as remedial. Though *the flesh* be destroyed it is in order that *the spirit may be saved*. That he means saved in the fullest sense is made clear by the addition *in the day of the Lord*. At the final day of judgment he expects to see the disciplined offender among the Lord's people.

iii. Exhortation to cleanse out all evil (v. 6–8). *Glorying* might be rendered 'boasting' (strictly the word applies to the matter of boasting, rather than to the act: 'what you boast about is not good'). It shows that the Corinthians did more than merely acquiesce in the situation. They were proud of their attitude. Paul says bluntly that their boasting is *not good*. He borrows an illustration from the kitchen to show the dangers inherent in their attitude. It requires only a very small quantity of yeast to leaven quite a large lump of dough (cf. Gal. v. 9). This applies in more ways than one. It applies to the Church. By keeping the offender within the fold they were retaining that bad influence which could not but spread and infect many. Moffatt cites Thomas Traherne, 'Souls to souls are like apples, one being rotten rots another.' It applies to the individuals. By their *glorying* they were admitting an evil into their own lives. It would in time work throughout their whole being. Sin must be put away rigorously, else in time the entire Christian life will be corrupted.

7. The metaphor is pursued. Paul calls upon them to 'clean out the old yeast' (the verb rendered *purge* has definitely the idea of cleansing). His point is that the old habits are not only bad ones—they are corrupting. Just like yeast they will work until the whole be permeated. The only thing to do is to get rid of them entirely. So Paul speaks of *a new lump*. The Christian Church is not just the old society patched up. It is radically new. The evil that characterizes worldly men has been taken away, and the apostle can say *ye are unleavened* (Weymouth, 'free from corruption'). He does not say 'You ought to be unleavened', but states a fact. That is what Christians actually are. The implication is that they have no business to be re-introducing the old yeast.

Gar, for, introduces the reason for his confident assertion about their state. *Christ our passover is sacrificed.* It is this that makes all things new for Christians. Christ has put away their sin by His death. He has made them to be *unleavened.* The passover was the annual commemoration of the deliverance from Egypt in ancient time. The Israelites had offered up their lamb or kid in order that the destroying angel might pass over them. They were delivered, and the slave rabble emerged from Egypt as the people of God. In using this imagery Paul reminds his readers that the death of Christ delivered them from deadly peril, and constituted them the people of God. In this context, however, the important thing is the emergence to new life. One feature of current passover observance was the solemn search for and destruction of all leaven before the festival began (for seven days unleavened bread only might be eaten). This purging out of all leaven was done before the *pascha,* the passover victim (either a kid or a lamb), was offered in the temple. But Paul points out that *Christ our passover* has already been sacrificed. It is time and more than time that all leaven was cleansed out.

8. The Christian life is likened to a continual festival (*let us keep* is present continuous). The Christian does not observe this feast according to the standards of the old life he has left. The *old leaven* is linked with *the leaven of malice and wickedness.* The old way of life is characterized by evil things. By contrast the Christian's perpetual festival is kept with *the unleavened bread of sincerity and truth. Sincerity* refers to purity of motive, and *truth* to purity of action. Both are so characteristic of the Christian as to be compared to his necessary food.

iv. A misunderstanding cleared up (v. 9–13). Some have understood *I wrote* as an epistolary aorist, in which case it would refer to the letter being written. But there seems little in favour of this, and it is better to see a reference to an earlier letter, now lost (see Introduction, p. 21). The verb *to company* is an expressive double compound found in the New Testament only in this passage and in 2 Thes. iii. 14.[1] The meaning is 'to mix up yourself with'. Paul had forbidden them to have familiar intercourse with sexual offenders of any kind.

But his directions in the earlier letter had been misunderstood or misrepresented. He had not meant that they were to have no contact whatever with this world's evil men, for that would necessitate leaving the world. *Not altogether* means 'not in all circumstances'. Circumstances would arise in which they must meet with gross sinners. He extends the list to include others than *fornicators*. The *covetous, pleonektai*, are those possessed by the desire to have more, the spirit of self-aggrandisement. From the spirit Paul passes to the deed. *Extortioners, harpages*, are those who seize something, i.e. robbers in any shape or form. These two are lumped together as one class, the two nouns being joined under a single article and linked by *kai*, while they are separated from the others by *ē*. These sinners have a wrong relation to man, and Paul includes *idolaters*, who have a wrong relation to God. Such evil men abound. It is impossible to live without having some contact with them. Paul had not meant to censure that.

11. There is a rather stronger case for thinking that *I have written* here is an epistolary aorist than was the case in verse 9. Yet it is not likely that Paul would use the same expression twice in different senses so soon and in such close connection. Even the *now* does not require this. The sense will be 'But now (you see) I wrote. . . .' His point had been that they must not maintain intimate fellowship (*to keep company* is the same pic-

[1]See the author's note on this verse in his commentary on 1 and 2 Thessalonians, Tyndale Press, 1956, p. 149.

turesque word as in verse 9) with one who professes to be a Christian (*that is called a brother*), but denies his profession by his manner of life. He is not really *a brother*, but *a fornicator* or the like. To the evils castigated in the previous verse Paul adds two more. A *railer, loidoros*, is one who abuses others (cf. Mt. v. 22). That such men should be found in the Christian Church indicates the background of some of the early converts. Small wonder that they found it difficult to enter all at once into the fulness of Christian experience. But Paul will not compromise for a moment. If they continue in such practices believers are to have no social intercourse with them at all. *No not to eat* will refer primarily to ordinary meals, and not to Holy Communion, though that, too, would be forbidden. When we reflect that our Lord ate with publicans and sinners, and that Paul regards it as permissible to accept invitations to eat in heathen homes (x. 27), the detailed application of this injunction is not easy. But the principle is plain. There is to be no close fellowship with anyone who claims to be a Christian, but whose life belies his profession.

12. There is a difference between those within and those outside the church. Paul makes it clear that it is not his function to act as judge of outsiders. In the next verse he goes on to say that it is God who is their judge. But it is a different matter altogether in the case of those within the church. Paul does not say that he should judge them, but *ye*, the Corinthians. It was their responsibility to take action in connection with their own members. The question form, *do not ye . . .?* is a way of making their duty in the matter even more plain.

13. If verse 12 insists on the necessity for the church to discipline its members, this verse limits the scope of such activity. It is no part of the church's function to discipline those who are not members. Them *God judgeth*. But Paul makes this the occasion for a final injunction to *put away . . . that wicked person* (cf. Dt. xvii. 7, etc.). They are to expel the offender, and leave him to God's judgment, he having now become one of *them that are without*.

The application of all this to the modern scene is not easy. Our different circumstances must be taken into account. But Paul's main point, that the church must not tolerate the presence of evil in its midst, is clearly of permanent relevance.

b. Lawsuits (vi. 1-11)

The reference to judgment brings Paul to a related matter. Some of the Corinthians were going to law with one another. He rebukes them for this (1-6), then for actually defrauding one another (7-8), and goes on to speak of the kind of contact which excludes men from the kingdom of God (9-11).

1. Paul recognizes that disputes between brethren will occur. But the first point he makes, with the use of a rhetorical question, is that when a dispute arises it should be settled within the brotherhood. Hodge cites the Rabbinical maxim: 'It is a statute which binds all Israelites, that if one Israelite has a cause against another, it must not be prosecuted before the Gentiles.' The Corinthians did not reach even the Jewish standard. The expression *having a matter against, pragma echōn pros*, is frequent in the papyri in the sense of a lawsuit. *The unjust* (or 'unrighteous'; in Greek one word does duty for both ideas) does not necessarily indicate that the courts at Corinth were corrupt. It is a term applied to all outside the Church. They did not regulate their thinking and living by the law of God. They were not 'justified', therefore 'not just'. Paul's complaint is not that the believers would not obtain justice in heathen courts, but that they had no business to appear there at all.

2. Further rhetorical questions remind them that *the saints* will assist in the final judgment of *the world*. This goes back to the teaching of our Lord, who associated the Twelve with Him in judgment (Mt. xix. 28; Lk. xxii. 28ff.; cf. also Dn. vii. 22).

There is no record of His having said that all believers (*the saints*) would share in this, but Paul appeals to it as a well-known fact. The reference to angels in verse 3 shows that *the world* has the same wide sense as in iv. 9, 'the entire universe of intelligent beings'. Some have felt that *judge* is to be taken in the Hebraic sense of 'rule'. This is possible, but the context is concerned with lawsuits, not government. The word rendered *matters*, *kritērion*, is different from that used in the previous verse. It denotes properly the instrument or means of judging, the rules by which one judges. It comes to signify the place of judging, and perhaps the panel of judges (Jas. ii. 6). The sense 'tribunal', 'court of justice' is common in the papyri (see MM). Here the sense will be, 'are you unworthy to judge in the least important courts?'

3. The rhetorical questions continue. *Angels* is without the article, which has the force of directing attention to their character or quality. They are by nature the highest class of created beings. Yet the saints will judge them. Accordingly the Corinthians should have known that they were capable of judging *things that pertain to this life*. This expression is the translation of one Greek word, *biōtika*. It points to the ordinary things of common life. *How much more, mētige*, is a strong expression (occurring only here in the New Testament). The conclusion is inescapable.

4. The if-construction (*ean* with the subjunctive; contrast *ei* with the indicative in verse 2) carries a delicate implication that such lawsuits should not arise. *Judgments* is the word rendered 'matters' in verse 2 (where see note). It may be that the sense of it here is 'lawsuits'. AG, on the basis of two inscriptions, accept this meaning, both here and in verse 2. This gives a better sense. But it is more in accordance with the usage of the word to take it in the sense of 'courts'. *Set them to judge* will mean 'If it is needed to have judgments on earthly things, set up the least of you, those who pass for the least intelligent: they will be good enough for this want' (Godet). But the verb is not necessarily an imperative. The words may be taken as a statement, 'you set them . . .', or as a question (as RV), 'do ye set them. . . .?' A decision is difficult. With hesitation I incline to RV. *Who are least esteemed, exouthenēmenous,* is a strong expression. In i. 28 it is rendered 'despised'. In accepting the standards of Christ Christians have deliberately set aside the standards of the world. These standards are nothing. Those who judge by them are nothing. Cf. Weymouth, 'men who are absolutely nothing in the Church—is it *they* whom you make your judges?'

5. In iv. 14 Paul made the point that he was not writing to shame his readers. But so strongly does he now feel that he does wish to move them to shame. When he dealt with the subject of wisdom early in the Epistle it appeared that the Corinthians had rather prided themselves on their wisdom. But now the apostle can ask whether they have even one *wise man* among them. *To judge* is an aorist infinitive with the meaning 'to give a decision' (rather than 'conduct a trial'). The word implies not litigation, but 'an amicable settlement by means of arbitration' (Grosheide). *Between his brethren* is actually a singular, 'between his brother'. We must supply 'and another', so that AV gives the sense of it.

6. A string of argumentative questions is typical of Paul's style, and this verse may be another in the chain, 'Does brother go to law, etc.?' The question is broken with *and that.* It is extraordinary that brother should want to go to law with brother at all. If he did, it was even more extraordinary that he should do so before *unbelievers.* This last word is without the article in Greek. It is their quality as lacking faith to which Paul draws attention.

7. *Now, ēdē,* means 'already'. *Fault, hēttēma,* is 'a worsening'. We should probably take it here as 'a defeat', as some of the early Fathers held. Paul's point is that to go to law with a brother is already to incur defeat, whatever the result of the legal process. *Because ye go to law one with another* might be rendered 'because you get judgments (*krimata*) among yourselves'. The gaining of the verdict signifies little. The cause is already lost when a Christian institutes a lawsuit. The injurious effects are implied in the pronoun 'yourselves'. Injury is to the body of Christ, not to outsiders. More biting questions drive home the point that a real victory might be obtained rather by choosing to *take wrong*, to *be defrauded*. Jesus had counselled His followers to turn the other cheek (Mt. v. 39). When they were sued at law for their coat He said they should yield up their cloke also (Mt. v. 40). But the Corinthians were far from basic Christian principles.

8. Indeed they were farther away even than all this implied. Not only were they not ready to suffer wrong, but Paul makes the accusation that they were actively doing wrong to others. They were defrauding them. Sharp practice is usual in society at large, but it should have no place among Christians. The addition, *and that your brethren*, does not imply that the sin was not very serious when committed against unbelievers. The sin is castigated against whomsoever committed. But it is the consistent New Testament teaching that in addition to that Christian love which the believer should exercise toward all men, there is a special 'love of the brethren'. Those in Christ should have a special care for one another. The Corinthians were committing a double sin. They were sinning against ethical standards, and they were sinning against brotherly love.

9. As in verses 2, 3, Paul appeals to what is common knowledge. *Unrighteous* is without the article in the Greek, the stress being on the character of these people, and not on the unrighteous as a class. People of this kind are excluded from the kingdom. The word-order brings the word *God* immediately after *unrighteous,* thus heightening the contrast. Unrighteous people cannot be expected in that kingdom which is *the kingdom of God. Klēronomeō, inherit,* as often in the New Testament, is not used in the strict sense, but with the wider meaning, 'enter into full possession of', without reference to the means. Paul goes on to particularize various forms of evil which are incompatible with the kingdom. *Fornicators* is the general term covering all forms of sexual sin (see on v. 1 for the cognate noun, 'fornication'). *Adulterers* are those specifically who violate the marriage bed. *Malakoi, effeminate,* means basically 'soft'. It comes to have the derogatory meaning of our translation. This part of the list gives prominence to those who sin against themselves by practising sexual vice. The inclusion of *idolaters* may point us to the immorality of much heathen worship of the day.

10. The second part of the list puts the emphasis on sins against others. *Thieves, kleptai,* are petty pilferers, sneak-thieves, rather than brigands. For *covetous* and *extortioners* see the notes on v. 10, and for *revilers* on v. 11 (the singular of which is there translated 'railer'). Once again Paul stresses that people who practise such vices will have no part in the kingdom of God.

11. The tremendous revolution brought about by the early preaching of the gospel is implied in the quiet words, *and such* (actually a little stronger, 'these') *were some of you.* It was no promising material that confronted the early preachers, but people whose values were exactly the opposite of those of Christ. It had required the mighty power of the Spirit of God to turn people like that away from their sins, and to make them members of Christ's Church. Three times Paul uses the strong adversative *alla, but,* to stress the contrast between the old life that they had left, and their experience in Christ. The verb *apelousasthe, ye are washed,* is in the middle voice, with a force something like 'you got yourselves washed' (as in Acts xxii. 16). Many commentators see a reference to baptism. This may be so, though there is nothing in the context to indicate it. The word may signify the kind of washing we see in Rev. i. 5, 'unto him that . . . washed us from our sins in his own blood'. The prefix *apo* points to the complete washing 'away' of sins. The tense is past, the aorist referring to a decisive action. *Ye are sanctified* is the same tense. They had been set apart to be God's. They had been the recipients of sanctifying power. *Ye are justified*, the third of the trio, is another aorist. It looks back to the time when they were accepted as just before God. The verb means 'to reckon as righteous', 'to declare righteous'. It is a legal term, used of the acquitted. Paul uses it for the act of God whereby, on the basis of Christ's atoning death, He declares believers to be just, and accepts them as His own. It is curious that this reference follows that to sanctification. It may be that Paul felt that sanctification required special stress. Or perhaps the point is that after sanctification has reminded them of the character implicit in Christian profession, justification stresses the divine action. The God who has justified them will surely provide them with the power needed to carry through their sanctification. Calvin maintained that all three terms refer to the same thing, though from different aspects.

The *name* brings before us all that is implied in the character of the Lord, while the full title, 'the Lord Jesus Christ' (so the better MSS) brings out the dignity of Him whom we serve. To this is joined *the Spirit of our God*. There is a power manifest in Christian living, and that power is not human. It is a divine power, given by the very Spirit of God Himself.

c. Fornication (vi. 12–20)

From lawsuits Paul turns to sexual laxity. He has already spoken of a specific case of incest (chapter v). Now he deals with the general principle. He does this in two stages. In the first (12–14) he shows that the Christian's bodily life is determined by what God has done for him. In the second (15–20) he applies this to the specific evil of sexual sin.

12. He first lays down the principle of Christian liberty, *all things are lawful unto me* (repeated in x. 23). The way he introduces this makes it seem as though the Corinthians had used the maxim to justify their conduct. Possibly they had derived it from Paul's teaching when he was among them. At any rate, Paul accepts it. Other religions prescribed rules which men must keep if they would be saved. Food laws were especially common. The abstaining from all unlawful things was a necessary part of attaining salvation. Not so with Christianity. The believer will avoid evil and unhelpful things, but this does not earn his salvation. Salvation is all of grace. It depends on what God has done in Christ. The believer is not hedged around with a multitude of restrictions. All things are lawful for him.

But if it is true that the Christian is not inhibited it is also true that he is not unmindful of moral issues: *all things are not expedient* ('helpful' or 'advisable'). There are some things which are not expressly forbidden, but whose results are such as to rule them out for the believer. A second reason for the exercise of caution in using Christian freedom Paul gives in the words, *I will not be brought under the power of any.* There is a play on words which Edwards renders (following Chrysostom), 'All things are in my power, but I shall not be overpowered by anything.' There is some emphasis on 'not I'. Paul would not allow himself to come under the sway of anyone or anything. How could he when he was 'the slave of Christ' (Rom. i. 1, etc.)? There is a danger that in claiming his Christian freedom a man may bring himself into bondage to the things he does.

13. *Meats for the belly, and the belly for meats* may be another expression used by the Corinthians. Eating is a natural function, and they apparently implied that one bodily function is much like another. Fornication is as natural as eating. Paul repudiates this with decision. The belly and food are transient. In due time God will do away with both. For

destroy see on i. 28. Both food and belly will be brought to
nothing. But the body is not destined to be destroyed. It is to
be transformed and glorified (Phil. iii. 21). There is no such
connection between *the body* and sensual lusts as between *the
belly* and food. Rather the connection is between *the body* and
the Lord. God did not design *the body* for *fornication* as He did
the belly for food. There has been much recent discussion of the
Pauline concept of the body. Most agree that whereas the
word *sarx*, 'flesh', expressed for Paul thoughts like those of man
in his weakness, his sin and his fallen estate, *sōma*, 'body', is
rather the whole personality, man as a person meant for God.
'While *sarx* stands for man, in the solidarity of creation, in his
distance from God, *sōma* stands for man, in the solidarity of
creation, as made for God.'[1] The body cannot be disregarded
as unimportant. The body is *for the Lord*. It is the instrument
wherein a man serves God. It is the means whereby he glorifies
God. *The Lord for the body* brings the thought that just as
food is necessary if the belly is to function, so is the Lord
necessary if the body is to function. It is only as God enables
that we can live the kind of bodily life for which we were
meant.

14. The resurrection dominated early Christian thinking, as
we see from the early chapters of the Acts, and, indeed, from
the whole New Testament. That the Father raised the Son
from the dead, and did not simply cause His soul to persist
through bodily dissolution, indicates something of the dignity
of the body. Bodily life enshrines permanent values. The
resurrection forbids us to take the body lightly. Here, as
usually in the New Testament, the resurrection is attributed
to the action of the Father, though occasionally we read of
Jesus rising. Closely connected is the future resurrection of
believers (note the *both* . . . *and*). Paul is to deal with this
question at greater length in chapter xv. Here it is enough
for him to draw attention to the fact of the resurrection as

[1] J. A. T. Robinson, *The Body*, London, 1952, p. 31.

indicating the importance of the body. If it is to be raised, it must not be disregarded as though it were to be destroyed. That this is due to the divine initiative is stressed in the reference to *his own power*. Notice the exact correspondence. Meats are for the belly and the belly for meats, and the destiny of both is destruction. The body is for the Lord and the Lord for the body, and resurrection is postulated of both.

15. As he has already done three times in this chapter, Paul employs the formula *know ye not?* to appeal to a matter of common knowledge. *Melē, members,* is the ordinary word for parts of the body (cf. its use in a similar sense in Rom. vi. 13ff.). Elsewhere the thought of the Church as the body of Christ is more fully developed (xii. 12ff.; Eph. v. 23ff.). For Paul believers are united to Christ in the closest fashion. They are 'in Christ'. They are members of His body. It is this which makes sexual vice so abhorrent. The word rendered *take, airō*, means 'take away'. The horrible thing about this sin is that *the members of Christ* are taken away from their proper use. They are taken away from their proper Lord. They are made *the members of an harlot*. The sinner is, of course, not a *member of an harlot* in the same sense as he is a *member of Christ*. But for Paul the sexual union is such an intimate union as virtually to make one body out of the two (see next verse). Thus there is a horrible profanation of that which should be used only for Christ. Paul recoils from this with an emphatic *God forbid*. This is a paraphrase of *mē genoito*, 'may it not be'. All but one of the New Testament occurrences of this expression are in the Pauline writings, though this is the only example in this Epistle. It is a strong repudiation of the suggestion that has been made. Paul will have nothing to do with it. 'Perish the thought.'

16. Once again Paul appeals to that which is common knowledge. The view he expounds of the nature of the sexual act was no private opinion, but one known and accepted by the Corinthians (*know ye not?*). The basis for the idea is in Gn. ii. 24. Paul understands the words *for two . . . shall be one flesh* (used there of man and wife) to signify the sexual act. This being so, any man who unites with a prostitute by that act becomes one with her. The Corinthians had not realized the implications of their view of sexual laxity. Paul drives home his point with this combination of an appeal to Scripture and to well-known fact.

17. He uses the same strong word, *kollōmenos*, for *joined*. The verb is used of close bonds of various kinds. In the literal sense it refers to the process of glueing. It comes to have metaphorical meanings, but clearly it points to a very close tie. In the previous verse Paul had thought of the physical bond, in the union with a harlot. Now he employs the same word for the spiritual tie which links the true believer to the Lord. Those who share the sexual act become 'one body'. Those joined by the spiritual tie become 'one spirit'. The believer is one with his Lord. He has 'the mind of Christ' (ii. 16). He will react the way the Lord would react.

18. *Flee fornication*, says Paul. The present imperative indicates the habitual action, 'Make it your habit to flee'. That is the only way to treat it. It cannot be satisfactorily dealt with by any less drastic measures. The Christian must not temporize with it, but flee the very thought. Paul goes on to develop the idea that this sin strikes at the very roots of a man's being. He does not say that this is the most serious of all sins. But its relation to the body is unique. Other sins will occur to us which have their effects on the body. But this sin, and this sin only, means that a man takes that body which is 'a member of Christ' and puts it into a union which 'blasts his own body' (Way). Other sins against the body, e.g. drunkenness or gluttony, involve the use of that which comes from without the body. The sexual appetite rises from within. They serve other purposes, e.g. conviviality. This has no other purpose than the gratification of the lusts. They are sinful in the excess. This is sinful in itself. And fornication involves a man in what Godet calls 'a degrading physical solidarity, incompatible with the believer's spiritual solidarity with Christ'. The sexual sinner sins *against his own body*. It is worth noting the interpretation suggested by Moule[1], that 'every sin that a man doeth is without the body' is the slogan of some of the Corinthians, meaning 'physical lust cannot touch the secure "personality" of the initiated'. To this Paul retorts: 'on the contrary: anyone who commits fornication *is* committing an offence against his very "personality".' The use of *hamartēma* for *sin*, rather than the more usual *hamartia*, puts the emphasis on the result, rather than the act.

19. For the sixth time in this chapter Paul drives home his appeal to what the Corinthians know so well with his argumentative question, *know ye not?* In iii. 16 he had referred to the Church as a whole as God's temple. Here *body* is singular. Each Christian is a *temple* in which God dwells. The word is *naos*, referring to the sacred shrine, the sanctuary, not *hieron*, which includes the entire precincts. This gives a dignity to the whole of life, such as nothing else could do. Wherever we go we are the bearers of the Holy Ghost, the temples in which it pleases God to dwell. This must rule out all such conduct as is not appropriate to the temple of God. Its application to the sin of fornication with which Paul has been dealing is obvious, but the principle is of far wider application. Nothing that would be amiss in God's temple is seemly in the body of the child of God.

This verse sheds light on the way the Spirit was regarded by Paul. Clearly he viewed the Spirit as divine in the fullest sense. The *temple* is the place where God dwells. That is its distinguishing characteristic. But the One who dwells in this *temple* is the Spirit. This is brought out also in the expression *which ye have of God*. The Spirit in man is the gift of God,

[1] *Idiom Book*, pp. 196f.

not the result of some man-induced experience. The last thought in this verse is that *the temple* belongs to God. Because he is God's temple, the believer cannot think of himself as independent, as belonging to himself.

20. The basic reason for the previous statement is now given. *Ye are bought with a price* (Goodspeed, 'you have been bought and paid for'). The verb is in the aorist tense, that is, it points to a single decisive action in time past. Paul does not mention the occasion or the price, but there is no need. We are immediately reminded of One who, on Calvary, gave His perfect life that sinners might be purchased. The imagery is that of redemption, probably of sacral manumission. By this process a slave would save the price of his freedom, pay it into the temple treasury, and then be purchased by the god. Technically he was the slave of the god. As far as men were concerned he was a free man. Paul applies this imagery to the dealings of Christ with men. Deissmann tells us that his words here are 'the very formula of the records' (LAE, p. 324). The price paid to purchase us from the slavery to sin (cf. Jn. viii. 34) was no pious fiction, but the very heavy price of the death of the Lord. The result is to bring us into a sphere where, as far as men are concerned, we are free (cf. 'all things are lawful unto me', verse 12). But we are God's slaves. We belong to Him. He has bought us to be His own.

The obligation resting upon believers as a consequence is that they should *glorify God*. Here we have the positive, where in 'flee fornication' we had the negative. The prime motive in the service of the Christian must be not the accomplishing of purposes which seem to him to be desirable, but the glory of God. All the words after *body* are absent from the better MSS. They express a true thought, but they form no part of the true text. At this point Paul is not concerned with the spirit of man (though that, as well as the body, belongs to God). His whole discussion centres on the use that should be made of the body. It is God's temple. It must be used solely for

God's glory. The particle *dē*, rendered *therefore*, is a shortened form of *ēdē*, which means 'already'. *Dē* is sometimes added to an imperative to give it a note of greater urgency. 'Do it so speedily that it is already done!' The use of the aorist, rather than the present imperative, accords with this. Paul does not want the command to glorify God to be taken as something that does not matter. There is an urgency about it. Let there be no delay in obeying.

IV. MARRIAGE (vii. 1-40)

a. The general principle (vii. 1-7)

Paul turns to the specific subjects on which the Corinthians had written to him. The first is marriage. In estimating what he says the situation must be borne in mind. There was in antiquity a widespread admiration for ascetic practices, including celibacy. Some, at least, of the Corinthians shared in this. Paul makes every concession to their point of view. He agrees that celibacy is 'good' and he points out some of its advantages. But he regards marriage as normal. From xi. 11 we see that, though there are some advantages in celibacy, there is a greater completeness in marriage. Celibacy requires a special gift from God. Paul remembers the stresses of living the Christian life in Corinth, with its constant pressure from the low standards of pagan sexual morality. He bears in mind the current emergency ('the present distress', verse 26; cf. verses 29f.). Though he himself prefers celibacy his advocacy of that state is very moderate. He does not command a celibate life for all who can sustain it. He never says that celibacy is morally superior to marriage. He regards marriage as the norm, but recognizes that there are some, to whom God has given a special gift, who should remain unmarried.

1. It is *good* (not 'necessary', nor 'morally better') for a man *not to touch a woman*. In this context *touch* refers to marriage. Paul's view is that the unmarried are free to serve God without the cares attendant on the married state (32ff.). But this does not imply that the married state is not also *good*. Our Lord commanded the rich young ruler to sell all that he had, but this does not imply that all ownership of goods is an evil.

2. The general rule is that men be married. The reasoning runs thus: Celibacy, as you say, is good. But temptation abounds. It is inevitable. The right solution is for *every man* to be married. *Let every man have* is not a permission. It is a command. There will be exceptions (verse 7), but Paul leaves no doubt as to what is normal. *Fornication* was rife at Corinth (the word is plural, pointing to many immoral acts). This made it harder for the unmarried to remain chaste. Harder, too, for them to persuade others that they were, in fact, chaste. Some have suggested that Paul here gives expression to a low view of marriage. The answer is that he is not expounding his view of the married state (cf. Eph. v. 28ff.), but dealing with a specific question in the light of an actual historical situation. Cf. Calvin: 'the question is not as to the reasons for which marriage has been instituted, but as to the persons for whom it is necessary.'

3. Marriage has its obligations. Paul reminds them that each partner has rights. The meaning of *tēn opheilēn* is not *due benevolence* (which rests on an inferior reading) but 'the debt'. Paul calls on each to pay what is due. Each owes duties to the other. Paul enjoins them to pay what they owe. He does not stress the duty of either partner at the expense of the other, but puts them on a level. The present imperative, *render*, indicates the habitual duty.

4. This is made more explicit. *Hath not power* translates a verb, *ouk exousiazei*, which means to exercise a full authority (cf. Lk. xxii. 25, 'they that exercise authority'). Neither wives nor husbands have the right to use their bodies completely as they will. They have obligations to each other. In view of the widespread exaltation of celibacy Paul's recognition of the indispensability of the sexual act in marriage is all the more noteworthy.

5. There may arise occasions when the partners to a marriage agree to abstain for a time from normal intercourse in order to give themselves the more wholeheartedly to *prayer* (*fasting* is absent from the better MSS). But this is clearly exceptional. Normally each belongs to the other so fully that Paul can call the withholding of the body an act of 'fraud'. *That ye may give yourselves* (*hina scholasōte*; we get our word 'school' from this verb) is literally 'that you may have leisure for'. Prayer must be unhurried. In the rush of life it may be necessary sometimes to take exceptional measures to secure a quiet, leisurely intercourse with God. But for married people the breaking off of normal relations even for such a holy purpose can be only by mutual consent. Then they must *come together again*. Otherwise, on account of their natural passions, they place themselves at Satan's mercy.

6. *This* will refer, not to the last provision, but to the whole of the foregoing, with its acceptance of marriage. Marriage is not a duty required of all. What has been said has been *by permission* (*sungnōmēn*, 'an opinion with', i.e., a concession as a result of fellow-feeling), *and not of commandment*. Paul has laid down the duties of all who are married, but he does not lay it down as a duty that all should be married.

7. Paul's own preference is that men should be celibate. In that state they serve the Lord without the distractions involved in marriage (32ff.). But *even as I myself* is emphatic. Paul had a number of special gifts (*charismata*), one of which enabled him to remain unmarried. He recognizes that continence is a special divine gift. Those who have not received it should not try to remain unmarried. Each has *his proper gift of God*. The question of marriage cannot be decided by applying one law to all. Each must consider what is God's will for him. And marriage, just as much as celibacy, is a gift from God.

b. The unmarried and the widow (vii. 8, 9)

8. Having laid down the general principle Paul now proceeds to deal with specific classes. He begins with those who have no marriage tie, whether *unmarried* or *widows*. Some have thought that the former term means 'unmarried men', others that it signifies 'widowers'. The reasoning in both cases is that it is set over against *widows*. This does not carry conviction. *Unmarried, agamois,* is a broad term. It includes all not bound by the married state. One group, the *widows*, is singled out for special mention (cf. 'and Peter', Mk. xvi. 7), perhaps because of the particular vulnerability of their position, and the consequent temptation to re-marry. Paul maintains that it is well for all such to remain as they are, just as he himself does.

9. But this depends on their having the gift of continence. If God has not given them this gift they are to marry. *Let them marry* is a command, not a permission. There is no advantage in celibacy if it means only that one is to *burn* (i.e. with sexual desire). Paul does not regard the suppression of sexual desire as itself meritorious, as some later writers have held.

c. The married (vii. 10, 11)

10, 11. To the *married* Paul is able to give an authoritative *command* (*parangellō*; see notes on I Thes. iv. 2, 11[1]). He stresses that this is not a personal direction. It is *the Lord* who commands (cf. Mt. xix. 6). The case envisaged is that of marriages where both partners are Christians. Paul directs the wife not to *depart* (the verb is passive, 'not to be separated'; MM say that in the papyri it 'has almost become a technical term in connexion with divorce'). *But and if she depart* ('be separated') envisages the possibility of disobedience to this injunction (or

[1]*Op. cit.,* pp. 73, 82.

perhaps of the action of the husband). The separated wife must then remain as she is, or else *be reconciled to her husband*. Similarly, the husband is not to divorce his wife. The verb *put away* is different from that used of the wife, but the result is the same. Paul does not mention the exception allowed by Christ on the grounds of fornication (Mt. v. 32, xix. 9). But he is not writing a systematic treatise on divorce. He is answering specific questions.

d. The Christian married to an unbeliever willing to live with the believer (vii. 12–14)

12, 13. It is noteworthy that Paul gives these directions under the heading, *speak I, not the Lord*. He does not mean, of course, that this is contrary to what the Lord would have ordered. But in verse 10 he had been able to quote an express command of Christ to suit the situation. On this occasion he has no such express command, and he makes the situation clear. He gives his direction without quoting Christ. But he does not think that what he says is unauthoritative. On the contrary, he ends the chapter by assuring his readers that he believes he has the Spirit of God. Moffatt points out that Paul's careful discrimination between a saying of the Lord and his own injunction tells strongly against those who maintain that the early Church was in the habit of producing the sayings it needed and then ascribing them to Christ. 'It is historically of high importance that he did not feel at liberty to create a saying of Jesus, even when, as here, it would have been highly convenient in order to settle a disputed point of Christian behaviour.'

The rest must indicate those not bound in ties of Christian marriage. Otherwise all the cases have been dealt with, the unmarried, the widows, and the married. But some were married before they became Christians (Paul does not envisage believers marrying unbelievers; they will marry 'only in the Lord', verse 39). Paul regards unions entered into as pagans as being on a footing different from those entered into as Christians. Here everything hinges on the attitude of the pagan partner. If the unbelieving wife *be pleased* (*suneudokei*, 'agrees with him') to continue the marriage, the *brother* (almost a technical term for a Christian) is not to divorce her. In exactly similar language Paul instructs the believing woman married to an unbelieving husband not to divorce him, if he is agreeable to the marriage being sustained.

14. Now comes a reason for the procedure Paul has outlined. Believers are 'saints'. They have been set apart for God (see on i. 2). The basic thought in *sanctified* is that of relation to God, not that of moral uprightness (though this should follow). The believer's state of being set apart for God is not diminished because, before believing, he had contracted a marriage with a continuing heathen. Rather, the good prevailing against the evil, his sanctification in some way covers his wife. It is not possible to give precise definition of what this signifies. But it is a scriptural principle that the blessings arising from fellowship with God are not confined to the immediate recipients, but extend to others (e.g. Gn. xv. 18, xvii. 7, xviii. 26ff.; 1 Ki. xv. 4; Is. xxxvii. 4). Paul teaches that the sanctification of the believing partner extends to the unbeliever. He reinforces this by citing the position of the children of the marriage. If the believer's sanctification extended no further than himself, his children would be *unclean*. The word is used of ceremonial uncleanness, 'that which may not be brought into contact with the divinity' (AG). This is an unthinkable position. Clearly Paul regards *now are they holy* as an axiom. Until he is old enough to take the responsibility upon himself, the child of a believing parent is to be regarded as Christian. The parent's 'holiness' extends to the child.

e. The Christian married to an unbeliever not willing to live with the believer (vii. 15, 16)

15. The case is different if the unbeliever is unwilling to continue the marriage. *Depart* is in the middle voice, 'take himself off'. It is the verb used in verses 10f. of the wife being separated from her husband. If the unbeliever takes the initiative in this way, then the believer *is not under bondage*. This seems to mean that the deserted partner is free to remarry.

But God hath called us to peace probably refers to the whole of the treatment of mixed marriages, and not simply to the last clause. Paul's point is that the believer is called by God into a state when *peace* in the widest sense is his concern. In this whole matter of mixed marriages the line should be followed which conduces to peace. In some cases it will mean living with the heathen partner, in some cases it will mean accepting the heathen partner's decision that the marriage is at an end. But the underlying concern for *peace* is the same in both cases.

16. It is uncertain whether a believing spouse will succeed in 'saving' the unbelieving if the marriage continues. Exactly opposite conclusions have been drawn as to the force of this. Some feel that it means that a marriage should be retained as long as possible in the hope of a conversion. Who can tell whether the other will not be saved? To others Paul's meaning is that marriage is not to be regarded simply as an instrument of evangelism. To cling to a marriage which the heathen is determined to end would lead to nothing but frustration and tension. The certain strain is not justified by the uncertain result. The guiding principle must be 'peace' (15). On the whole the latter seems more likely to be right than the former.

f. Lead the life God assigns to you (vii. 17–24)

Paul leaves the question of marriage and deals for a time with the wider question of living contentedly in whatever state one is. He relates this on the one hand to the divine equipment and call of every man, and on the other to circumcision and to slavery, the great religious and social distinctions which divided the world of his day.

17. *But* translates *ei mē*, an unexpected conjunction. It means 'save', 'except'. Probably we should understand it here as putting the opposite of the preceding. Paul has asserted the freedom of the Christian (15). But freedom is not licence. Over against the liberty which the believer has in respect of certain marriage regulations, Paul sets the maintenance of one's present state as the normal Christian practice. In accordance with the better MSS the positions of *Lord* and *God* should be interchanged (the New Testament habitually thinks of the Father as calling men). *Walk* is a favourite metaphor with Paul for the living out of the whole of life, more particularly for the Christian. Its idea of steady progress is very applicable. Men should continue their lives according to God's order for them. *Every man* and *every one* are both in emphatic positions. The duty of the individual is stressed. The verb *memeriken*, *hath distributed*, is often used of dividing things between people, though usually the things divided are mentioned. It points us here to the thought of the divine endowment of every man. Men are not self-made. *Hath called* reminds us of the priority of the divine call in salvation. Men do not choose God. He chooses them. When therefore God gives men certain gifts, and calls them in a certain state, it is for them to live the life He sets before them, using the gifts He gives them. This is no novelty enunciated for the special benefit of the Corinthians. Paul is accustomed to ordering affairs in this manner *in all churches*.

18, 19. The bearing of this principle on the great religious division into circumcised and uncircumcised is now brought out. The Jews, of course, insisted upon circumcision, and during the Maccabean struggle the performance of the rite had assumed a paramount place. The uncircumcised were, for them, outside the covenant of God. They were cut off from the blessings God had for His people. In a sense circumcision could be said to be everything. For many of the Gentiles, on the other hand, circumcision was something to be looked down on. It was the mark of the religion of a despised people. For them it was a sign of emancipation when, as sometimes happened, a Jewish youth, by undergoing a surgical operation (e.g. 1 Macc. i. 15), tried to efface the marks of his circumcision in order to take his place in the wider world of Hellenistic culture.

Paul calls on men to take no notice of these distinctions. They do not matter. The *circumcised* are not to *become uncircumcised*. Those *called in uncircumcision* are not to be *circumcised*. The thing is indifferent. A man should not change his state. Though *circumcision* had originally been instituted by divine ordinance, yet Paul can lay it down that both *circumcision* and *uncircumcision* are *nothing* at all. Over against both he sets *the keeping of the commandments of God* (cf. Gal. v. 6). It was this that made the former statement true. No matter of ritual can be set alongside the keeping of the commandments.

20. The principle of verse 17 is stated another way. *Calling*, *klēsis*, signifies the act of call, the invitation. Here it means the call taken in conjunction with all the external circumstances. Men should serve God in that place in life in which it pleases Him to call them. *Abide* is present imperative, with the thought of continuance.

21. Paul turns from religious to social divisions. *Art thou called* is really the same tense as in the previous verse, 'were you called?' It looks back to the time when God first spoke to the man. A *servant, doulos,* is rather what we would call a 'slave'. The important thing is to serve God, and the slave should not worry unduly about the fact that he is a slave. If God has called him as a slave, He will give him grace to live as a slave. If however the opportunity of becoming *free* occurs, Paul suggests that he *use it*. The meaning of this last verb, *chrēsai*, is disputed. Some think the sense of it is, in Goodspeed's translation, 'Even if you can gain your freedom, make the most of your present condition instead'. In favour of this can be urged the fact that elsewhere in this chapter Paul counsels people to remain in whatever state they are in.

Against it is the aorist imperative, which more naturally signifies the beginning of a new 'use' than the continuing of the old. It is also difficult to think that Paul, who held that marriage introduced difficulties in the way of Christian service, could have thought otherwise about slavery, which introduced much more serious difficulties. It seems to me that Paul is saying: 'Your state is not of first importance. If you are a slave, do not worry. If you can be made free, then make use of your new status. But remember the slave is the Lord's freeman, and the freeman is the Lord's slave.'

22. Paul employs paradoxical language to emphasize his point that the outward state of a man matters little. The slave who is *called* enters the glorious liberty of the sons of God. This divine liberty matters so much more than his outward circumstances that he can think of himself as *the Lord's freeman*. Being *called in the Lord* is an unusual expression. *Called* is usually sufficient. The addition emphasizes the presence of that wonderful Being, the divine Lord. It is not without interest and importance that this emphasis should be directed towards the slave, the least esteemed of all men in the first century. With this goes the other truth that the freeman who *is called* is *Christ's servant* ('slave'). Once more the point is that outward circumstances matter little. The important thing for such a one is that his life is lived in the service of his Master. It is the relation to the Lord which is primary. Nothing matters alongside this.

23. For *ye are bought with a price* see the notes on vi. 20, where exactly the same expression occurs. Believers have been purchased by Christ's blood. They belong to the Lord. They should not henceforth be the slaves of men. Deissmann reminds us that it was specifically provided in many documents of manumission that the person who had been bought by the god to be the god's freeman should never again be brought into slavery (LAE, p. 325). Paul may have had this law in

. mind. No one could bring the Corinthians into slavery again. Let them not make themselves the slaves of men. It is unlikely that it is literal slavery that is meant. But to live as a free man demands a special temper of mind and spirit. It is easy to accept unquestioningly what others lay down, and thus display the mentality of a slave. This is not the Christian way.

24. The section concludes with the reiteration of the principle already laid down in verses 17, 20, that *every man* (note the individual application) should content himself by remaining in that state in which God has called him. This does not forbid a man to better himself. But it cautions him not to seek a change simply because he is a Christian. In passing it is worth noticing that this principle is still valid. Conversion is not the signal for a man to leave his occupation (unless it is one plainly incompatible with Christianity) and seek some other. All of life is God's. We should serve God where we are until He calls us elsewhere. As throughout the passage, *is called* is in the aorist, and looks back to the time of God's call. *Abide* is present continuous. The concluding *with God* rounds off the whole passage. Paul is not counselling some passive resignation, an acceptance of the established order at all costs. He is pointing his friends to that God who is willing to be with them whatever their circumstances. It is for them, then, to seek first and always to abide with Him.

g. Virgins (vii. 25–38)

25. *Now concerning, peri de,* indicates that this is another matter on which the Corinthians had asked a specific question. *Virgins* usually refers to females, though in Rev. xiv. 4 it is used of males. The whole tenor of this passage makes it clear that Paul is referring to women only. The manner of his refer-ence is dictated by the fact that the decision of a girl's parent or guardian largely determined whether she should marry or not. As before, where he has no saying of the Lord to quote, he makes the position quite clear. His description of himself in terms of the mercy shown him emphasizes at one and the same time his own shortcomings, and the centrality of his Lord. The perfect (*eleēmenos*) indicates the permanence of the Lord's mercies, and the following *to be faithful* the obligations this lays on the recipients of God's good gifts.

26. The reference to *the present distress* is important. We do not know what this distress was. The word is a strong one (cf. its use in Lk. xxi. 23), signifying a pressing constraint. Some pressing care lay hard on the Corinthians at the time of writing. Some have understood this to mean the troubles heralding the second advent. There seems little to be said in favour of this. Paul often refers to Christ's return, but he does not associate a *present distress* with it. Others think it means no more than the opposition the Christian always encounters. But the language is too strong for this. It is most naturally taken as indicating that Paul's friends were at that time in unusually difficult circumstances. In view of the troubled times Paul felt it best for men to stay as they were. When high seas are raging it is no time for changing ships.

27. He makes plain what he means. The man who has entered into the bonds of matrimony should not seek to loose them. The man who has not, should not seek them. The verbs *art . . . bound* and *art . . . loosed* are both in the perfect tense. They indicate settled states.

28. Paul has consistently maintained that, while circumstances existed in which it was good for some not to marry, yet marriage is the normal state. There is nothing sinful about it. This truth he now repeats. Even though the prevailing distress made it inadvisable for a man to seek marriage, there was no sin if he did decide to marry. And so with a virgin. Paul's reason for not advocating marriage is that *such shall have trouble in the flesh. Such* is masculine, so that it embraces all cases, and is not confined to *virgins*. He does not define the nature of the *trouble*. Robertson and Plummer appropriately cite Bacon, 'He that hath wife and children hath given hostages to fortune', and 'children sweeten labours, but they make misfortunes more bitter'. Marriage implies responsibility, and marriage in times of distress must lead to trouble of some sort. Paul's tenderness comes out in his refusal to pursue the matter further. *But I* is emphatic. He, for his part, would *spare* them the difficulties involved in marriage.

29. *But this I say* gives what follows a certain heightened solemnity. *Brethren* is an affectionate address. *Short* is a perfect participle. 'The time has been shortened' is the sense of it. Evidently the Corinthians understood what Paul meant, but the reference is not clear enough for us to ascertain it with certainty. Calvin thought that the approach of death is meant, but it is difficult to see how this justifies the following instructions. Many see a reference to the second advent. This may be right, but, though he often refers to the Lord's return, Paul never elsewhere gives this kind of counsel. Both in his earlier and his later Epistles he uses the second advent to inspire men to blameless conduct (e.g. 1 Thes. v. 1–11, Phil. 1: 9–11). The note of present crisis, so marked here, is absent. It is probably best to see a reference to circumstances at Corinth (as in the case of the 'distress' of verse 26). The crisis was not far off. The result is that all sorts of human values are transformed. In particular, *they that have wives* must be *as though they had none*. The folly of marriage under such circumstances is obvious.

30. Other groups are singled out for mention. Mourners are apt to be engrossed in their mourning. Those that rejoice are usually taken up with their happiness. Those that buy concentrate on their new possessions. In the prevailing distress and the shortened times all will be jolted out of their usual attitudes. The Christian should accordingly not be preoccupied with his earthly circumstances. As far as possible he should be detached from them all.

31. The whole is summed up in the expression *they that use this world*. The construction is unusual (*chraomai* with the accusative, only here in the New Testament), but the meaning is clear. Paul speaks of those who make any use at all of the things of time and sense. *Abusing* translates the compound verb, *katachraomai*, of which the uncompounded form has just been employed. The preposition *kata* sometimes gives the simple verb a sinister twist ('use wrongly', 'abuse'). But it often simply intensifies the meaning ('use to the full'), though the intensification may not be very marked (i.e. the simple and compounded verbs may differ little). In view of the context the latter is probably Paul's meaning. Those who make use of the things of this world should not be engrossed in them. They must bear in mind the importance of eternal things, and the transitoriness of earthly things. *The fashion of this world passeth away*. *Schēma, fashion*, denotes the outward form, especially when there is some idea that this is changeable. It is adapted to the thought of fickleness, the changing fashion. There is nothing solid and lasting in this world system. It is its nature to pass away.

32. Paul reiterates his thought of verses 27f. that he wishes to spare his friends trouble in these difficult days. *Without carefulness* signifies 'without anxiety'. The trying nature of the times meant that the married must have anxious thought for their partners. Cf. Lightfoot, 'A man who is a hero in himself becomes a coward when he thinks of his widowed wife and his orphaned children' (on verse 26). This concern would distract from that perfect service of the Lord which Paul longed to see. The unmarried man can concentrate on *the things that belong to the Lord*. He is able to give himself over to the question of *how he may please the Lord*. As MM show, the verb *areskō, please*, includes the thought of service in the interests of another, in this case, of God. This is the extent of Paul's preference for celibacy. He longs to see men given over to the service of God with no distraction.

33. The married man, by contrast, must have a certain concern for *the things that are of the world*. This does not, of course, denote 'worldliness' in the technical sense of that term. It is rather a reminder that the married man must have regard to the interests of his family. He has obligations which he must discharge. And their discharge demands some attention to the things of this world. He must face the question *how he may please his wife* (the expression is exactly the same as the one he has just used of 'pleasing the Lord'). It is possible that we should add 'and is divided' (as RV mg.), in which case Paul is saying that the man's purposes are twofold. He wants to please the Lord, and he wants to please his wife.

34. The question is a complicated one. EVV take the verb *memeristai* with this verse, and understand it as 'differ'. This yields a good sense, though in this context we might expect it to mean 'is divided'. There is also the point that the verb is singular, where we should anticipate a plural for the meaning 'the wife and the virgin differ'. To meet this it is suggested that we read, 'the woman also is divided, the virgin who is unmarried . . .' But this is not very natural either. Fortunately our uncertainty as to details does not extend to the sense of the passage. In verses 32f. Paul shows the difference between married and unmarried men. In this verse he shows that there is the same kind of difference between married and unmarried women. The unmarried woman is able to concentrate on the things of God. Without distraction she may give herself over to being *holy both in body and in spirit*. *Holy*, of course, refers not to ethical achievement, but to consecration. The virgin is no more righteous than the wife. But her consecration is unmodified by any earthly commitment. The married woman, by contrast, must take into account the needs of her husband. Just as he does, she must give attention to the things of this world in order to please her partner.

35. Once again the apostle insists that he has in mind the best interests of the Corinthians themselves. He is not trying to confine them within some cramping straitjacket. He is seeking what is to their *profit* (or 'advantage'). The course he urges is best for them. A *snare, brochos,* is a 'noose'. The metaphor is from hunting. Paul is not trying to capture and constrain them. *Comely (euschēmon,* 'of good shape') signifies that which is proper, that which makes for good order. *That ye may attend upon the Lord* is a paraphrase of an expression stressing constancy (*euparedron*). There need be no intermission in the service offered to the Lord by the unmarried, no *distraction* of any sort.

36. As he has done repeatedly, Paul qualifies a statement pointing to the advantages of celibacy by making it clear that marriage is not to be despised. There is no sin if the *virgin* gets married. The interpretation of this verse is beset with difficulties. One explanation is as follows. The *man* is a general term for the parent or guardian of a girl. *Behaveth himself uncomely* means treating her dishonourably, in this case failing to provide for her marriage. He has acted on the principles Paul has just been outlining, but it is borne in on him that he is not doing the proper thing by the girl. To withhold marriage from a girl of marriageable age, and anxious to marry, would have been to court disaster, especially in first-century Corinth. *If she pass the flower of her age* renders a very unusual expression, *ean ē huperakmos.* It seems to mean 'if she passes the stage of being fully developed' (*akmē* = 'highest point', 'prime'; Plato speaks of a woman as at her *akmē* at the age of twenty, *Rep.* V. 460). That is to say she is of an age when marriage is most natural, perhaps even past such an age. Paul adds the point about there being *need* (lit. 'and so it ought to be done'). This will refer to the absence of the gift of continence. If the guardian sees all this, he may do what he wants, there is no sin. *Let them marry.* The principal objections to this view are two. *His virgin* is not common for 'his daughter' (but it does occur; LS cite Sophocles as saying 'my virgins' for 'my daughters'). But it would be a quick way of referring to guardians as well as parents. The other is that *let them marry* is most naturally taken as referring to the man and the virgin spoken of in the earlier part of the verse.

A second explanation is that the case is one of a man and his fiancée (cf. rsv, 'his betrothed'). The pair first agree to remain celibate. Paul tells them that there is no sin if they change their mind. But why should people become engaged if they do not intend to marry? The whole point of betrothal is marriage. Moreover it is difficult to put meaning into *behaveth himself uncomely* on this hypothesis. There is nothing *uncomely* in his not marrying a girl he has agreed not to marry. Again, *his virgin* is a very strange designation for a man's fiancée.

Most recent writers think that Paul is probably referring to 'spiritual marriage', whereby people went through a form of marriage, but lived together as brother and sister. From highly spiritual motives they abstained from sexual inter-course. They sought a union of spirit, but not of bodies. Paul gives permission to such to marry if they find the strain too great. The decisive objection to this is verse 5. Paul regards the withholding of sexual relations by married people as an act of fraud. Though it may be done by agreement, this must be only 'for a time', and the couple must 'come together again'. There is also the fact that, while the custom did exist, the earliest date at which it is at present attested is toward the end of the second century. We have no reason for thinking that it existed within the Christian Church as early as this. Then this view has to adopt an unnatural understanding of the verb *gamizō*, 'give in marriage', in verse 38 (where see note). Robertson and Plummer regard this objection as 'decisive'. Again, *huperakmos* must on this view be taken in the sense 'over-passionate', which is more than doubtful. Moffatt renders, 'if his passions be strong', and says the word denotes 'the surge of sexual passion'. However he gives no reason for this rendering, which does not seem a natural one. It is per-haps inevitable if we feel that there is no change of subject, and that therefore it must apply to the man. But we would not expect such a meaning for the word.

None of the suggested explanations is free from difficulty. But there seem fewest objections to the first, which accordingly we adopt.

37. Paul reaffirms his preference that the *virgin* be not given in marriage. He carefully lists the circumstances when this course may be followed. The man must stand *stedfast*, i.e. not think he is behaving 'uncomely'. He must have no *necessity*, which may point to some external obligation, such as a marriage contract. *Power* is *exousia*, 'authority', 'right', so that *power over his own will* means 'the right to give effect to his own purpose' (Parry). Slaves, for example, would not have this right. If under all these circumstances a man has come to a firm decision (*kekriken*) to keep his virgin unmarried, Paul thinks that he *doeth well*.

38. He sums up the matter with the thought that the man who gives his virgin in marriage *doeth well*, while he who does not *doeth better*. The verb *giveth in marriage* is *gamizō*, a word which is found rarely outside the New Testament. The *-izō* termination points to a meaning like that of AV, which does not accord with the idea that the passage refers to fianceés or to 'spiritual brides'. Those who hold such views must maintain that *gamizō* here has the same meaning as *gameō* in earlier verses. But this raises problems. Why should Paul change his verb? Why should he do it just here? Why should he use a verb which elsewhere always means 'give a woman in marriage'?

h. Widows (vii. 39, 40)

39. The indissolubility of marriage, other than by death, is at the basis of this verse. A wife is bound to her husband as long as he lives. If he dies (*koimēthē*, 'falls asleep'), she is free to remarry if she will, the one restriction being, *only in the Lord*.

In marriage, as in all else, the Christian must be mindful that he acts as a member of Christ's body.

40. Right to the end Paul refrains from saying anything to indicate that there is something morally higher about celibacy. He thinks that the widow will be *happier* if she refrains from remarriage. We must read this in the light of the special circumstances he has mentioned earlier in the chapter.

But there is nothing tentative about the authority with which Paul speaks. He has throughout this discussion made it clear when he is quoting a saying of Christ's, and when he is not. Now he gives his firm opinion that in what he says he has *the Spirit of God*. He is conscious of the divine enablement. What he says is more than the opinion merely of a private individual.

V. MEAT SACRIFICED TO IDOLS
(viii. 1–xi. 1)

a. Knowledge about idols (viii. 1–6)

Christians today are apt to find it a little strange that there was any doubt as to the attitude of Christians to meat which had been offered to idols. It seems to us so obvious that they could have no truck with idolatry. But it was not so easy as that to a new convert at Corinth in the first century. The situation was complicated by two facts. First, it was an accepted social practice to have meals in a temple, or in some place associated with an idol. 'It was all part and parcel of the formal etiquette in society' (Moffatt). The kind of occasion, public or private, when people were likely to come together socially was the kind of occasion when a sacrifice was appropriate. To have nothing to do with such gatherings was to cut oneself off from most social intercourse with one's fellows. Immature believers, firmly convinced that there was but one God, might well reason, 'How can there possibly be any harm in eating before a block of wood or stone? What difference can it make if meat has been offered to a non-existent deity?' Secondly, most of the meat sold in the shops had first been offered in sacrifice. Part of the victim was always offered on the altar to the god, part went to the priests, and usually part to the worshippers. The priests customarily sold what they could not use. It would often be very difficult to know for sure whether meat in a given shop had been part of a sacrifice or not. Notice that there are two separate questions: the taking part in idol feasts, and the eating of meat bought in the shops, but previously part of a sacrifice. Many things might be said. Paul begins with the obligations of Christian love.

1. *Now as touching* is the same formula as that rendered 'Now concerning' in vii. 1. It indicates that this is another matter which had been raised in the letter from the Corinthians. *We know that we all have knowledge* associates Paul with his friends. It is not unlikely that their letter had stressed the place of knowledge. Paul may even be quoting from it. At any rate he agrees with the importance of knowledge, and joins himself with them in its exercise. The use of *all* may be a gentle reminder that the knowledge on which the Corinthians prided themselves was by no means unusual, but the common possession of Christians. Paul proceeds to contrast knowledge with love. *Knowledge puffeth up* (for this verb see note on iv. 6). Pride so often accompanies knowledge, but it is the very antithesis of the genuine Christian spirit. The word *agapē*, translated *charity*, is better rendered 'love'. Whereas knowledge puffs up, love builds up (cf. Phillips, 'while knowledge may make a man look big, it is only love that can make him grow to his full stature'). *Edifieth* translates a verb, *oikodomei*, properly applying to the erection of buildings (cf. 'edifice'). Paul is very fond of using it metaphorically of the building up of Christian character. (See note on 1 Thes. v. 11.[1])

[1] *Op. cit.*, p. 97.

2. Paul's second point is that knowledge here on earth is, at best, incomplete. No matter what a man thinks he knows (the perfect tense implies full and complete knowledge), he does not yet know as he *ought* (lit. 'must', *dei*). There is no point in priding oneself on what inevitably is partial and incomplete. There is probably also the thought that he who thinks he knows really does not know (cf. iii. 18). As Kay says, 'Knowledge is proud that it has learnt so much. Wisdom is humble that it knows no more'.

3. Love, by contrast, has permanent effects. There is a typical Pauline turn of construction here. After 'If anyone thinks he knows something he knows nothing. If anyone loves God' we would expect something like, 'he has real knowledge'. Instead, Paul says, *the same is known of* God. The really important thing is not that we know God, but that He knows us. 'The Lord knoweth them that are his' (2 Tim. ii. 19; cf. Gal. iv. 9). When a man truly loves God he is brought within the sphere of those on whom God is graciously pleased to set His knowledge.

What Paul has done in these three verses is to give a very gentle rebuke to those who gave too high a place to knowledge. Love rather than knowledge should be the Christian's determining consideration.

4. Returning to the subject of idol meats, Paul agrees with the Corinthians that *an idol is nothing in the world* (or, perhaps, 'there is no idol in all the world'). Many think that he is quoting from the Corinthians' letter again, and this may well be the case. He is certainly not giving his own full ideas on the matter, for he later says that what is sacrificed to idols is actually sacrificed to devils (x. 20). There are spiritual beings behind the idols, though not the ones their worshippers thought. But here this is not the point. Paul is prepared to agree with his correspondents that the gods the heathen worship are no gods. In all this ordered universe there is no reality corresponding to idols. This is a necessary consequence of the assertion that *there is none other God but one*. One of the first things a little Jewish boy was taught was the *Shema*, 'Hear O Israel: The Lord our God is one Lord' (Dt. vi. 4). It was absolutely fundamental, and the Jew clung to it with a fierce tenacity. The Christian was no less sure of it than the Jew.

5. The nature of idols is further examined. Paul allows that there are those *that are called gods*. Idol worshippers referred to the objects of their worship as 'gods', and really believed them to be such. But the reference to their being *called* gods indicates their unreality. All are included in the condemnation, whether their abode was thought to be *in heaven or in earth*. There is probably no difference meant between *gods many* and *lords many*. *Lord* was the usual way of referring to the deity in the various cults of the time (which makes Paul's frequent application of it to Jesus Christ significant). Paul simply makes it clear that the heathen world worshipped a multitude of deities, and he puts no difference between them.

6. *But* is the strong adversative *alla*, and *to us* is in an emphatic position. Christians contrast sharply with the idolaters. They are essentially monotheistic. *There is but one God*. He is given His characteristic title, *the Father*, partly as denoting His relationship to the Son, and partly as denoting His tender care for His people (both being mentioned in the following clauses). The heathen divided up creation between their many gods and goddesses, each of whom had his proper sphere. But the one God, says Paul, is responsible for *all things*. All is from Him. *We in him* is better as AV mg., 'for him', or as RV, 'unto him'. The preposition *eis* indicates the set of one's life. The Christian lives for God. He lives only to do Him service.

Together with the Father, Paul thinks of the Son. He is described as *one Lord Jesus Christ*. Again *one* draws attention to Christian monotheism over against the plurality of the gods of the heathen, and *Lord* points to the deity of Christ. So, of course, does the fact that He is mentioned in this way in the same breath as the Father. Paul does not trouble to examine the relationship between them. But clearly he is laying down the proposition that there is but one God, and just as clearly he is including the Lord Jesus within that one Godhead (cf. Moffatt, 'For Paul, the *one Lord* is vitally one with the *one God*'). *By* (lit. 'through') *whom are all things* points to Christ as the Agent in creation. While all things originated from the Father, they came 'through' the Son (cf. Col. i. 15f.; Jn. i. 3). *We by* ('through' again) *him* indicates that we Christians have our being only through Him. It is a reference to the new creation in Christ (cf. 2 Cor. v. 17).

b. The weak brother (viii. 7–13)

7. Paul has been speaking of that knowledge which enables a man to regard an idol as a thing of naught. Now he makes the point that such knowledge is not universal among Christians. There is no contradiction with verse 1. There Paul said that this knowledge was not confined to the Corinthian élite. He did not mean that every Christian, without exception, had it. Now he points out that there are some weaker brethren who have not risen to this knowledge. From their pre-Christian days they were so accustomed to thinking of the idol as real that they could not completely shake off such thoughts. It is like the situation in the modern mission field, where some converts find it very hard to rid themselves completely of a belief in witchcraft. *With conscience of the idol* does not seem to be the true reading. For *suneidēsei, conscience*, we should substitute *sunētheia*, a word which means first 'intimacy', and then 'custom', a 'being accustomed to'. 'Through being long accustomed to idols' (Goodspeed) is the sense of it. *Unto this hour* ('until now') means that they still had the old associations, though now they were Christians. *Their conscience being weak is defiled.* Not being able to shake off the feeling that the idol was somehow real, they felt that they were doing wrong when they ate what had been offered to it.

8. The word *brōma, meat,* means rather 'food' (so also in verse 13). The eating of any particular kind of food is really a very minor matter. Those who wish to eat are not contending for some great principle (as Paul was when he stoutly refused to accept circumcision as necessary). The eating of *meat* is a thing indifferent. *Commendeth* is not a good translation of the verb *paristēmi,* which means rather 'present' (as in Rom. vi. 13, RV), or 'bring near to' (cf. Acts xxvii. 24). Some MSS have the present tense, yielding the meaning, 'the eating of meat does not bring a man near to God'. Others have the future, which may look to bringing a man before God for praise or blame at the day of judgment. The eating of meat does not 'make us abound', it 'gives us no advantage' (so, rather than *are we the better, perisseuomen*). If we abstain from it, 'we have no lack' (*husteroumetha*; cf. Phil. iv. 12 for both verbs). Many think that this verse is another quotation of a saying used by the Corinthians. If so, Paul endorses it.

9. The requirement that the strong have a care for the weak becomes explicit. *Liberty* is *exousia,* which means 'authority', or 'right'. The Corinthians claimed the 'right' to do as they pleased in the matter of idols. Paul reminds them that no Christian is at liberty to assert his 'rights' if that means doing harm to other people, a principle of wide application. A *stumblingblock, proskomma,* is a stone in the pathway, an obstacle, something that trips one up and makes progress difficult. The actions of the strong must not be such as to afford a hindrance to the progress of the weak. What is right for one man may well be wrong for another. No one should try to force his standards of right and wrong on to others, whose conscience reacts differently.

10. The inevitable consequence of the strong exercising their rights without regard to the weak is made clear. The man with *knowledge* is pictured as taking part in a feast in the temple of an idol. *Sit at meat* is the ordinary word for 'recline'.

It indicates a leisurely meal. The man is taking his ease at some festival. The result is that the conscience of the weak is *emboldened*. The word is that rendered 'edifieth' in verse 1. Here it is ironical. Evidently the strong among the Corinthians had spoken of the necessity of 'building up' the weak by encouraging them to do such actions. Paul takes up their word, and with a rhetorical question points out the harm. 'By setting such an example will you not "build up" the weak brother? You will "build him up" only to destruction!'

11. It is likely that the question terminates at the end of verse 10 (as RV). This verse gives the consequences (*and* is really 'for', *gar*). The *knowledge* on which the strong pride themselves is the means of doing tremendous harm to the weak. *Perish, apollutai*, is a strong term (cf. Phillips, 'bring spiritual disaster to'). The action of the strong may well inflict ruinous damage on the weak, by inducing him to sin where he otherwise would not. The better MSS have the present tense, not the future. Paul sees him as even now perishing. The word-order is unusual. Paul emphasizes 'the brother for whose sake (*di' hon*) Christ died', by putting it right at the end. Robertson and Plummer comment: 'The last clause could hardly be more forcible in its appeal; every word tells; "the brother," not a mere stranger; "for the sake of whom," precisely to rescue him from destruction; "Christ," no less than He; "died," no less than that.'

12. The harm done to the weak is not the whole story. To sin *against the brethren* means nothing less than to sin *against Christ* (a lesson brought home to Paul long since, on the Damascus road, Acts ix. 4f.). They are 'in Christ', and anything done against them is accordingly done against Him (cf. Mt. xxv. 40, 45). There is a high dignity in the Christian calling. It is always easy to think of certain church members as unimportant. But they are not so. Christ lives in them. We should honour them as members of Christ, and beware of sinning against the Lord. *Wound* renders the verb *tuptō*. This is the only place in the New Testament where it is used metaphorically. Its customary use is for striking vigorous blows, for beating. It stresses the harm done by the strong.

13. Paul's conclusion from all this is that he will do his utmost to see that he does not hinder the weak brother. In this context he might well have referred to 'meat offered to idols', but he prefers to leave *meat* ('food', see on verse 8) unqualified. If need be, he will eat no *flesh* (i.e. 'meat' in our sense of the word) of any sort. The important thing is not his own rights, nor his own comforts, but the well-being of the brotherhood. Notice the emphasis on *brother*. It occurs four times in the last three verses. *Make . . . to offend* renders *skandalizei*, a word difficult to translate. It really means something like 'to set off a trap' (from *skandalon*, the stick which triggers off the trap, i.e. the stick which sets the trap in motion when a bird or animal touches it). It is used metaphorically for trouble of various kinds. Paul's negative is the emphatic *ou mē*, the double negative. *While the world standeth* is literally 'into the age', i.e. lasting into the coming age. It is the usual expression for 'for ever'.

The principle laid down in this chapter is one of great practical importance. It is always easy for the strong Christian to see no harm whatever in actions which would be sin if performed by the weak. While it would not be true to say that the robust Christianity of the New Testament envisages the strong as permanently shackled by the weak, yet the strong must always act towards the weak with consideration and Christian love. In cases like the one here dealt with the strong must adapt their behaviour to the consciences of the weak. No good purpose is served by their asserting what they call their 'rights'. Cf. Paul's treatment of the same general subject in Rom. xiv.

c. The example of Paul (ix. 1–27)

i. His rights (ix. 1–14). At first sight this appears to be a different subject altogether. Accordingly, not a few have thought that this is an insertion from some other letter, or that it is a parenthesis in which Paul temporarily leaves his subject. There is no need for such hypotheses. Paul has been dealing with people who asserted their rights to the detriment of others. He has told them that this is wrong. He now proceeds to show that he himself has consistently applied this principle. He practises what he preaches.

1. The order of the two opening questions is reversed in the better MSS, which also omit *Christ* in the third. Paul asks, 'Have not I the liberty of a Christian?' and advances to 'Have not I the rights of an apostle?' The order hints that he does more than he has been urging the Corinthians to do. He forgoes not only the general rights all Christians have, but his special rights as an apostle as well. It is rare to find the name *Jesus* in Paul's writings without *Christ.* Here we must assume that he wishes to place some emphasis on the human nature of the Lord. That he has seen the Lord brings out one of his qualifications to be an apostle. Apostles were authoritative witnesses to the facts of the gospel, more especially to the resurrection (Acts i. 21f., ii. 32, iii. 15, iv. 33, etc.; notice the significance of Ananias' words to Paul, 'The God of our fathers hath chosen thee, that thou shouldest . . . see that Just One', Acts xxii. 14). As Paul was not one of the original apostolic band some may have questioned his right to bear such witness. But on the Damascus road he was granted a special privilege— he saw the Lord. This qualified him to bear witness to the resurrection. The *not* in this question is more emphatic than in the others (*ouchi*), so that Paul lays stress on his having seen Christ. The addition, *in the Lord,* to the reference to the Corinthians as his *work* arises from the consideration emphasized in iii. 5–7. It is not the minister, but the Lord who 'gave the increase'. Cf. Calvin: 'We must always speak of the efficacy of the ministry in such a manner that the entire praise of the work may be reserved for God alone.'

2. Others might call Paul's apostleship in question, but the Corinthians ought to be the last to do that. No one else had the same relationship to them as did he. They were a living proof of the effectiveness of his work. A *seal* was important in an age when many could not read. A mark stamped on clay, or wax, or some similar substance, was first of all a mark of ownership, and then a means of authentication. All could see the mark, and know what it signified. The Corinthians had been won for Christ by Paul, and they were thus the sign that attested his apostleship (Goodspeed translates, 'the certificate of my apostleship'). Their very existence as Christians proved his point.

3. In the Greek these words can be taken either with what precedes or with what follows. They seem to me to go better with the preceding. What follows does not attest Paul's apostleship, but represents some of the consequences that follow when that apostleship is attested. *Apologia*, translated *answer*, signifies properly a legal defence against a charge. *Examine* is *anakrinousin*, another legal word, for which see note on ii. 15. Both *mine* and *me* are emphatic.

4. *Power* is *exousia*, the word used of the Corinthians in viii. 9 (see note); it means 'authority' or 'right'. As the previous chapter has been concerned with the eating of certain foods it may be that Paul is reminding his friends that he himself has full rights in such matters. But in the context it seems more probable that we should understand after *to eat and to drink*, the phrase 'at the church's expense'. It is the right to maintenance of which Paul speaks. The use of the plural is curious. It is possible that Paul wishes to associate Barnabas with him in what follows. More probably what he says concerns himself, the *we* being what is termed an 'epistolary plural'. It is often difficult to be certain whether *we* in Paul's letters extends to others than the apostle.

5. This verse does not assert the right of apostles to marry. Nobody in the apostolic age would have queried this. It affirms rather the right *to lead about* a wife. It was accepted that an apostle ought to be maintained by those to whom he ministered. Paul asserts here the right of the apostle, if married, to take his wife with him, the implication being that she, too, would be supported by the church. There is an article before *other*, so that we should read, 'the other apostles'. We would have expected that most were married, and this indicates that this was indeed so. *Cephas* (Peter) is singled out as a specially important case. The most natural interpretation of *the brethren of the Lord* is that they were the children of Joseph and Mary. The views that they were the children of Joseph by a former marriage, or cousins of the Lord, do not rest on evidence, but are conjectures based on the assumption that it would not have been seemly for Mary to have children other than the Lord. But the repeated use of *brethren* without qualification is against such views.

6. *Only* is singular, which makes it seem as though *Barnabas* was added as an afterthought. This in turn militates against the idea that there is significance in the plural *we* of the previous verses. Paul singles out Barnabas and himself as two apostles who did not refrain from earning their own living while preaching. This makes it seem as though it was the custom of all the others to do so.

7. From three diverse human activities Paul shows his right to be maintained. The soldier, the man who plants a vineyard, and the shepherd all draw their sustenance from their occupation. The inference is that Christian apostles are entitled to do the same. Notice the differing status of the three Paul selects. The soldier was commonly paid wages, the man who plants a vineyard here seems to be the owner (he does not eat *of* the fruit as AV, but 'the fruit'; only the proprietor would be in a position to do that), while the shepherd, more often than not, was a slave. Yet all were fed from their occupation. *Charges*, *opsōniois*, means 'wages' (the word originally signified 'rations').

8. The argumentative questions continue. The first is introduced by *mē*, indicating that a negative answer is expected. Paul repudiates the thought that the principle he is enunciating and illustrating from various fields of human endeavour rests simply on human wisdom. In speaking in this fashion he does not speak *as a man* simply. He can show the same thing in *the law* (an affirmative answer to the second question is implied). This term properly applied among the Jews to the first five books of our Old Testament, though sometimes it is used loosely to denote the whole of sacred Scripture. But whichever be the usage, it is always regarded as authoritative.

9. Paul quotes from Dt. xxv. 4 the prohibition to muzzle the ox when engaged in treading out the corn for threshing. The animal trampled the corn, thus shaking the grain loose from the husks. The mixture was then tossed up in a breeze, and the wind blew the chaff away, while the heavier grain fell straight down. While the ox trod the grain he was not to be muzzled, which meant that he could take some mouthfuls of the grain. The question *Doth God take care for oxen?* expects the answer 'No'. This must be understood carefully. It does not mean that Paul held that God was indifferent to the needs of oxen, nor that the verse does not apply to them. Yet in connection with this last point we should notice that it occurs not in a passage dealing with animals, but in one dealing with human activities. It may well have been meant figuratively from the very first. However that may be, many of the Rabbis distinguished a spiritual, as well as a literal sense, in much of

Scripture. Paul is doing something rather like that. He is asking where the primary application of the words lies, and denying that it is with oxen.

10. He answers his question with another question and an interpretation. The words he has quoted apply first and foremost to the preacher of the gospel. The force of *pantōs, altogether,* we may gather from Knox's rendering, 'Is it not clear that he says it for our sakes?' So the Christian worker, be he ploughman or reaper (cf. iii. 6), should do his work in hope. God provides for his needs from the fruits of his labour.

11. The application becomes specific. The opening conditional clause implies that the condition has been fulfilled. 'If, as is the case, we sowed . . .' Paul had preached the gospel at Corinth, and had been the means of starting the Corinthian Christians on the way. He speaks of sowing, though he might equally have added that he did some reaping. But the precise function exercised is not important at this point. Here he is concerned with the fact that the man who labours to produce the harvest is entitled to his share of the proceeds. Paul had laboured in *spiritual* things among the Corinthians. He was fully entitled to receive of them *carnal* (i.e. material) rewards.

12. Others, it would appear, had in fact exercised the right Paul speaks of. It may be that Peter or Apollos and others had received gifts from the Corinthians. Paul did not, and some of them evidently regarded this as proof of Paul's inferiority. Perhaps they said that Paul implicitly recognized his inferiority by not attempting to obtain sustenance. Paul maintains that the founder of the church at Corinth had far more right to this sort of thing than anyone else. *We* is emphatic. He goes on to give his reason for not exercising his right. He had not wished to *hinder the gospel of Christ. Hinder* is a graphic and somewhat unusual word (only here in the New Testament). It means literally 'a cutting into', and was used of breaking up a road to prevent the enemy's advance. Paul had avoided doing anything which might prevent a clear road for the gospel advance. *Suffer, stegomen,* is suffer in the sense of 'endure'

13. Another illustration of the principle is brought forward. It was well known that those whose work was in sacred things received their livelihood therefrom. More particularly, those who *wait at* (lit. 'sit beside'; the word denotes habitual service) *the altar* receive their portion of what is offered on the altar (see Lv. vii. 6, 8–10, 14, 28–36, etc.).

14. In conformity with this *the Lord,* none less, *ordained that they which preach the gospel should live of the gospel.* The highest authority is given to the command, since it came from Christ. At the same time the preceding has shown that it is not an arbitrary command, but one which accords with practice in many occupations. No command of the Lord in precisely these terms has been preserved. One may have been given, or Paul may be thinking of such words as 'the labourer is worthy of his hire' (Lk. x. 7).

ii. His refusal to exercise his rights (ix. 15–18). Paul was in no doubt about his rights. But he had not used them. Nor was it his purpose in writing in this strain to establish a claim for the future. So fiercely did he hold his convictions in this matter that he can say, *better for me to die, than*——. The text here is difficult. The best interpretation is that Paul breaks off his sentence and does not complete it. What follows is an exclamation, 'No man will make this boast of mine an empty one!' The break in construction marks Paul's deep emotion, and his emotion indicates the importance he ascribed to his practice.

16. Preaching the gospel is no matter for boasting. Paul feels that he can claim no particular credit in that. *Necessity* 'presses upon' (so, rather than *is laid upon, epikeitai*) him. And necessity presses upon all who have experienced the power of the gospel in their lives. Not all are called to a ministry like Paul's. But none is exempt from the requirement of letting the grace of God be known. Paul thinks of some undefined disaster as coming to him if he does not preach. The nature of the *woe* is not explained, and perhaps it is all the more effective for that. In these days we are not good at emphasizing duty, and we do not like the thought of punishment. But Paul clear-sightedly gives expression to both.

17. There is more than one way of understanding this difficult verse. Paul may mean that the man who preaches with a willing spirit merits a reward, whereas if he is unwilling he is not excused. He must still discharge his stewardship. Or he may be starting from the premise of verse 16 that 'necessity presses upon me'. If he preached of his own free choice he would merit a reward. As it is, it is not his own choice. He must preach. The next verse would then be understood as, 'What reward is possible under these circumstances?' There is nothing of grace in *misthos*, *reward*, which rather signifies 'wages', 'the payment of what is due'. For *dispensation* (*oikonomia*) see the note on 'steward' (*oikonomos*) on iv. 1. The thought is that of Paul's responsibility to God for discharging the commission entrusted to him.

18. Paul had to preach. But he did not have to preach without charge. To do this is his *reward*, as in verse 15 it was his ground for boasting. This is not only strategy with him. It is a source of pride. It is his *reward*: his highest pay is to serve without pay! *Abuse* renders the verb *katachraomai*, for which see note on vii. 31. Here, as there, it probably means 'use to the full'. *Power* is *exousia*, 'right'. Paul aimed, then, at not making full use of his rights.

iii. His service of all men (ix. 19–23). The extent of Paul's abandonment of his rights in the interests of the gospel is brought out. He had the status of a free man (he was proud of his Roman citizenship), but he became a 'slave' (so rather than *servant*) to all, so that he might *gain the more*.

20. To the Jews he *became as a Jew*. The sort of thing that is in mind is his conduct in circumcising Timothy. He would not needlessly antagonize his own nation. He respected Jewish scruples. *The law* is the law of Moses. Paul was not himself bound to that law. The true text adds, 'not being myself under the law', after as *under the law* (so RV). 'Christ is the end of the law' (Rom. x. 4). The Christian is 'not under the law, but under grace' (Rom. vi. 14). Yet Paul conformed to practices which would enable him to approach *them that are under the law* with greater acceptability.

21. *Them that are without law* does not mean 'outlaws' or anything like that. In this context it is practically equivalent to 'Gentiles'. It is those not bound by the law mentioned in the previous verse. Paul did not come among them as bound by all the Jewish regulations. He met them on their own ground. When he says that he was *as without law* he does not wish to give the impression that he was under no restraint. So he adds that he is *not without law to God*, and that he is *under the law to Christ*. Both expressions indicate that he was no free agent, but the servant of God. But as far as this service would allow he conformed to Gentile practice, that he might *gain them that are without law*.

22. This whole discussion has underlined Paul's tender concern for *the weak*. It helps us to see how he respected their scruples, and conformed his behaviour to theirs. He sums it all up with *I am made all things to all men*. This does not, of course, mean that his conduct was unprincipled. On occasion Paul could be very stubborn in following courses of action in the teeth of strong opposition. But where no principle was at stake he was prepared to go to extreme lengths to meet people. Personal considerations are totally submerged in the great aim of by all means saving some.

23. The better MSS read 'all things' for *this* of AV. Paul's whole conduct was determined by the gospel. That was what mattered, not the preacher. Yet he is not unmindful of his own need, and he brings in one small reference to it. He looks to being *a partaker*, i.e. to being a sharer with others in the blessing of salvation. Even here he thinks of others, for his word stresses the thought of partnership.

iv. His self-control (ix. 24–27). Athletic contests were common in the Greek world, and the Isthmian Games (second only to the Olympic Games) were held every three years at Corinth. Paul often, as here, uses imagery drawn from the Games. His first point is that a foot race yields but one winner. Therefore the runners put forth every effort. In like manner the Christian must strain every nerve to produce his finest effort.

25. *Striveth for the mastery* renders a verb, *agōnizomai*, which means 'to compete in the Games'. It gives us the word 'agony', from which we see that no half-hearted effort is meant. Every competitor had to undergo strict training for ten months. He was *temperate in all things*. Yet his reward, if successful, was *a corruptible crown* (in the Isthmian Games this was a pine wreath). The Christian has before him a much more worthwhile crown, namely an *incorruptible* one (cf. 2 Tim. iv. 8). The strenuous self-denial of the athlete in training for his fleeting reward is a rebuke to all half-hearted, flabby Christian service. Notice that the athlete denies himself many lawful pleasures. The Christian must avoid not only definite sin, but anything that hinders his complete effectiveness.

26. The imagery is still drawn from the Games. Paul is not like a runner who does not know where the finishing line is.

He is not as a boxer who strikes but the air (either 'shadow-sparring' or missing the opponent). Paul's Christianity is purposeful. He puts everything into direct and forceful Christian endeavour.

27. He refuses to be bound by bodily desires. In picturesque language Paul speaks of the way he disciplines the flesh. *Keep under* renders *hupopiazō*, but the better reading is the similar *hupōpiazō*. This is a verb from boxing, with the meaning 'give a black eye to'. *Bring into subjection, doulagōgō*, is 'bring into slavery'. Paul leaves no doubt as to the vigour with which he subdues the flesh. *Castaway* is too strong for *adokimos*. The word means 'which has not stood the test', and in this context refers to disqualification. Paul's fear was not that he might lose his salvation, but that he might lose his crown through failing to satisfy his Lord (cf. iii. 15).

d. The example of the Israelites (x. 1–13)

i. A reference to history (x. 1–5). Paul continues to rebuke the complacency of the Corinthians. He leaves his own example and turns to the history of the people of God recorded in the Scriptures to show that the enjoyment of high privileges does not guarantee entry into final blessing. The Israelites experienced redemption, baptism and God's continuing succour. Yet nearly all perished in the wilderness.

1. *Moreover* should read 'For'. The section is closely linked with the preceding. The danger just spoken of is not imaginary, as the case of the Israelites in the wilderness demonstrates. For the formula, *I would not that ye should be ignorant*, see the note on 1 Thes. iv. 13.[1] Notice the fivefold repetition in these verses of the word *all*. Stress is thus laid on the fact that without exception the Israelites received the tokens of God's good hand upon them. This gives greater force to the reminder in verse 5 that most perished. The reference is to the

[1]*Op. cit.*, p. 84.

events associated with the Exodus. *The cloud* is the cloud which was the means of divine guidance (Ex. xiii. 21, 22, xiv. 19, 24, etc.).

2. The experiences of being guided by the cloud, and of passing through the Red Sea (Ex. xiv) had the effect of uniting the people to Moses in such a way that they are said to have been *baptized unto Moses* (the Greek seems to imply a willingness to get themselves baptized in this way; cf. Goodspeed, 'all, as it were, accepted baptism as followers of Moses'). It is startling for the Christian, who is 'baptized unto Christ', to find such a reference to baptism. Probably we are to think of Moses as a type of Christ. Just as baptism has as one effect, the bringing of a man under the leadership of Christ, so did the participation in the great events of the Exodus bring the Israelites under the leadership of Moses (Ex. xiv. 31 can say, 'they believed in the Lord, and in his servant Moses', RV). They were united to him, though we should not press this as though any other union can be anything like as close as the union between the Christian and the Christ. All the Israelites shared this common baptism.

3. They likewise were all sustained by the manna (Ex. xvi. 4, 13ff.), here referred to as *spiritual meat* (the word means 'food', not 'meat' in our sense of the term). The adjective does not mean that Paul is calling in question the physical reality of the manna. It is his way of directing attention to the heavenly origin of this food (cf. Ps. lxxviii. 24); RSV renders 'supernatural'.

4. Just as they had spiritual food, so they had *spiritual drink*. Paul adds an explanation, as he did not do with the reference to food. There was a Jewish legend that a rock followed the Israelites throughout their wilderness wanderings. Paul may have had this legend at the back of his mind, but certainly he does not refer directly to it. He refers to Christ. In doing so he transfers to the Lord the title, 'the

Rock', used in the Old Testament of Jehovah (Dt. xxxii. 15; Ps. xviii. 2, etc.; notice the implications for Christology both of this transfer, and of the clear implication of the pre-existence of Christ). There is obviously a reminiscence of the smiting of the rock to obtain water (Ex. xvii. 6; Nu. xx. 1ff.). The allusion, however, is not a simple one, for there is no hint in those passages of a movable rock. But Paul understands Christ to have been the source of all the blessings the Israelites received as they journeyed. So he can think of the Rock, Christ, as following them, and continually giving them drink. The reference to spiritual food and drink may well, as Calvin and others have thought, be made in the light of the Holy Communion. Israel had her equivalents of both sacraments.

5. *But* (the strong adversative, *alla*), although God had given them such signal manifestations of His power and good-will towards them, the majority failed to enter the Promised Land. God was not *well pleased* with them. *Many of them* is rather 'the majority'. This is a masterly understatement. Of all the hosts of Israel only two men entered the Promised Land. The rest perished in the wilderness, or, as Paul puts it, they *were overthrown*. The verb *katastrōnnumi* lends a pictur-esque touch. It really means 'to spread out'. Paul pictures the wilderness as strewn with corpses. This is not simply natural death. It is God's sentence against the rebels.

ii. Idolatry and its lessons (x. 6–13). *These things* are not to be regarded simply as history. They were history. They really happened. But they were more than that. They hap-pened as *examples* (*tupoi*; for this word see note on 1 Thes. i. 7[1]). God had a purpose in them. *Lust* is strong desire of any sort, but in the New Testament it is more commonly used of evil passions than good desires.

7. The warning against idolatry is very much in point in view of the trouble at Corinth with which Paul is dealing. He

---

[1] *Op. cit.*, p. 38.

quotes Ex. xxxii. 6, where the reference to eating and drinking and playing (i.e. dancing) point to a typical idol festival. Often such a festival would degenerate into a debauch. There was no sense of serious purpose associated with idol worship (how could there be?). Thus men's lowest passions might be, and often were, unleashed in the very act of worship.

8. This is not a new subject, for *fornication* formed part of much idol worship. Sacred prostitutes were found at many shrines, and Corinth had an unenviable notoriety in this respect. But Paul's primary reference is to the incident recorded in Nu. xxv where Israel 'began to commit whoredom with the daughters of Moab' (verse 1), and 'joined himself unto Baal-peor' (verse 3). Judgment came in the form of a plague, and twenty-four thousand people perished (Nu. xxv. 9). Paul speaks of twenty-three thousand. Obviously both are simply round numbers, and in addition Paul may be making some allowance for those slain by the judges (Nu. xxv. 5). This verse is a reminder of the serious danger to which indulgence in idolatry exposes men.

9. The verb *peirazō* meant originally 'to test', but usually to test with a view to the person failing in the test. Thus its secondary meaning is 'to tempt' (another verb meaning 'to test', *dokimazō*, is test with a view to the person passing the test, and so comes to mean 'prove', 'approve'). The idea in 'tempting' God is that of putting Him to the test, of seeing how far one can go. Paul urges the Corinthians not to *tempt* Christ (or 'the Lord' as many mss read) in this way. The reference is to the people's complaint about food, as the result of which complaint God sent fiery serpents among them (Nu. xxi. 5f.).

10. The verb *murmur* is regularly used, as here, in the sense of 'to mutter against', and so 'to complain'. Thus in Nu. xiv. 2, 36, xvi. 11, 41, we read of such murmuring, and on each occasion there was an appropriate punishment. In this verse the reference is probably to the overthrow of the company of Korah in Nu. xvi. *The destroyer* (Phillips, 'the Angel of Death') does not occur in exactly that form in the Old Testament, though a similar expression is rendered 'the destroyer' in Ex. xii. 23 (cf. also 2 Sa. xxiv. 16). But the application is clear enough. Murmuring calls down divine punishment.

11. The foregoing is summed up. All these things happened to teach us *upon whom* 'the ends of the ages' *are come*. This curious expression appears to mean that the culmination of all past ages has arrived. They are completed, and the lessons they teach are manifest. We should reap the fruits of the experience of these ages. Possibly there is also the thought that the coming of Christ has decisive significance. He has brought all previous ages to an end.

12. The application is made clear. The Corinthians were cocksure of their position. But then, so had the Israelites been, and they had reaped nothing but disaster. Let the self-confident take heed, *lest he fall*.

13. *Temptation* here may be used in the sense of temptation to sin, but it seems to have the broader sense of 'testing', and to include trials of every kind. Either way, nothing exceptional had happened to the Corinthians. They experienced only what is *common to man*. God will always make *a way to escape*. This word, *ekbasis*, may denote a mountain defile. The imagery is that of an army trapped in the mountains, which escapes from an impossible situation through a pass. The assurance of this verse is a permanent comfort and source of strength to believers. Our trust is in the faithfulness of God.

e. The incompatibility of Christian and idol feasts (x. 14–22)

14. Paul proceeds to the heart of the problem. *Dioper, wherefore*, is a stronger particle than that used in verse 12. It indicates a very close logical sequence. The address, *my dearly be-loved*, is not a common one. It indicates something of Paul's deep emotion as he urges his dear friends to take the right course. As he had counselled them in vi. 18 to 'flee fornication', so now he says *flee from idolatry*. Here, as there, the present imperative gives the thought of the habitual practice. There is to be no leisurely contemplation of sin, thinking that one can go so far, and is safe from going further. The only wise course is to have nothing to do with it. 'They must not try how near they can go, but how far they can fly' (Robertson and Plummer). Paul has just been assuring them of God's help in time of temptation. Now he wants them to see that that does not give them licence to dally needlessly with it. Flee from it.

15. The Corinthians prided themselves on their wisdom. Paul appeals to it. If they are *wise* men they will appreciate the force of what he says. *Wise* is not the word used in the notable discussion in i. 20ff., but *phronimos*, which signifies 'intelligent', 'sensible'. *Ye* is emphatic. Paul does not need to demonstrate the point. They can see it for themselves.

16. *The cup of blessing* was the name given to the third cup in the passover feast. This may well have been the cup with which our Lord instituted the sacrament of Holy Communion, hence the appropriateness of the name. *Bless* does not refer to the attaching of some blessing to the cup, but to the kind of prayer that was used over it, though we may well hold that the effect of the prayer is to 'consecrate' the cup, i.e. set it apart for a holy use. Among the Jews the usual prayer of thanksgiving was one beginning, 'Blessed art Thou, O Lord'. After this came the matter for thanksgiving. Grace before meals, for example, began in this way. The reference then is to the prayer of thanksgiving said over the cup. Beet cites Chrysostom: 'A cup of blessing He called it; since, holding it in our hands, in this way we sing praise to Him.' It is interesting to find the cup mentioned before the bread, though when

Paul deals with the institution (xi. 23ff.) the bread comes first. The order here may be due to a desire to stress the shedding of the blood of the Lord. Or, it may be due to the prominence of the cup and the insignificance of bread in the pagan sacrifices to which Paul is leading up. The word *koinōnia, communion,* might be rendered 'participation in' (as RV mg.), or 'fellowship in' (cf. Goodspeed, 'in drinking it we share in the blood of Christ'). The meaning is that those who rightly receive the cup receive Christ. They are bound together in fellowship with Christ. As Calvin says, 'the soul has as truly *communion in the blood,* as we drink wine with the mouth'. Such reception is, of course, a spiritual process, and therefore takes place by faith. Paul affirms that the faithful communicant receives Christ. But he says nothing as to the 'how' of it. Hodge points out that Roman Catholics, Lutherans, and Reformed all agree 'that a participation of the cup is a participation of the blood of Christ'. But doctrines like transubstantiation or consubstantiation cannot be demonstrated from this passage. 'All that the passage asserts is the fact of a participation, the nature of that participation must be determined from other sources.' The statement about *the bread* is to be understood similarly. The broken loaf is a participation in *the body of Christ.*

17. This is a difficult verse to interpret in detail, but the stress on unity is clear. A single loaf was used at Communion, and Paul speaks of this as symbolizing and bringing about unity. Though believers are *many,* yet are they *one bread, and one body.* The place of Holy Communion in bringing about unity is indicated by the *for.* The sacrament springs from unity, and creates unity.

18. From specifically Christian observances Paul turns to those of the Jews, *Israel after the flesh.* This expression distinguishes the nation Israel from the true Israel, the Christian Church. In the Jewish system those who *eat of the sacrifices* by that very fact are *partakers* (the word is cognate with 'communion' in verse 16) *of the altar.* Those who receive the food of sacrifice enter into fellowship with all that the altar stands for.

19. Paul is now right back at the problem before the Corinthians. The order of the questions in AV is the opposite of that in the better MSS. Paul first asks, 'Is idol meat anything?' and then goes on to, 'Is even an idol anything?' The vigorous questions imply that both were shams.

20. *But* is the strong adversative *alla.* Far from the preceding, Paul affirms something which is nearly its opposite. He will not dispute the contention of the Corinthians that an idol is not a god at all. But he will not agree that therefore idols can safely be treated as nothing more than so many blocks of wood and stone. The *devils* make use of men's readiness to worship idols. Thus, when men sacrifice to idols, it cannot be said that they are engaging in some neutral activity that has no meaning. They are in fact sacrificing to evil spirits, like the people spoken of in Dt. xxxii. 17. To share food is to establish fellowship. Thus they are entering into *fellowship* with *devils.* Paul does not wish this to happen to his Corinthian friends.

21. He puts the alternatives in stark contrast. It is just not possible for men to be participants both in the Holy Communion and in idol feasts if they realize what they are doing. The one necessarily excludes the other. *The Lord's table* reminds us that the Lord is the host at the sacrament. By parity of reasoning *the table of devils* indicates that there may be other hosts. But if a man accepts the Lord's invitation he cannot in good conscience also accept the invitation of devils. If he is really in fellowship with the Lord he cannot also be in fellowship with devils. Some have thought that the reference to the two tables in close connection like this points to the Holy Communion as being essentially sacrificial in nature. Thus support is found for the doctrine of the Eucharistic sacrifice. This however is not a valid inference. The stress is on *koinōnia*, 'fellowship'. All that Paul is saying is that the Holy Communion, in one aspect, is a feeding at the table of the Lord, an enjoyment of fellowship with Him. Similarly, participation in an idol feast means having fellowship with demons. There may be many other aspects to either. Identity of principle is neither asserted nor implied.

22. The 'Or' at the beginning of this verse in the better MSS brings us to an alternative. Paul has been assuming that the Corinthians do not realize the significance of taking part in idol feasts. He has accordingly explained it. But suppose they do not understand the significance of all this. Then they would be wilfully provoking the Lord. A second question brings home the weakness of all men before their Maker and, therefore, the incredible folly of the kind of action of which he speaks.

f. The practical outcome (x. 23–xi. 1)

23. *All things are lawful* . . . repeats a statement already made in vi. 12 (where see notes). This time Paul says it twice, and adds *but all things edify not*. For *edify* see on viii. 1. There are some things that are not wise. They do not build men up in the faith. It is more important to avoid such matters than to assert one's rights.

24. It is important that every Christian have a concern for the well-being of others. There is no word in the Greek corresponding to *wealth*, and perhaps our translators could have chosen a better word (cf. RSV). Paul means that each Christian must seek to promote the best interests of other people, not selfishly seek his own.

25. In the preceding section the matter of attendance at idol feasts has been dealt with. Paul refused to countenance this in any shape or form. But buying meat in the *shambles* ('shops'; RSV, 'meat market') was a different matter. There, as we noted before on viii. 1–6, it would be difficult, if not impossible, to know whether a particular piece of meat had or had not been offered to an idol. There is no point in pressing one's scruples in such a situation. 'Don't ask fussy questions for conscience's sake' as Barclay translates. Over-scrupulousness is to be discouraged. It hinders rather than helps in such a situation.

26. The reason, given in a quotation from Ps. xxiv. 1, is that everything belongs to the Lord. Though the heathen may offer the meat to his idol, the Christian knows that it comes from the goodness of the Lord, and from no other source. Therefore, even though there may be some doubt as to what has happened to it on the way, the divine origin makes it all right for the Christian to eat.

27. A similar ruling is given on accepting an invitation to a meal. A meal in a private home is meant, for eating in idol temples has been dealt with above. When invited by a heathen, a Christian is at liberty to accept, and to eat whatever is provided without asking questions as to its origin, even though the meat might have come from a sacrifice.

28. The situation is different if someone expressly says, *This is offered in sacrifice unto idols.* The meat is now not simply a gift of God which has passed through unknown channels. It is the end-product of idolatry and is known to be such. To eat under such circumstances, some would think, would be to countenance idolatry. The Christian accordingly must not eat *for conscience sake.* The words which follow are absent from the better MSS, and seem to be a mechanical repetition from verses 25f.

29. Paul makes it clear that it is not the conscience of the eater that he means. He is writing of the strong Christian, who knows that offering meat to an idol cannot really alter its character. But the man who speaks to him, or some other in the company, may well not see it so. Out of consideration for the weaker conscience of such a one the strong should abstain from eating. The meaning of the latter part of the verse may be seen in Godet's explanation of the *hina ti* with which it begins, 'For what advantage can there be in my liberty being condemned. . . .' The action which to the strong is a simple exercise of *liberty* must not be made the means of offence to another.

30. It is only *by grace* (or perhaps, 'with thanksgiving') that the strong is able to partake of such meat. It is a gift of God, and he gives thanks for it. Paul does not wish that an action done in this spirit should be the means of bringing forth evil-speaking from others who do not see it in the same light. It is better to abstain rather than allow that to happen.

31. The principle is clear. The Christian is not concerned with the assertion of his rights, but with *the glory of God*. Eating, or drinking, or anything else, must be subordinated to this major consideration.

32. Paul urges his friends to have a tender concern for all, *Jews, Gentiles,* and *the church of God*. Their conduct might have repercussions in any of these groups, and they should endeavour to give no offence to any.

33, xi. 1. Paul concludes by appealing to his own example. No personal advantage determines his guiding aim. He seeks that *many* may be *saved*. He does not do the things that are pleasing to himself. So he calls on the converts to be *followers* (better, as RV, 'imitators') of him. Yet in the very act of saying this he points them away from himself. The only reason they should imitate him is that he imitates Christ. He trusts that his example will point them to the Saviour.

VI. DISORDERS IN PUBLIC WORSHIP
(xi. 2–xiv. 40)

a. The veiling of women (xi. 2–16)

The next subject to be dealt with is that of public worship. The Corinthians had asked Paul about one aspect of this subject at least (as we see from the 'now concerning' of xii. 1). Paul makes comments on other aspects also. He had evidently heard that some 'emancipated' Corinthian women had dispensed with the veil in public worship, and he argues that women should be veiled. For a woman to appear in public bareheaded was to act in what we would call a 'barefaced' manner. It was the mark of a woman of loose morals. It outraged the proprieties. Paul accordingly rejects it with decision. It is no part of the life of the Christian needlessly to flout the conventions.

2. First comes a word of praise, as is Paul's habit where this can in good conscience be done. We do not know what is behind *ye remember me in all things*, but it looks as though the reference is to directions Paul had given for public worship. *Paradoseis*, translated *ordinances*, is better 'traditions'. The reference is to that oral teaching which formed such an important part of early Christian instruction. The article points to the well-known Christian traditions. They were not Paul's own. The teachings had been handed down to Paul, and he passed them on to the converts. The term stresses the derivative nature of the gospel. It does not originate in the fertile mind of the teacher. See further on 2 Thes. ii. 15.[1]

3. *The head* indicates a relationship of superior authority, but it does not define that authority with precision (none of the relationships mentioned in this verse is exactly the same as any of the others). Bedale reminds us that the functions of the nervous system were not known to the ancients, who,

[1] *Op. cit.*, p. 138.

accordingly, did not view the *head* as we do (they held that man thinks with the midriff, the *phrēn*). Bedale argues that the use of this term here conveys much the same meaning as does verse 8: woman derives her being from man, and to that extent is subordinate to him.[1] It is this subordination that is the important point for Paul. Yet we should notice that he is not arguing for anything other than a partnership (cf. verse 11), though a partnership in which the man is the head of his household.[2]

4. A man ought to pray with his head uncovered. This was something new for Paul the Christian. Jewish men always prayed with their heads covered (as they still do). Greek women, as well as their menfolk, prayed with heads uncovered. Christians adopted a distinctive practice of their own. The covering of the head is the sign of being under authority to another. As a man is not in this way subject to any creature, he *dishonoureth his head* if he covers it when he prays. See below on verse 7. *Head* is primarily the physical head, but there may also be a reference to Christ (verse 3). For *prophesying* see on xii. 10.

5. Paul has argued that in the order of creation there is a sense in which the woman is subordinate to the man. This should be recognized in worship. The woman should wear something on her head. For her to pray or to prophesy without such a covering means that she *dishonoureth her head*. Paul uses forceful language. He maintains that it is as bad for her to pray in this way as it would be if she were *shaven*. The dishonour is the same.

6. The point is driven home. If a woman will not cover her head, then let that head be shorn. If she counts it *a shame* for

[1] JTS, Oct. 1954, pp. 211–215.
[2] C. S. Lewis has some very pertinent observations on this subject, *Mere Christianity*, London, 1955, pp. 99f.

her head to be shorn, let her understand that it is equally a shame to have her head uncovered. Thus Paul urges his point in the strongest terms.

7. The reason the man ought not to cover his head is that he is *the image and glory of God*. The reference is to Gn. i. 26, 27, where in the creation story it is said that God made man in His own image. There no distinction is made between the sexes, but Paul understands it particularly of the male. *Glory* is not mentioned in the Genesis account. It is Paul's understanding of the case. If man is the summit of creation, then he shows forth God's glory as does nothing else. Because of this high dignity Paul feels it right that there should be no sign of subordination about man when he worships. The woman has a place of her own, but it is not the man's place. She stands to the man in such a relation as does nothing else, and so she is called *the glory of the man*. This expression at one and the same time assures her of a high place in the scheme of things, and ensures that it is not man's place.

8, 9. When Paul says *the man is not of the woman* he means that man did not take his origin from woman (*ek*, *of*, denotes the source). *But the woman of the man* refers to Gn. ii. 21ff., where we read of Eve's being made from a rib taken from Adam's side. It is the same story which supplies the background to *neither was the man created for the woman* etc., for God said, 'It is not good that the man should be alone; I will make him an help meet for him' (Gn. ii. 18). Neither in her origin, nor in the purpose for which she was created can the woman claim priority, or even equality.

10. The first major point of difficulty in this verse is the reference to *power on her head*. The word *power* is *exousia*, which means 'authority'. The difficulty is that the context seems to demand a meaning like 'a symbol of subjection' (Moffatt) whereas the Greek word seems to mean rather 'a sign of her authority'. Indeed, Ramsay pours scorn on the idea that the term can indicate woman's subjection (which nevertheless in substance is the idea conveyed by most translators). He says it is 'a preposterous idea which a Greek scholar would laugh at anywhere except in the N.T.' He gives this explanation: 'In Oriental lands the veil is the power and the honour and dignity of the woman. With the veil on her head she can go anywhere in security and profound respect. She is not seen; it is a mark of thoroughly bad manners to observe a veiled woman in the street. She is alone. The rest of the people around are non-existent to her, as she is to them. She is supreme in the crowd. . . . But without the veil the woman is a thing of nought, whom any one may insult. . . . A woman's authority and dignity vanish along with the all-covering veil that she discards' (cited in Robertson and Plummer). Paul's meaning then, is that by covering her head the woman secures her own place of dignity and authority. At the same time she recognizes her subordination.

The second difficulty is the expression *because of the angels*. The probability is that Paul means that good angels are always with us, and especially at worship. It is not only a matter of what the men and women in the congregation see and·think. The angels will observe what the woman does. She must not be unseemly before them.[1] This is the more appropriate in that angels serve men (Heb. i. 14), yet they do not rebel. The celestial observers may also be thought of as the agents of God in punishing and the like (cf. Moffatt, *the angels* 'here are more than a periphrasis for the divine Being; they are the divine executive'). Some have thought the meaning to be that bad angels will lust against unveiled women in the spirit of Gn. vi. 2. This seems unlikely. *The angels* without qualification would not be understood of evil spirits. More-

---

[1] J. A. Fitzmyer draws attention to passages in the Dead Sea Scrolls in which men with any blemish (cripples, diseased, etc.) are excluded from the army or from the assembly, because of the presence of angels (*New Testament Studies*, vol. IV, pp. 48–58). No unseemliness must come before them.

over there seems no reason why such angels should be tempted only during worship.

11. What Paul has been saying might easily be understood of an undue subordination of women. This is far from his thought. There is a partnership between the sexes and *in the Lord* neither exists without the other. The man must not vaunt his place.

12. Earlier Paul had made the point that woman took her origin from man. Now he supplements that by pointing out that *the man is also by* (*dia*) *the woman*. The reference is no longer, of course, to the Genesis story, but to the ordinary processes of birth. In this sense every man is *by the woman*. The addition, *but all things of God*, is a typical Pauline reminder of the priority of the divine. *Of* is *ek* once more, so that we have the thought that the source of all things, the origin of all things, is God. The man and the woman are not to be thought of as independent beings. The implications for conduct are plain.

13. Paul makes an appeal to the Corinthians' own understanding. *Yourselves* is emphatic, both from its position, and because *autois* is added to *humin*. They can see for themselves. They need not rely on Paul's direction to them. *Is it comely, prepon*, is an appeal to the fitness of things.

14, 15. *Long hair*, reasons the apostle, is a *shame* to a man. This had not universally been the case. Some among the ancient Greeks, notably the Spartans, and some philosophers, had had long hair. But generally speaking what Paul says held among mankind. Exceptions were local and temporary. It certainly must have held in first-century Corinth, and in the places known to the men living there, else Paul could never have couched his appeal in this way. By contrast, long hair is *a glory* to a woman. The precise length is not specified, and is not important. Woman's hair is longer than man's, and distinctively so. This fact points to nature as giving in symbol the need for a woman to have her head covered on appropriate occasions. Indeed, her hair is *given her for a covering*.

16. But Paul has no intention of arguing the matter with any who is given to wordy battles (*contentious, philoneikos*, is one who loves strife). Such are capable of prolonging an argument indefinitely. In the face of such an attitude Paul points to universal custom. *We have no such custom*, i.e. such as women praying or prophesying with head uncovered. Exactly who he means by *we* is not clear, but the addition, *neither the churches of God*, shows that what he has just outlined is the habit throughout the Christian churches.

Behind all that Paul says in this section is the principle that the Christian should always act in a seemly manner (cf. xiv. 40, 'Let all things be done decently and in order'). The application of this principle to the situation at Corinth yields the direction that women must have their heads covered when they worship. The principle is of permanent validity, but we may well feel that the application of it to the contemporary scene need not yield the same result. In other words, in the light of totally different social customs, we may well hold that the fullest acceptance of the principle underlying this chapter does not require that in Western lands in the twentieth century women must always wear hats when they pray. 'We must remember that when Paul spoke about women as he did in the letters to the Corinthians, he was writing to the most licentious city in the ancient world, and that in such a place modesty had to be observed and more than observed; and that it is quite unfair to wrest a local ruling from the circumstances in which it was given, and to make it a universal principle.'[1]

b. The Lord's supper (xi. 17–34)

i. The offences (xi. 17–22). Accustomed as we are to the service of Holy Communion being the most solemn and

[1] W. Barclay, *Letters to the Seven Churches*, London, 1957, p. 75.

dignified of services, this passage comes as something of a surprise. Clearly the service was far from being edifying, or even dignified, in first-century Corinth. The passage is important as throwing light on the way the service was conducted, and as giving us important teaching on the theology of Holy Communion.

17. *In this that I declare unto you* means rather, 'commanding you this'. The verb, *parangellō*, is that for an authoritative charge. The situation is serious, and Paul is not simply offering a few academic comments. He commands that it be set right. Introducing the previous section he had been able to praise the Corinthians for the way they kept 'the traditions'. When he comes to deal with the Communion service he finds himself unable to *praise*. He gives voice to the supreme condemnation of any assembly for worship: they *come together not for the better, but for the worse*. Instead of the Communion being supremely an act of edification, it was having a disruptive effect.

18. Paul begins with *first of all*, but, as there is no 'secondly' answering to it, this is probably a way of stressing the importance of what he has to say. There is no article with *church* in the Greek, so that the expression is rather like our 'in church'. But even there, in the assembly for worship, Paul hears of *divisions*. The word is *schismata*, which he used in i. 10, of the dissensions which had rent the church into factions. These intruded into the holiest of worshipping actions. *I partly believe it* is a reminder that Paul was not credulous. He did not accept every tale that he heard. On this occasion he recognized that there was some exaggeration in the account that had reached him, but he recognized also an unpleasant amount of truth.

19. Philosophically he accepts the inevitability of *heresies, haireseis*. This word comes from a root stressing the idea of choosing. It comes to mean the choice of a group of opinions, and so those who have chosen in a like way. There is at first no necessarily derogative significance attaching to it. It is used of the Sadducees (Acts v. 17), the Pharisees (Acts xv. 5), and the Christians (Acts xxiv. 5, 14). But it can be one of 'the works of the flesh' (Gal. v. 20), and this is the sense of it here. It is the same kind of thing as the 'divisions' of verse 18. It is only as those who choose in a self-willed manner make their appearance that *they which are approved may be made manifest*. The idea in *approved, dokimoi*, is that of having stood the test. Obviously if such people are to appear the test is necessary.

20. The adjective *kuriakon*, translated *the Lord's*, is found in the New Testament only here and in Rev. i. 10. It stresses the connection with the Lord. The disorders at Corinth are so serious that when the church meets for the sacrament it is not *the Lord's* supper that is eaten. The disorders have given it a different character. It is no longer *the Lord's*.

21. This verse reveals that at Corinth the Holy Communion was not simply a token meal as with us, but an actual meal. Moreover it seems clear that it was a meal to which each of the participants brought food. Such common meals, in which the rich shared with the poor, sometimes occurred in heathen religions, where they were called *eranoi*. For a time there was in the early Church in association with the Holy Communion a meal called the *agapē* or 'love-feast' (2 Pet. ii. 13; Jude 12; see RV). But at Corinth what took place was a travesty of love. The Corinthians did not even reach the standards of the heathen. Each put his provisions in front of him and proceeded to eat them. Indeed, he ate *before* his neighbour, which gives a picture of an undignified scramble, or perhaps of some who had brought food impatiently starting before others had arrived (slaves would often be unable to arrive early). The upshot was that some, who were poor, went hungry, and some, who were rich, drank too much. There is a sharp contrast between the hungry poor (lacking even necessary food), and the drunken rich. There was no pretence at making the meal a common one, with real sharing. We see that the divisions of verse 18 were on the grounds of wealth and social position.

22. A typical series of rhetorical questions hammers at the evil of the practice. Home is the place to satisfy one's hunger and thirst. To behave like the Corinthians is to despise *the church*, that *church* whose dignity is brought out with the addition *of God*. It is to shame the poor. There is no place whatever for praise.

ii. A reminder of the institution (xi. 23–26). It is practically certain that this Epistle was written before any of the Gospels, which means that this is the earliest account we have of the institution of the Holy Communion. Indeed, it is the earliest record of any words of our Lord. It is one of the very few incidents in the earthly life of our Lord which Paul describes in detail. There are some features of this account which we do not find elsewhere, for example, the command to continue the service 'till he come' (verse 26) Other points are indicated in the notes.

23. The verbs *received* and *delivered* (*paralambanō* and *paradidōmi*) are almost technical terms for receiving and passing on the Christian traditions (cf. verse 2). This, taken with the general probability, leads most commentators to feel that Paul should not be taken as meaning that he had a personal revelation from the Lord on this matter. Against this is the emphatic *I*, *egō*, which begins this verse. There seems no reason why Paul should say, '*I* received of the Lord', if he means, 'I received from other men a tradition deriving ultimately from the Lord'. There are several references to revelations made directly to Paul (Acts xviii. 9f., xxii. 18, xxiii. 11, xxvii. 23–5; Gal. i. 12, ii. 2; 2 Cor. xii. 7). It seems as though this is another such case. The use of *apo* rather than *para* for *from* does not necessarily indicate an indirect report (though it would be consistent with it), for it refers to direct communication in Col. i. 7, iii. 24; 1 Jn. i. 5. The night when the sacrament was instituted is designated *the same night in which he was betrayed* (better, 'he was being betrayed'). Paul brings out the poignancy of the institution of that feast of love which was to bring such strength and consolation to Christians, at the very time when human malignancy was engaged in betraying the Saviour to His enemies.

24. An interesting minor point is that Matthew and Mark use the verb 'bless' of the bread, though Luke employs the same verb that Paul uses. All three use 'give thanks' of the wine. There is no important difference between these expressions, for the prayer of thanksgiving would have begun, 'Blessed art Thou, O Lord' (see note on x. 16). We should probably omit the words *Take, eat*. They are not in the better mss, and they are the kind of harmonizing addition which scribes would naturally make. Jesus broke the bread, and said, *This is my body* (Moffatt, 'This means my body'). These words have been made the proof text for doctrines like transubstantiation and consubstantiation with their realistic identification of the bread with the body of Christ. However, *is* can denote various kinds of identification, as we see from the use in passages like Jn. viii. 12, x. 9; 1 Cor. x. 4, to name no others. Moreover in the next verse the cup is not 'my blood', but, 'the new covenant in my blood'. The words will not prove all that advocates of such theories would wish. On the other hand, they should not be minimized into giving us a 'Zwinglian' view, that the service is nothing more than an occasion when we think of Christ. There is a very real gift of the Saviour in the sacrament, none the less real for being essentially spiritual. 'The sacrament is a medium of communion with the body and blood of Christ, and a real means whereby faith appropriates the blessings which flow from the glorified Christ in virtue of His death' (Edwards).

The next words are *which is for you*. The MSS on which AV depends have inserted *broken*, others 'given', or 'bruised'. Paul's account leaves the word to be supplied. The emphasis is on the vicarious work of Christ. What happened to the body was *for* us. There was purpose in His suffering, and that purpose was directed towards His people. *This do* is present continuous: 'Keep on doing this.' This is important, for there is some textual doubt about Lk. xxii. 19. If it be judged that the latter part of that verse is no part of the true text, this is the sole record of the command to continue the Communion, though we should not pass over the significance of the regular practice of the Church from the very first (Acts ii. 42). *Remembrance* is *anamnēsis*, which means the activity of calling to mind. By breaking and receiving the bread we recall Christ's sufferings for us. *Of me* is emphatic (*emēn*, not *mou*). It stresses the Christ-centred nature of the service.

25. There is no verb *took* in the Greek, though this may give the sense of it. The language is terse and vivid. The impression left is that the bread was broken and shared during the course of the meal, and the cup was taken at the end. The word *diathēkē, testament*, presents some problems, too complex to be discussed here.[1] Briefly, *diathēkē* is the usual Greek word for 'last will and testament' (hence AV). This is practically the only meaning it has in Greek writings generally, and it has it with great frequency. But in the Greek Old Testament the word is used regularly to translate the Hebrew for 'covenant' (277 times). The question in the New Testament is, 'Is *diathēkē* to be understood as in Greek generally, or as in the Greek Old Testament?' Probably the answer differs from passage to passage. Here the meaning will be 'covenant'. Jesus is referring to the 'new covenant' prophesied in Je. xxxi. 31ff. The idea of covenant dominates the Old Testament. The people entered into a covenant with the Lord (as nar-

[1]The word is discussed in chapter II of my *The Apostolic Preaching of the Cross* (London, 1955).

rated in Ex. xxiv), and from then on they were God's people. The prophecy of Jeremiah shows that this was not permanent, but that the old covenant in due time would be replaced by a new one, based on forgiveness of sins, and with the law of God written in the hearts of the people. Jesus is saying, then, that the shedding of His blood is the means of establishing the new covenant. It provides forgiveness of sins, and opens the way for the activity of the Holy Spirit in the heart of the believer. The whole Jewish system is replaced by the Christian, and everything centres on the death of the Lord, which establishes the new covenant. *My* is the emphatic *emos*. The place of the Lord is absolutely central.

26. The importance of obeying Christ's command to continue the observance of the feast is brought out. The important word here is that rendered *shew* (*katangellō*). This has sometimes been made the proof text for positions like that expressed in W. Bright's hymn,

'We here present, we here spread forth to Thee
That only Offering perfect in Thine eyes,
The one true, pure, immortal Sacrifice.'

This, however, is quite unscriptural. In the Communion we receive Christ. We present neither Him nor His sacrifice to the Father. We present, and can present, only ourselves. *Katangellō* means 'announce', 'proclaim'. In the New Testament it is used mostly of preaching the gospel. Always it denotes an activity exercised towards men, and never one exercised towards God. Thus here it means that the solemn observance of the service of Holy Communion is a vivid proclamation of the Lord's death. In word and symbol Christ's death for men is set forth before them. 'The Eucharist is an *acted* sermon, an *acted* proclamation of the death which it commemorates' (Robertson and Plummer). *Till he come* reminds us of the eschatological aspect of Holy Communion.

It looks forward to the day when the Lord will come again. It will not be necessary in the new order that will then appear. But till then it keeps us mindful not only of the Lord's first coming, when He suffered for our sins, but also of His second advent, when He will come to take us unto Himself.

iii. The practical outcome (xi. 27–34). Paul now goes on to speak of the way in which the service should be conducted. The exposition of the meaning of the service he has just given lifts the question from the realm of liturgical minutiae. It is the observance of a most solemn rite, instituted by the Lord Himself, and charged with deep and sacred meaning. As such it should be observed with unfailing reverence.

27. *Wherefore, hōste*, stresses consequence. It is because of the significance just outlined that men must observe the service with due care. There is a sense in which all must partake *unworthily*, for none can ever be worthy of the goodness of Christ to us. But in another sense we can come *worthily*, i.e. in faith, and with a due performance of all that is fitting for so solemn a rite. To neglect this is to come *unworthily* in the sense castigated here. A man who does this is *guilty of the body and blood of the Lord*. The greatness of the gift that is offered is the measure of the greatness of his guilt.

28. *Examine* is *dokimazetō*, 'test'. It is often used of the testing of metals. Paul means that nobody should take the Holy Communion as a matter of course, as just another service. It is a solemn rite, instituted by the Lord Himself, charged with deep significance. Before taking part in such a service, the very least that we can do is to conduct a rigorous self-examination. Failure to do so will result in communicating 'unworthily' (verse 27). In passing we notice that the reference to *bread* at the moment of reception (not 'the body of the Lord') does not accord with theories like transubstantiation. The bread remains bread.

29. *Unworthily* seems to be no part of the true text, and the sense is as RV. *Damnation* is too strong a translation for *krima*, which means rather 'condemnation'. Paul does not mean that a person who communicates wrongly incurs eternal damnation, but that he comes under the measure of condemnation appropriate to his act. *Not discerning the Lord's body* is difficult. The verb *diakrinō* means 'to distinguish', and so 'to discern', 'to separate'. Here it will mean distinguishing the Lord's supper from other meals, i.e. not regarding it as like any other meal. The true text reads 'the body', not 'the Lord's body', though, of course, there is no difference in sense. Some think the *body* to be the Church, as in xii. 13; Col. i. 18. But there seems no real reason for thinking that the term means anything different from what it meant in verse 27. At the same time there is a marked stress throughout this whole passage on the corporate nature of the rite, and on the responsibility of each to all.

30. Spiritual ills may have physical results. Paul informs his friends that the reason for the ill health and even the death of some of their number goes back to a wrong attitude to this most solemn service. Some see a reference to the results of excessive drinking (verse 21). But what Paul means is probably not what we should call the 'natural' results of excesses, but the chastening hand of the Lord (verse 32).

31, 32. The Corinthians evidently thought there was little amiss with them. But Paul points out the value of systematic right judging of ourselves. We should make a practice (such is the force of the imperfect tense) of 'distinguishing ourselves' (so, rather than *judge ourselves*), i.e. distinguishing between what we are and what we ought to be (the verb is *diakrinō* as in verse 29). Barclay renders it, 'if we truly discerned what we are like'. Then we should not find ourselves *judged*, i.e. the objects of the kind of judgment Paul has spoken of in the previous verse. *We are chastened of the Lord* means that these disasters are not nameless evils, but the tokens of God's love. They are sent to bring us back from the wrong way, so that we shall not share in the condemnation of *the world*.

33, 34. Arising out of this discussion (*hōste, wherefore*) Paul gives the conclusion of the matter. He urges them to *tarry one for another* when it comes to eating. That is to say he wants the disgraceful scramble of verse 21 to cease. Indeed the purpose of the Lord's supper is not to satisfy physical hunger at all. If a man is hungry, *let him eat at home*. So Paul urges them to avoid condemnation. These are the urgent things. Apparently he felt that there were other matters concerning the administration of the sacrament which were not so urgent. They could wait until such time as Paul came to Corinth. Incidentally, *when* is the indefinite *hōs an*. He did not know when it would be.

c. Spiritual gifts (xii. 1–xiv. 40)

It was universally accepted in antiquity that some people, who were in specially close touch with the divine, had special spiritual endowments. Usually this was understood in terms of trances, ecstatic speech, and the like. From the day of Pentecost on, there were some within the Christian Church who manifested such spiritual gifts. While the Holy Spirit was given to all believers (Rom. viii. 9, 14), yet He came to some in a special way, so that they did unusual things such as speaking in a tongue they did not understand. To many early believers this kind of thing was pre-eminently the hallmark of a 'spiritual' man. By comparison the practice of Christian virtue seemed staid and colourless. Paul's discussion of this subject is epoch-making. He begins by showing that it is the Lordship of Christ that is important. All spiritual gifts must be brought to this touchstone. If their exercise is inimical to Christ, they are not of God. Then he makes the point that there are many gifts of the Spirit, and all are necessary. He lists some of them, but then proceeds to the 'more excellent

way', the way of Christian love. The use of spectacular gifts
has its place. Paul does not deny it. But he insists that the important thing is the manifestation of ethical qualities, especially love, which the presence of the Spirit in the heart of the
believer makes possible (cf. Gal. v. 22ff.). Then Paul goes on
to relate the exercise of the spectacular gifts to the conduct of
public worship, and he insists that all must be done in orderly
fashion. It is clear that he assigns to the so-called 'spiritual'
gifts no such place of eminence as they were accorded in
popular esteem.

i. The variety of gifts (xii. 1–11). *Now concerning* is the
expression used in vii. 1, viii. 1, in introducing subjects mentioned in the letter from the Corinthians to Paul. Here is
another topic on which they had asked direction. Whether
gifts should be added after *spiritual* (as AV) is not certain. The
word *pneumatikōn* is of indeterminate gender. It could accordingly denote 'spiritual men' or 'spiritual things'. Usually it is
held to refer here to 'spiritual things', i.e. the spiritual 'gifts',
and this is likely, though we should notice that the immediate
context is full of references to persons. However there is not a
great deal of difference, for both Paul and the Corinthians
are thinking of the men who exercised the gifts. The word
pneumatikos is not the usual one for the spiritual gifts, *charisma*
being the common term. Notice the affectionate *brethren*, introducing a section where there may be much rebuke. For the
formula *I would not have you ignorant*, cf. 1 Thes. iv. 13, and the
note there.[1] It indicates that the subject introduced is an
important one.

2. As it stands this verse in the Greek is ungrammatical.
Two possibilities have been suggested with some plausibility.
The one is Hort's suggestion, that for *hote* we should read *pote*,
when the sense would be, 'You know that formerly you were
Gentiles, carried away. . . .' The other is that we supply

---

[1]*Op. cit.*, p. 84.

another *ye were* (*ēte*) with the participle *apagomenoi, carried away*, which in the Greek is at the end of the sentence. This would yield the meaning, 'You know that, when-you were Gentiles, you were carried away. . . .' The difference is not great, and it does not matter much which we adopt. *Gentiles* is used in the sense 'heathen'. Usually in the New Testament the word means non-Jews, but sometimes it means all who are not Christian (e.g. 1 Thes. iv. 5), and this is the case here. The characteristic of these *Gentiles* is that they are *carried away* to idols. The verb is often used of leading away a prisoner or condemned person (e.g. Mk. xiv. 44, xv. 16). The heathen are pictured, not as men freely following the gods their intellects have fully approved, but as under constraint, as helpless, as men who know no better. There is something pathetic about idol worship. *Dumb idols* characterizes their deities as totally unable to answer those who call upon them. They could give no revelation. They could make nothing known to their worshippers. *Even as ye were led* is probably, 'how ye were led whenever the occasion happened' (Edwards). The construction is unusual (Moulton says it is one of only three places in the New Testament where the old iterative use of *an* survives[1]), and serves to underline the plight of the heathen. Far from reaching the dignity of the sons of God, they were continually led about. And no matter how they were led, they were brought only to dumb deities.

3. Because of this background the Corinthians could not be expected to know everything about Christianity, and more particularly about 'spiritual men'. So Paul lays down his first point that the genuinely spiritual man is to be known by his utterances. *Anathema*, translated *accursed*, is a word which meant originally 'something laid up', i.e. laid up in a sacred place. So it came to mean that which is given to a deity. Since what is thus given is totally lost to the giver, the word came to have the meaning of 'that which is destroyed'.

[1]*Prolegomena*, p. 167.

Particularly was this the case when the destruction was itself a religious act, for example, when Jericho was totally destroyed at the command of the Lord. So the meaning passes over to 'accursed', and this is the usual sense of the term in New Testament days. That someone had called Jesus accursed is the natural inference from these words, but how or why we cannot say. Elsewhere Paul says that Christ was 'made a curse for us' (Gal. iii. 13). It is not beyond the bounds of possibility that some excitable and imperfectly instructed Corinthian had distorted the thought in an ecstatic utterance. If Paul is referring to an exclamation made by a non-Christian, a Jew is more likely to have used the term *anathema* than a Gentile. The Corinthians may have wondered whether the excitement with which such a statement was made did not indicate divine inspiration. Paul firmly denies this. The expression is a denial of the lordship of Christ. It asserts that Jesus is rejected of God. That is not the way the Spirit leads men. The Spirit leads men to ascribe lordship to Christ. It is only *by the Holy Ghost* that a man can really speak of Christ as Lord. This does not mean that it is impossible for an unbeliever to say the words *Jesus is the Lord*. Obviously he can do this in mockery. But the words can be said with full meaning only under the influence of the Holy Spirit. Paul means that it is not a human discovery that *Jesus is the Lord*. It is a discovery that can be made only when the Spirit works in a man's heart.

4. *Daireseis, diversities*, is from a root expressing the idea of a division. The noun might thus mean 'apportionment', 'allotment' (the corresponding verb is used in this sense in verse 11), though most take it as AV. *Charismatōn, gifts*, is the usual word for one of the extraordinary endowments the Spirit confers on men. The word is from the same root as the great Christian word 'grace', *charis*. Basically it stresses the freeness, the bounty of the gift. It might be used in a general sense of God's gifts to men (Rom. xi. 29), or of the 'spiritual gift' that Paul wished to impart to the Romans (Rom. i. 11).

But characteristically it is used, as here, for the special operations of the Holy Spirit within men. The Corinthians had apparently used the *gifts* as a means of fomenting division. They regarded the possession of such *gifts* as a matter for pride, and set up one against another on the basis of the possession or otherwise of this or that gift. Paul insists that this is the wrong attitude. Though he recognizes that there is diversity in the endowments conferred by the Spirit, yet it is *the same Spirit.* The Spirit does not fight against Himself. The gifts He gives to one are to set forward the same divine purpose as the different gifts He gives to another.

5. The Greek word translated *differences* is the same as that rendered 'diversities' in the preceding and following verses. *Administrations, diakoniōn,* expresses the idea of service (see note on the cognate word *diakonos* in iii. 5). There are different ways of serving. But the differences are not important. It is *the same Lord. Lord,* as usually in Paul, refers to Christ. This passage reveals something of the high place Paul assigns to Him, for He is mentioned between the Holy Spirit and God the Father. Paul does not formally enunciate the doctrine of the Trinity, but passages like this are distinctly Trinitarian in character. The thought of service might be that of service rendered to Christ. But, since in the previous and the following sections it is the action of the divine within the believer that is described, we should probably understand this verse of the service that the indwelling Christ enables His people to render, or perhaps of the service to which He calls them. Though this service differs from person to person it is *the same Lord* in them that does the work.

6. *Operations* translates *energēmatōn.* This derives from the usual word for 'work' (the verb from this root is rendered *worketh* in this very verse). It means something like 'activity'. The thought is that of God's power in action. The divine activities are manifold, *but it is the same God.* For the third time

Paul brings out his point that there can be no division among men on the ground of the 'gifts', because it is one and the same God who provides the 'gifts' in all their diversity. This time he adds, *which worketh all in all*. The first *all* is neuter, and means 'all things'. The second might be either masculine or neuter, 'all things in all men', or, 'all things in all things'. As the emphasis in this passage is on the working of God within men the former is to be preferred.

7. It is not clear whether we should understand *the manifestation of the Spirit* as meaning 'that which the Spirit makes manifest', or 'that which makes the Spirit manifest'. Either way the thought is of the spiritual gifts, and of the exercise of the spiritual gifts as something public and open, which others than their possessors perceive. *To every man* (rather, as RSV, 'to each') probably indicates that the gifts of the Spirit are not reserved for a few outstanding men. Some gift is given to each. These gifts are not for rivalry and jealousy, but *to profit withal*. This might in English be understood to mean 'that he might profit thereby', but the Greek is more indefinite, 'for profit'. While it is true that a man who has a spiritual gift is thereby profited, the advantage is wider. Other people are also profited. Indeed, that is the point of it. Spiritual gifts are always given to be used, and the use is for the edification of the whole body of believers, not some individual possessor of the gift.

8. What has been put shortly in verses 4–6 is now expanded, with the mention of a number of gifts which the Spirit gives. This leads up to the reiteration of the truth that it is the one Spirit who provides all these. The first two gifts enumerated present us with a problem, for it is not easy to see the distinction Paul intends between *the word of wisdom* (*sophia*), and *the word of knowledge* (*gnōsis*). *Word* (there is no article) will signify 'utterance'. The Spirit gives the power to utter *wisdom* or *knowledge* as the case may be. The former term denotes the highest mental excellence (see further on i. 24). AG point out that Paul associates *knowledge* with mysteries, revelations and prophecy (xiii. 2, xiv. 6). They suggest that he thus 'invests the term with the significance of supernatural mystical knowledge', a meaning which is common in Hellenistic Greek, more especially among the mystery religions. Paul thinks of all *wisdom* and *knowledge* that the Christian may have as coming from the Spirit.

9. The difficulty here is that whereas *faith* is the characteristic of all Christians (they may be spoken of simply as 'believers'), Paul is limiting it to a certain group to whom it comes as a special gift. There is no difficulty about the idea of faith being a gift; all faith must be reckoned as God's good gift to men. The difficulty is in seeing what this special faith is over against the common faith that all believers have. Unfortunately there is little to guide us. Paul proceeds to speak of things like healing and the working of miracles, so that probably he has in mind a special faith which is associated with miraculous operations (cf. xiii. 2, 'though I have all faith, so that I could remove mountains'). There is no article with *gifts of healing* (nor with any other item in this list). The effect of this is to fasten attention on the quality of the gift, rather than its individuality. *Healing* is plural in the Greek, which perhaps means that there were 'healings' for various kinds of sickness and disease.

10. *Working* translates the Greek word rendered 'operations' in verse 6. Here, as there, it is plural. *Miracles* is *dunameōn*, a word which stresses the element of power in the 'mighty works'. It is often used of the miracles of Jesus. We can only conjecture what the term is meant to cover. As it is mentioned immediately after healings, and preceded by *to another* it would seem that miraculous cures are not meant. Jesus Himself did miracles other than healings, like the stilling of the storm, and the feeding of the multitudes, but there is no record of His followers doing such things. We should, however, notice that Mk. xvi. 17f. prophesies that believers would cast out devils, 'take up serpents', and drink poisons without coming to harm. Calvin thinks we see the kind of thing that is meant in the smiting of Elymas with blindness (Acts xiii. 11), and the deaths of Ananias and Sapphira (Acts v. 1–10).

Prophecy is inspired speech. In the Old Testament the prophets were men who spoke the word of God to their generation. Nowadays the element of prediction in their prophecies is often minimized, but it should not be overlooked. On occasion the ability to predict the future accurately might be regarded as the mark of the true prophet. Yet the emphasis is not on prediction, but on setting forth what God has said. This, too, is the function of the prophets of the New Testament. Prophecy might be occasional (Acts xix. 6), or a settled office (verses 28f.). Here Paul probably has mostly in mind the second class, though his expression is broad enough to include both. His point is that the Spirit gives to some the ability to utter inspired words, which convey the message of God to the hearers.

Discerning of spirits is something that every Christian must practise in a measure (1 Jn. iv. 1). But there must have been occasions in the early Church when it was very difficult to know the origin of spirits, and from this verse we find that some had a special gift of discernment in this matter.

Tongues appears to have been a special form of ecstatic speech when the person uttering the words did not know what they meant (unless he had also the gift of interpretation). On the day of Pentecost mentioned in Acts ii there was an unusual manifestation, when Peter and others were understood by people from many places speaking many languages. Some commentators (e.g. Hodge) think that it is this gift of speaking in other languages which is meant here. This is an attractive solution, but nobody reading 1 Corinthians would think that this is what Paul had in mind. The gift is not part of the evangelistic programme of the Church, but is exercised among believers. It is not understood by folk speaking other languages, but requires a special gift of interpretation. Without the gift of interpretation its possessor is to speak 'to himself, and to God' (xiv. 28), which is a strange way to treat one of the world's recognized languages. The gift of which Paul speaks was not one whereby men might the more easily be understood by others, but one wherein they did not even understand themselves. Ecstatic utterance in no known language, and under the influence of the Spirit, seems to be Paul's meaning. After this gift Paul speaks of *the interpretation of tongues*. This was the gift whereby God made intelligible what was hidden from all in the ecstatic utterances just referred to.

11. The variety of gifts is stressed with the emphatic position of *all these*. The unity of the divine purpose comes out in the expression *that one and the selfsame Spirit*. Previously Paul has spoken only of 'the same' (verses 4, 5, 6), but the stronger form here underlies the truth that the divergent gifts do not point to divergent divine purposes. It is the one God who gives all these gifts. The inference is that the gifts are not to be set over against one another, with the possessors appearing as rivals. *Every man severally* is a reminder that God deals with us as individuals. He does not deal out His gifts indiscriminately, but meets the needs and the capacities of each man. The personality of the Spirit is brought out with the concluding *as he will*. The New Testament thinks of the Spirit as a person, not simply a power; as 'He', not 'It'.

ii. Diversity in unity illustrated from the human body (**xii. 12–31**). In verse 12 Paul outlines the thesis that he is about to expound. It takes many different *members* to make up one human body. The members differ inevitably. But their differences do not affect the fact that there is a fundamental unity. *So also is Christ*. The thought of Christ as the Head of the body is not explicit here as in Eph. v. 23; Col. i. 18, etc.

But Paul's favourite thought that the Christian is 'in Christ' (for this phrase see note on i. 30) is at the basis of his statement. Since all believers are in Him, they are one body. As with the human body so with Christ. There is unity in diversity.

13. Baptism symbolizes this truth. Already in i. 13ff. Paul has appealed to the one baptism into Christ as pointing the Corinthians away from their factions and rivalries to the essential unity of believers in Christ. The same thought is put in a different form here. *Jews or Gentiles*, . . . *bond* (i.e. 'slaves') *or free*, all alike are baptized into *one body*. This unity transcends any distinctions that may exist. Notice the emphasis on the *Spirit*. *By one Spirit* is really 'in one Spirit', the construction being the same as that in Mt. iii. 11 ('with water', 'with the Holy Ghost'). It points to the Spirit as the element 'in' which they were baptized. Those baptized are brought within the sphere of the Spirit. It is only as there is an activity of the Spirit that baptism has meaning. But the Spirit is not thought of as external. All Christians have been *made to drink one Spirit* (there is no *into* in the better MSS.). The Spirit has entered their innermost being. In all Christians it is the same Spirit that is at work in the deepest recesses of their personality. The verb is sometimes used of irrigating, whence comes the thought of abundant supply (cf. Goodspeed, 'we have all been saturated with one Spirit').

14. Diversity is not an accidental attribute of the body. It is of its very essence. No one member is to be equated with the body. It takes many members to make up one body.

15, 16. Evidently the disputes at Corinth had depressed some of the less gifted members of the Church. They wondered whether they had any right to belong to so august a body as the Church, including as it did men who possessed very wonderful and spectacular gifts. Paul gives encouragement to such first of all. *The foot* may very well be depressed at its inability to exercise the complicated functions of a *hand* (there is no article with *hand* in the Greek). But that does not put it outside *the body*. The latter part of both verses is probably to be taken as a statement rather than as a question, 'it is not therefore not of the body'. As with *foot* and *hand*, so with *ear* and *eye*. Though *the ear* is not an *eye* that does not put it outside the body. Bodies need feet as well as hands, ears as well as eyes. Chrysostom acutely points out that the foot contrasts itself not with the eye, but with the hand. We are prone to envy those who surpass us a little, rather than those who are patently in a different class.

17. We should omit *an*, and read, 'if all the body were eye...' The necessity for differing functions is stressed. There is also an implication that no member of the body can perform the function of another member. The ear cannot see, but then the eye cannot hear either. Both hearing and seeing are necessary if the body is to function normally. So with *hearing* and *smelling*.

18. The whole is placed on the highest level with the reminder that *the members* are not in the body at haphazard. They are *set . . . in the body* by God. Their place and their function derive from the divine appointment, and not from anything lower than that. *Hath* before *set* should be omitted. The verb is in the aorist, and the reference is to creation. God made things so. *Every one of them* brings out the point that God's care does not extend only to the more important and spectacular. He has extended His oversight and His arrangement to every member of the body. *As it hath pleased him* is really 'as He willed'. This is the way God has planned things. There is a finality about the arrangement.

19, 20. The incongruity of the exaggerated reverence the Corinthians had for one or other of the members is brought out by a rhetorical question. No matter how important any one member may be, there can be no body formed from it alone. *But now*, as things are, there are *many members*, who together make up but *one body*. This emphatic reiteration of the theme of unity in diversity concludes this part of the discussion.

21. In verses 15f. Paul has been dealing with the humbler members of the church, who felt that their lack of the spectacular gifts might well put them out of the body. Now he looks at the other side of the same situation. Evidently those who possessed the greater gifts looked down on their less gifted brethren. In their lofty eminence they thought that they could manage well enough without the unimportant contributions of lowly people. But *the eye* cannot do without *the hand*, nor *the head* without *the feet*. The fact that one member of the body discharges its own function well does not mean that it can dispense with the services of other members which discharge other services. Barclay reminds us that we cannot think in terms of relative importance. 'Whenever we begin to think about our own importance in the Christian Church, the possibility of really Christian work is gone.'

22. From the negative Paul proceeds to the positive. Not only can no member do without other members, but even the *more feeble* members are *necessary*. *Feeble* is from *asthenēs*, which basically means 'sick'. So it comes to mean 'sickly', 'feeble'. The word emphasizes the complete unimportance of the members so indicated. Yet, even so, Paul does not speak of them as an 'addition' or even 'a welcome addition'. He says they are *necessary*. They cannot be dispensed with if we are to have a body. Robertson and Plummer comment that in society the humbler workers are more necessary that those with higher gifts. 'We can spare this artizan better than this poet; but we can spare all the poets better than all the artizans.'

23. Paul has probably in mind the use of clothing here. There are some parts of the body deemed to be *less honourable*.

These are clothed in seemly fashion and given *more abundant honour* (the verb rendered *bestow* is often used of clothing people, e.g. Mt. xxvii. 28). In the same way our uncomely members are given a *comeliness* that by nature they lacked (rsv, 'our unpresentable parts are treated with greater modesty').

24. *Our comely parts* are our presentable parts, our good-looking parts. These need no aid, and thus we do not adorn them as we do the other parts of the body. This expression probably belongs to the preceding sentence. We should put a full stop after *need.* What follows is a slightly different aspect of the subject. It is no longer what we do, but what God does. As in verse 18, Paul brings out the thought that the arrangement of the body is not by chance, but is due to God's ordering. Now it is God's giving of honour to those parts of the body that naturally would lack it that Paul brings out. *Tempered* signifies a harmonious blending (the word may be used of mixing colours). God's arrangement of the members in the body does away with clashing and blends all into one harmonious whole.

25. This action of God is directed to the prevention of *schism*. The meaning of this last word is not so much schism in our sense of the term as 'dissension'. Paul has already used the word in i. 10 of the dissensions which caused factions within the Corinthian church. In His perfect blending of the parts of the human body it was God's plan to prevent such dissension. *But* is the strong adversative *alla*. Far from this, God planned that the members should *care one for another*. The insertion of *same* guards against partiality. In the body all the members without distinction work for the good of the whole. No special care is lavished on one member to the detriment of other members. *Merimnaō*, the word for *care*, often has the notion of anxiety. It is a strong term, and denotes no tepid emotion.

26. The unity of the body is seen in suffering and in honour. The suffering of any member means that the whole body suffers. It is impossible to think of one part of the body as being in pain, and the remainder of the body as being at peace. The existence of one trouble centre means that the whole body is involved. Similarly when one part of the body is *honoured*, the remainder shares in the joy. Paul does not speak of sharing in the honour, but in the rejoicing. His choice of word emphasizes the impossibility of rivalry within the body.

27. *Ye* comes first with emphasis. *Body* is without the article, which indicates that it is the characteristic of the Corinthian believers that they belong to Christ's body (the use of the article would distinguish this body from other bodies). The effect of all this is to put a strong emphasis on the fact that they, the Corinthians, are members of nothing less than Christ's body. All that Paul has been saying refers to them, because they are members *in particular*. This last expression, *ek merous*, means literally 'in part', which is the way it is translated in xiii. 9. From this it gets the meaning 'individually'. Paul's meaning is that each one of them belongs to the body. None can claim to be the whole, but none is excluded.

28. Some of the different parts of the body of Christ are now listed. Paul has insisted that in the natural body God arranges the parts (verses 18, 24). It is the same with the body of Christ. Men do not choose to be *apostles, prophets*, etc., but God sets them in the Church. Paul's *first, secondarily, thirdly*, rank these various gifts to the Church in order of honour (cf. the similar list in Eph. iv. 11). We cannot press the order throughout the list, but it is probably significant that *tongues*, which the Corinthians valued so highly, are mentioned last of all. *Apostles* were originally chosen by Christ to be with Him, and that He might send them to teach and to cast out devils (Mk. iii. 14f.). In time there were others than the Twelve, for example, Barnabas, James, and Paul himself. Always they appear to have been held in high esteem as custodians of the authentic gospel. For their functions as witnesses see on ix. 1f. For *prophecy* see on verse 10. We would not have expected that *teachers* would rank so high. The fact that they do indicates the importance attached to teaching in the apostolic age. We must bear in mind that the cost of hand-copied books was high, so high that, according to A. Q. Morton's estimate, 'a gospel represents in papyrus alone a year's wages and a New Testament about eight years' pay of a skilled workman'.[1] Few believers could look forward to owning a Bible. The function of the teacher in such a church must have been tremendously important.

From this point on Paul does not speak of the persons exercising the gifts, but of the gifts themselves. *Helps* and *governments* present us with a problem. Neither term occurs elsewhere in the New Testament. *Helps* points to the general function of assisting those in need (cf. the use of the corresponding verb in Acts xx. 35). Some have thought this indicates a general work, to be accomplished by all believers. Against this is the fact that it occurs here in a list of 'gifts'. Others think of the work of deacons, which is possible. But we really do not know. *Kubernēseis*, rendered *governments*, denotes the activity of the steersman of a ship, the man who pilots his vessel through the dangerous shoals and brings her safe to port (a cognate word is used in Acts xxvii. 11; Rev. xviii. 17 of the 'master' of a ship). The function is obviously one of direction, and may be the work of the elders. But we have no way of knowing. The expressions are a reminder of the immense amount about life in the apostolic Church of which we are ignorant. *Diversities of tongues* is the expression translated 'divers kinds of tongues' in verse 10 (where see note).

29, 30. All the questions in these two verses are introduced with the particle *mē*, indicating that the answer 'No' is expected. The series of rhetorical questions, quite in Paul's argumentative style, hammers home the fact of diversity. It is very

[1] *Penguin Science News*, No. 43, London, 1957, p. 26.

obvious that Christians differ from one another in the gifts they have received from God. No gift can be despised on the grounds that all have it, for all differ. In his questions Paul does not include a reference to either 'helps' or 'governments', which he has mentioned in the previous verse. Contrariwise he does include a reference to the interpretation of tongues, although he did not mention them previously.

31. *Covet* is our rendering of *zēloute*, which means 'be zealous for', 'desire earnestly' (often in a bad sense). Paul has not hesitated to rank certain gifts of God in order. He has indicated in this chapter that even the humble parts of the body are necessary, and that all are set in the body by God. It is not inconsistent with this to suggest that the Corinthians do well to desire the greater gifts. Yet there is something higher than the greatest of these gifts, and something that is within the reach of the humblest and most ordinary believer. So Paul proceeds to unfold the *more excellent way*. Some feel that Paul means that love is the more excellent way to the gifts. This is possible grammatically, but Paul's treatment of love does not leave the impression that it is simply a means to an end. Love is to be pursued for its own sake.

iii. A hymn in praise of love (xiii. 1–13). Paul's 'more excellent way' is the way of love, which he proceeds to expound in a passage of singular beauty and power. Robertson and Plummer cite Harnack as speaking of this chapter as 'the greatest, strongest, deepest thing Paul ever wrote', and few would be prepared to contest this verdict. The chapter is not, as some have thought, a digression from the argument. Paul has not finished with the 'gifts', and he has much to say about them in the following chapter. But here he is concerned to insist that the central thing is not the exercise of any of the 'gifts'. It is the practice of Christian love. Throughout this passage AV renders the word *agapē* by 'charity' (as also does Knox), but 'love' is the English equivalent. AV probably derives it from Wycliffe, who in turn took it from the *caritas* of the Vulgate. Jerome used this rendering because he recognized the unsuitability of the Latin *amor* as a rendering of the Greek *agapē*. *Agapē* (for which see note on 1 Thes. i. 3[1]) was not in common use before the New Testament, but the Christians took it up and made it their characteristic word for love. It is a new word for a new idea. Whereas the best concept of love before the New Testament was that of a love for the best one knows, the Christians thought of love as that quality we see displayed in the cross. It is a love for the utterly unworthy, a love which proceeds from a God who is love. It is a love lavished upon others without a thought of whether they are worthy to receive it or not. It proceeds rather from the nature of the lover, than from any merit in the beloved. The Christian who has experienced God's love to him while he was yet a sinner has been transformed by the experience. Now he sees men in a measure as God sees them. He sees them as the objects of God's love, as those for whom Christ died. Accordingly his attitude towards them is one of love, of self-giving *agapē*. He comes to practise the love which seeks nothing for itself, but only the good of the loved one. It is this love which Paul unfolds.

1. *Though* is perhaps too strong for *ean* (as also in verses 2, 3), which is rather 'if'. What follows is put forward as a hypothetical possibility. *The tongues of men and of angels* is almost certainly a reference to the gift of 'tongues'. The expression is made as far-reaching as it well can be. No language in earth or heaven is to be compared with the practice of love. While Paul's starting point is the ecstatic speech of some of the Corinthians, his words are general enough to cover speech of any kind. It is easy enough to be fascinated by eloquent discourse, to be hypnotized by the magic of words, and to pass over that which matters. The man who is taken up with saying, rather than doing, has become nothing more than

[1]*Op. cit.*, pp. 34f.

sound. Paul chooses the gong and the cymbal for his illustration. *Brass* denotes first of all the metal, copper, and then any object made from it. Here the object is almost certainly a gong (though a few take it to mean a trumpet). In parenthesis we might note that *brass* is usually incorrect for any object coming down from antiquity. The term properly denotes an alloy of copper and zinc, and this the ancients used but rarely. The correct term is 'bronze', an alloy of copper and tin. *Sounding* we might render 'resounding', the verb being *ēcheō* (from which we derive our word 'echo'. Knox translates 'echoing bronze'). There may be plenty of noise in a gong, but there is nothing more. *Tinkling, alalazon,* is better 'clashing'. It describes the clanging of metal to produce a loud, but harsh sound. The sound of gongs and cymbals would have been familiar at Corinth from their frequent use by devotees of Dionysus or Cybele. Phillips perhaps has this sort of thing in mind with his unusual rendering: 'If I were to speak with the combined eloquence of men and angels I should stir men like a fanfare of trumpets or the crashing of cymbals, but unless I had love, I should do nothing more.' The best speech of earth or heaven, without love, is but a noise.

2. Paul's first example was taken from the ecstatic gifts. His second represents those concerned with knowledge, as his third is to be connected with administration. For *prophecy* see on xii. 10. Paul has just ranked *prophecy* as second only to the apostolate (xii. 28), so that he cannot be accused of minimizing its importance. But loveless *prophecy* must be condemned. For *mysteries* see on ii. 7. *All mysteries, and all knowledge* point us to the sum of all wisdom, human and divine. It includes the knowledge that men may gather for themselves (*gnōsis, knowledge*, sometimes has a meaning not unlike our 'science'), and what is attainable only by revelation. *Mysteries* are truths that men could never penetrate for themselves, but know only because it has pleased God to reveal them. *Faith* is the basic Christian attitude, but we have noticed in xii. 9 that the term is used also for a special gift of the Spirit. Here it is clearly the latter that is meant, and it is the kind of faith that can accomplish miracles (cf. Mk. xi. 22f.). *All* indicates the presence of this kind of *faith* in the fullest degree. The Corinthians clearly thought that the possessors of certain gifts were extremely important persons. Paul stoutly maintains that if they have even the highest of gifts, and that in full amount, but lack love, not only are they unimportant, but they are actually *nothing*. The choice of word is very impressive.

3. From knowledge and deeds of power Paul turns to deeds of mercy and dedication. *Bestow . . . to food* renders the verb *psōmizō*. This is connected with *psōmion*, 'a morsel', used, for example, of the 'sop' which Jesus dipped and gave to Judas (Jn. xiii. 26f.). Paul is speaking of giving one's goods in small amounts, i.e. to large numbers of people. Edwards thinks that the verb also conveys the idea that 'every gift is made by the man himself'. The verb is in the aorist tense, pointing to a once-for-all action, the action of a man who, in one grand sweeping gesture, sells all that he has and gives it away. It is sobering to reflect that one may be generous to the point of beggary, and yet completely lack the spirit of love. The Greek has nothing corresponding to *the poor*. The emphasis is on the giver, not the recipients. Giving the *body to be burned* is an expression reminiscent of Dn. iii. 28 (LXX), where it is used of the three youths giving their bodies to the fire. It is possible that Paul has this in mind, or some other specific allusion. Lightfoot thinks of the Indian who burned himself alive at Athens, and whose tomb was a well-known sight.[1] Whether Paul had such a case in mind or not, the general sense is clear enough. Burning stands for the worst that can happen to the body. A man may have such a sense of dedication to a high ideal that he will give himself up to a death as painful as this, but if he lacks love he is nothing profited. Men of the first century commonly saw great merit in deeds of charity and

[1]*Colossians*, p. 394, n. 2.

suffering. Paul totally rejects those ideas. Love is the one thing needful. Nothing can make up for its lack.

4. From the negative Paul turns to the positive. He has shown that even the highest gifts without love avail nothing at all. Now he expounds love's virtues. Love *suffereth long*. Love has an infinite capacity for endurance. It is not readily put out, but endures patiently. The word points to patience with people, rather than patience with circumstances (as Barclay notes). It is eloquent of love's self-restraint. The other side of this is that love *is kind*. It reacts with goodness towards those who ill-treat it. Love gives itself in the service of others. *Envieth* is a verb which occasionally is used in a good sense (as in xii. 31, 'covet'), but more usually it denotes a strong passion of jealousy or the like. It has such a meaning here, and we are reminded that love is not displeased at the success of others. *Vaunteth not itself* employs a picturesque word, the root pointing to what AG define as a 'wind-bag'. For *puffed up* see note on iv. 6. There are many ways of manifesting pride, and love is incompatible with them all. Love is concerned rather to give itself than to assert itself.

5. *Behave . . . unseemly* has the idea of what is not according to due form, and thus anything disgraceful, dishonourable, indecent. It is a general term with a wide range of meaning. Love avoids the whole range of unseemliness. Similarly love *seeketh not her own*. Love is the very antithesis of self-seeking. *Is not provoked* points to the equability of true love. 'It is not touchy' (Phillips), not ready to take offence. *Thinketh no evil* leads on from that. Love is always ready to think the best of people, and does not impute evil to them. *Thinketh* is *logizetai* (which Paul uses frequently in the sense of the reckoning or imputing of righteousness to the believer). It is connected with the keeping of accounts, noting a thing down and reckoning it to someone. Love does not impute evil. Love takes no account of evil. Love does not harbour a sense of injury.

6. It is all too characteristic of human nature to take pleasure in the misfortunes of others. Much of the news columns of our daily papers is taken up with the recounting of *iniquity*, either in the sense of disaster, or in that of evil deeds. Plainly there is that in man to which reports of this kind appeal. But love is not like that. Love takes no joy in evil of any kind. Rather its joy is *in the truth*. Actually this might be rendered 'with the truth'. It is when truth rejoices that love rejoices. Love shares truth's joy. It is a reminder that even love cannot rejoice when the truth is denied. There is a stern moral element throughout the New Testament, and nothing is ever said to obscure this. Love is not to be thought of as indifferent to moral considerations. It must see truth victorious if it is to rejoice. Truth is often thought of in close connection with the very heart of Christianity (cf. Jesus' saying 'I am . . . the truth', Jn. xiv. 6; Paul's words, 'as the truth is in Jesus', Eph. iv. 21). In 2 Thes. ii. 10, 12, as in this verse, *truth* is set over against 'unrighteousness' (the same Greek word as is here rendered 'iniquity'). We should probably understand the wider use here. Love rejoices in the truth of God, in the truth of the gospel (cf. Jn. viii. 56).

7. After some resounding negatives come some glorious positives. Love *beareth all things*. The verb *stegō* has the basic idea of 'cover'. Thence it comes to mean, 'to hide by covering', or 'to ward off by covering', 'to endure'. It is possible that it has the former meaning here. Love conceals what is displeasing in another. But it is more likely that it has the latter meaning (as it has in ix. 12, 'suffer all things'). Love does not easily give way; it endures. *Believeth all things* points to that quality which is always ready to allow for circumstances, and to see the best in others (cf. Moffatt, 'always eager to believe the best'). It is easy to think the worst, but love retains its faith. It is not implied that love is deceived by the pretences of any rogue, but that love is always ready to give the benefit of the doubt. *Hopeth all things* is the forward look. The thought is not that of an unreasoning optimism, which fails to take account of reality. It is rather a refusal to take failure as final. Following on from *believeth all things* it is the confidence which looks to ultimate triumph by the grace of God. *Endureth all things* brings the thought of steadfastness. The verb *hupomenō* denotes not a patient, resigned acquiescence, but an active, positive fortitude. It is the endurance of the soldier who in the thick of the battle is undismayed, but continues to lay about him lustily. Love is not overwhelmed, but manfully plays its part whatever the difficulties.

8. The permanence of love is stressed. Love *never faileth*, the verb being that in common use for 'to fall'. It comes to be used in the sense of 'collapse', 'suffer ruin'. Love will never suffer such a fate. 'Many waters cannot quench love' (Ct. viii. 7). Over against this permanence of love Paul sets the certain passing away of gifts on which the Corinthians set much store. Prophecies will *fail*. This verb is not the same as that rendered *faileth* in the earlier part of the verse, but *katargeō*, for which see note on i. 28. *Prophecies* are the setting forth of what God says to men through the prophet. But when we stand before God there will be no place for the prophet. *Prophecies* will then have no place, they will be completely without force. *Tongues*, which mattered so greatly to some of the Corinthians, will likewise *cease*. The same line of reasoning applies here. In the very presence of God there will be no reason and no place for ecstatic speech. *Knowledge*, the painfully acquired knowledge of earthly things, will *vanish away* in the light of the immediate knowledge of God. The verb *vanish away* is *katargeō* once more, the same verb as that used of *prophecies*. AV in this verse is somewhat confusing, translating two different Greek words by the one English word 'fail', and translating the same Greek word by two different English words. Reasonable variation in translation is, of course, not only permissible, but necessary (it is the mark of a thoroughly bad translation slavishly to render a given Greek word, whatever its shade of meaning, by one standard English equivalent). But the reader of AV must exercise care here if he is to grasp Paul's precise meaning.

9, 10. All earthly knowledge is partial, which is easy enough to follow. What is meant by *we prophesy in part* is not quite so clear. It probably means that God does not reveal everything, so that the prophet, no less than the sage, gives but a partial glimpse of truth. *That which is perfect* renders *to teleion*, which has the idea of the destined end or aim. It points to God's plan. When the consummation is reached, all that is partial will *be done away* (the verb is *katargeō* again; see notes on previous verse and on i. 28).

11. The contrast between the partial and the complete is illustrated from the life of man. It is natural enough for a child to act like a child, as Paul points out from his own experience. The term *phroneō, understood*, denotes thought in general. RV and some others take it in the sense 'feel', but this does not seem correct. The word has to do with the intellect rather than the emotions. *Thought, logizomai*, is an advance on the preceding word. It means 'to reckon' (often in the sense 'impute'; see note on verse 5), from which we get the general idea of 'working things out', 'reasoning' which is the sense here. With all this Paul contrasts man's estate. As someone has said, he was no Peter Pan, refusing to grow up. He determinedly exercised the functions of adulthood. *Put away* is *katargeō* once more, this being the fourth occurrence (and the fourth different translation!) of this verb since verse 8 (where see note). Paul does not mean simply that childish things passed away with the passing of time. His choice of verb indicates a determination on his part that he would not be ruled by childish attitudes. The tense is perfect, which shows that Paul put away childish things with decision and finality.

12. *Esoptron*, here rendered *glass*, means a mirror, which in those days would have been of polished metal. Corinth was famous for its mirrors, but few Christians would have been able to afford a mirror of good quality. In the nature of the case the reflection would not usually have been very good, which gives point to the statement that we see, *en ainigmati, darkly*. The noun properly means 'a riddle' (we derive our word 'enigma' from it), so that the expression means 'in a riddle', i.e. 'indistinctly' (cf. Weymouth, 'For the present we see things as if in a mirror, and are puzzled'). While we live out our lives on this earth our sight of things eternal is, at best, indistinct. *But then*, says Paul, it will be *face to face*. He does not define his *then* but there is really no need. Likewise he does not say with whom we shall be *face to face*; but Christ was so central to Paul's thinking that there is no real doubt about that.

As with seeing, so with knowing. All earthly knowledge is partial, a truth Paul has already laid down in verse 9. Over against it he sets the perfect knowledge when we shall know as we are known. The first *know* is *ginōskō*, but on the second occasion Paul employs the compound *epiginōskō* (which is used also when he says *I am known*). The use of the compound verb often signifies no more than that one's knowledge is directed towards (*epi*) a particular object. But it may have the thought of a full and complete knowledge[1] and that would seem to be the force of it here. *I am known* is in the aorist tense, which points in the same direction. The knowledge that God has of Paul is not something growing and becoming more and more perfect. God knows him through and through, and God's knowledge of His servant is complete.

13. If *and now* is understood in a temporal sense, 'now, at this present', Paul is contrasting life in the here and now with that in the hereafter. This, however, seems unlikely. He is not saying that faith, hope and love continue throughout this life, for that could be said of prophecy, tongues, and the like with which he is contrasting them. It is more probable that the

---

[1]See Moulton, *Prolegomena*, p. 113. He paraphrases the present passage thus: 'Now I am acquiring knowledge which is only partial at best: then I shall have learnt my lesson, shall *know*, as God in my mortal life knew me'.

words are to be taken in the logical sense, 'now as things are', 'now in conclusion'. Over against the things which are temporary Paul sets these eternal verities. The verb *abideth* is singular. If this is significant Paul is regarding the three as in some sense one. They form a unity. His adding *these three* after his listing of their names is an effective way of setting them apart from everything else. These are pre-eminent. Nothing may stand with them. Incidentally the three are often linked together in the New Testament, as in Rom. v. 2–5; Gal. v. 5f.; Col. i. 4f.; 1 Thes. i. 3, v. 8; Heb. vi. 10–12; 1 Pet. i, 21f. Apparently it was an accepted practice in the early Church to think of these three together.

Faith is one of Paul's dominant themes. He could write 'The life which I now live in the flesh I live by the faith of the Son of God' (Gal. ii. 20). The faith that was central to his living was central to his teaching, as even a cursory knowledge of his Epistles will reveal. It is a little surprising that *hope* should figure in this short list. And yet—men cannot live without hope. In the first centuries Christianity made a habit of taking people from the depressed classes, slaves, women, outcasts, and giving them a living hope. It is not a gain, but a grievous loss that so often today Christians are men whose hope is nothing other than the hope that worldly men have. We must learn that *hope* in the New Testament sense is one of the great abiding realities.

The last word in this chapter fittingly is *agapē*. Love occupies the supreme place. We should not press Paul's comparison too closely, and waste our time inquiring into the precise manner in which love surpasses faith or hope (though it may not be without significance that in verse 7 he has spoken of the other two as modes of love's outworking). It is not Paul's intention to rank these three in order. In the face of the regard the Corinthians had for the spectacular he is saying, 'The really important things are not "tongues" and the like, but faith, hope and love. And there is nothing greater than love.'

The commentator cannot finish writing on this chapter without a sense that clumsy hands have touched a thing of exquisite beauty and holiness. Here what is true of all Scripture is true in especial measure, that no comment can be adequate to so great a theme. Yet no commentator can excuse himself from the duty of trying to make plain what these matchless words have come to signify for him. And no Christian can excuse himself from the duty of trying to show in his life what these words have come to mean for him.

iv. Prophesying is superior to 'tongues' (xiv. 1–25).

Having dealt with the variety of spiritual gifts, and the essential unity of their possessors in the body of Christ, Paul went on to show that love is pre-eminent above all else. Now he is in a position to deal specifically with the question of 'tongues'. He is at pains to make clear that the exercise of this gift is legitimate. But at the same time he curbs the exaggerated respect the Corinthians paid to it. Throughout this passage he steadily insists that the gift of prophecy is much to be preferred to it. 'Tongues' should not be exercised in public unless there is an interpreter. Edification must be the prime consideration. Note that throughout the discussion Paul refers to speaking in 'a tongue' or 'tongues'. There is nothing in the Greek corresponding to *unknown* in verses 2, 4, 14, 19, 27.

1. Paul's opening words sum up his whole position in this matter. The first thing is the pursuit of love, as he has been emphasizing throughout the previous chapter. *Follow*, *diōkete*, has the idea of pursuit with persistence; it 'indicates a never terminating action' (Grosheide). It is right to *desire* (the word is that rendered 'covet earnestly' in xii. 31) *spiritual gifts*. But among these *gifts* Paul gives the first place to prophecy (for which see note on xii. 10). It denotes something rather like our preaching, but it is not identical with it. It is not the delivery of a carefully prepared sermon, but the uttering of words directly inspired of God.

2. The reason for the inferiority of 'tongues' is its unintelligibility. The man exercising this gift is engaged in private communion with God. *No man understandeth him* makes it plain that the gift spoken of here is different from that in Acts ii, where all men understood. *In the spirit* probably refers to the man's own spirit, not the Holy Spirit. It is an activity of the *spirit* of man, but not of his understanding. *Mysteries* in the New Testament are things which man could never have known, but usually there is also the thought that God has now revealed them (see note on ii. 7). Here it is the element of secrecy that is uppermost. Apart from a special gift of interpretation, what is spoken in 'tongues' is quite unknowable to men.

3. By contrast the prophet edifies, exhorts, comforts. For *edification* see note on the cognate verb in viii. 1. *Exhortation* conveys the notion of a strengthening, an encouraging (see on 1 Thes. iii. 2[1], where the cognate verb, *parakaleō*, is discussed). *Paramuthia*, translated *comfort*, is found only here in the New Testament, but the cognate verb is used in Jn. xi. 19, 31, of comforting the bereaved. Prophecy, then, is a means of building up Christian character, of strengthening men, of giving them comfort in their distress.

4. Paul does not deny that 'tongues' have a value for edification. But it is only the person who exercises the gift who is edified, whereas *he that prophesieth* builds up the whole church.

5. Once again Paul stresses the importance of edification. He would like to see all the Corinthians speak with 'tongues'. Consistently he refuses to speak disparagingly of this gift. But even more than this would he wish to see them all prophesying. As we have seen in several places there is evidence that the Corinthians exaggerated the importance of speaking

[1]*Op. cit.*, pp. 62f.

with 'tongues'. The spectacular character of ecstatic utterance seems to have appealed to them greatly. Paul roundly affirms the superiority of prophecy to 'tongues', unless the speaker also has the gift of interpretation. The criterion is simply that of edification. If 'tongues' are interpreted, the hearers are edified, and there is then no great difference from prophecy. Both are inspired speech, and both now convey a message to men.

6. As often, Paul softens his rebuke with the affectionate address, *brethren*. The construction is very condensed, being a mixture of 'If I come . . . what shall I profit you?' and 'What shall I profit you, except I speak . . . ?' Paul pictures his next visit to Corinth, and shows that it would be futile were he to speak only *with tongues*. His criterion is still edification. The inferiority of 'tongues' is manifest, for this gift does not *profit* the hearers. The things which do profit are *revelation* and the like. This word is often used in the wide sense, of God's revelation of Himself to men. In this chapter there appears to be a narrower use to denote some specific matter that God might reveal to one of the brethren, which he might then pass on to the others (cf. verse 26). From verses 29–31 *revelation* in this sense would seem to be closely related to prophecy. For *knowledge, gnōsis*, see on xii. 8. *Doctrine* is *didachē*, 'teaching', instruction in the Christian faith.

7. Paul's point is now illustrated from other spheres, first of all that of music. *Aulos*, rendered a *pipe*, is a flute. Here it will stand for all wind instruments, and *kithara* (from which we get 'guitar'), *harp*, for all stringed instruments. Neither flute nor harp makes sense unless there is a meaningful variation in the sounds produced. A melody finely played speaks to a man's very soul. An aimless jangle means nothing.

8. So in the military realm. *The trumpet* conveys the commands of the leader to men remote from him. But it is of the first importance that *the trumpet* should be blown so that it can be understood. If the sound is *uncertain* the blowing of the trumpet has failed in its purpose. It is useless.

9. *Ye* is emphatic. What Paul is saying applies to the Corinthians. *By the tongue* is also in an emphatic position, which stresses the tongue's connection with intelligibility. The Corinthians had delighted rather to connect it with unintelligibility. Speech is either intelligible or nothing more than speaking *into the air*.

10. There are some obscurities in the Greek here. *It may be translates ei tuchoi,* an expression meaning, according to AG, 'if it should turn out that way, perhaps'. Its use with numerals is to make them indefinite. Here it is probably meant to modify *so many kinds* (which it follows in the Greek). *Voices* is probably used in the sense of 'languages', so that the meaning of the whole expression is, 'There are probably ever so many different languages in the world' (Goodspeed). *Without signification* is *aphōnon,* 'dumb'. There is a play on words with *phōnōn, voices.* There is no real difference between unintelligibility and dumbness. The whole point of language is that it is used to communicate meaning.

11. *Meaning* is *dunamis,* 'force', 'power'. Speech is an effective instrument of communication, but speech that is not understood is of no power at all. *Barbaros, barbarian,* is an example of onomatopoeia. It denotes a man whose language sounds like 'bar bar', i.e. whose language makes no sense. The word is often used in a derogatory fashion, of those beyond the pale of civilization (just as is the case with the English equivalent). Here Paul's primary thought is that of the unintelligibility of such a person's speech, but the derogatory associations of *barbarian* are in mind also. The ecstatic speech which seemed to the Corinthians a matter for such pride turns out to be the means of making them nothing more than *barbarians.* This would be even worse for a Greek than for us.

12. Once again Paul has an emphatic *ye* to drive home the relevance of what he says to his correspondents. *Zealous* is really a noun, 'zealots'. It is from the same root as the verb used in verse 1, 'desire', and xii. 31, 'covet earnestly'. There is this difference that, whereas the verb is often used in a bad sense, the noun is usually used in a good sense. *Spiritual gifts* is really 'spirits' (*pneumatōn*) but there is probably little difference. This word stresses a little more the truth that the gifts for which the Corinthians were 'zealots' had their origin in the Holy Spirit. Paul does not censure their desire, but takes it as the basis for urging them to seek to *excel to the edifying of the church*. Right through this passage he keeps coming back to this thought. The great thing for the Christian is that he may be able to edify others. While it is right for him to desire to excel in the exercise of spiritual gifts, he should seek those gifts which are useful for edification. Others are comparatively unimportant.

13. The man who has the gift of 'tongues' should not rest content with the gift. Realizing its limited value, he should pray for the gift of interpretation, so that what he says may be useful for edification. These words show that there was nothing static about possession of the gifts. A man who had the gift of 'tongues' need not take that as his end state. He might later receive other gifts, more particularly that of interpretation. He should pray to this end.

14, 15. Up till this point Paul has concentrated on the value of the gifts to others than those who exercise them. Now he points out that a man who prays in a *tongue* is not using his *understanding* (the word is *nous*, which stands for the mind, the intellect). The Christian life is considerably more than a mental exercise. But the man whose mind is *unfruitful* is not being true to his Christian calling. This passage is very important for its insistence on the rightful place of the intellect. Notice that this is secured without any diminution of spiritual fervour. Paul is not arguing for a barren intellectualism. There is a place for the fervour so strikingly exemplified in the use of 'tongues'. But it must be allied to the use of the mind, and this 'tongues' does not provide. The two activities Paul singles out for mention are prayer and singing, functions specially appropriate to public worship (*sing, psallō*, properly means, 'sing to the accompaniment of a musical instrument', but here it is probably used in a general sense). It is still worth emphasis that these activities must be such that worshippers can enter into them wholeheartedly, with the mind as well as with the spirit. All too often prayers are offered in a kind of emotional jargon, and hymns are chosen on the basis of attractive tunes rather than sound theology.

16, 17. Paul turns attention to him *that occupieth the room of the unlearned.* This last word is *idiōtēs* (from *idios*, 'one's own'), and denotes a private person. MM cite examples of the use of the word for laymen over against priests, private citizens over against those in public life such as magistrates, men without military rank ('privates') over against officers. It would be easy to understand the term here of those who are not Christians were it not for the fact that verse 23 seems to distinguish between 'unlearned' and 'unbelievers'. Some hold that the word denotes an ignorant or unskilful person, and that here it means a man without the gift of tongues (cf. RV mg., 'him that is without gifts'). The objection to this is that in verse 23 the *idiōtēs* is distinguished from 'the whole church', so that he cannot be a Christian. In verses 24f. the same marks of conversion are seen in him as in the unbeliever. AG tell us that *idiōtēs* was used in some religious associations for 'non-members who may participate in the sacrifices'. This may give us the clue. Paul speaks of *the room* (i.e. 'place') of these people, which indicates that they had their place in the Christian assembly. They would be 'inquirers', people who had not committed themselves to Christianity, but who were interested. They had ceased to be simply outsiders, but were not yet Christians. Such people would not be able to give assent to a prayer of thanksgiving uttered in a 'tongue', for they would not understand it. *Amen* is our transliteration from the Greek of what was already a transliteration from the Hebrew. *Amēn* is the participle of the verb 'to confirm', used adverbially in the sense 'truly'. It was employed as the congregational response to prayers (e.g. Ne. viii. 6), and that is its meaning here. It is the expression whereby the worshipper makes his own a prayer uttered by someone else. The *idiōtēs* is unable to do this, since he is ignorant of the content of the prayer. Others would be in the same position, but probably everyone had a special concern for the *idiōtēs*, the man who might be won. Paul insists that there may be nothing at all wrong with the prayer (*thou verily givest thanks well*), but unintelligibility results in there being no edification. And that, as he has been saying throughout this whole discussion, is the condemnation of 'tongues'.

18, 19. What Paul has been saying is not due to 'sour grapes'. Paul himself exercises the gift of *tongues* more than all the Corinthians. Moreover it is not something he regards with indifference. He thanks God for it. But *in church* (there is no *the* in the Greek) he would prefer to speak five intelligible words than to utter a torrent of words in a *tongue*. *In church*, of course, refers to the Christian assembly, and not to a building, as we might take it in English. There were no Christian church buildings at this period.

20. The address *brethren* is a further reminder of Paul's affection, and it also serves to slow up the progress of the argument and focus attention on the following statement. The force of the present imperative is 'stop being children in understanding'. *Understanding* is not the same word that Paul has used hitherto, but the plural of *phrēn*, 'the midriff', 'the diaphragm'. The ancients located thought in this part of the body, so that the word came to mean much the same as our 'mind'. There is not really a great deal of difference between this and *nous*, which Paul has used hitherto. Paul exhorts his readers to be no longer infantile in their thinking. Godet comments: 'It is indeed the characteristic of the child to prefer the amusing to the useful, the brilliant to the solid. And this is what the Corinthians did by their marked taste for glossolalia' (glossolalia = speaking with tongues). *Howbeit* is the strong adversative *alla*. In contrast to the preceding is the state of affairs Paul wishes to see. *Be ye children* is a somewhat stronger expression than that in the earlier part of the verse; 'be not children . . . be babes'. Paul's point is that there is a place for the childlike attitude, but it is with respect to *malice*, not thought. *Be men is teleioi ginesthe*. It would probably not be right to press the force of *ginesthe* as 'become' rather than 'be' (it is the same verb in the first part of the verse). But *teleioi* is not so much *men* as 'mature'. It indicates that which has reached its end or aim, and the word is often used to contrast the mature with the immature (see note on ii. 6).

21. *The law* here is the Old Testament in general, and not specifically the Pentateuch. The quotation is from Is. xxviii. 11f. There the reference is to the failure of the men of Israel to heed the prophet. Their judgment will be to be delivered over to men of strange speech (the Assyrian invaders). The connection with the present argument is not obvious. Perhaps Paul means that, as those who had refused to heed the prophet were punished by hearing speech that was not intelligible to them, so would it be in his day. Those who would not believe would hear 'tongues', and not be able to understand their wonderful meaning.

22. Considered in this way *tongues* are *for a sign* to unbelievers. They point to God's judgment. Prophecy, by contrast, is directed to believers. It brings them the veritable message of God.

197

23. From another point of view *tongues* are not helpful to the non-Christian. Paul imagines the whole church assembled and speaking *with tongues,* and pictures the effect on *unlearned, or unbelievers.* For *unlearned* see note on verse 16. If a man is not a Christian, whether he is interested in the faith or a rank unbeliever, the effect of a display of *tongues* will be only to convince him that believers *are mad.*

24, 25. The effect of prophecy is different. This time Paul uses the singular for him *that believeth not,* and the *unlearned* (he employed the plural in the previous verse), but the change is probably not significant. The effect of a display of prophecy on such an outsider is given in striking terms. We must bear in mind that prophecy meant the uttering of words direct from God (see note on xii. 10). The divine message will have powerful effects. *Elenchetai,* translated *convinced,* means 'convicted'. It is used in Jn. xvi. 8 of the Holy Spirit's work in convicting the world 'of sin, and of righteousness, and of judgment'. The divine word comes to the non-Christian with convicting power. For *judged, anakrinetai,* see note on ii. 14f. The effect of the prophetic word is to reveal to the man his state. His whole inner being is searched out. Those things he fondly imagined to be locked within *his heart* he finds reproved and judged, and he can only ascribe this to the activity of God. The exercise of prophecy results thus in the man coming to *worship God,* and to recognize the presence of God in His Church. The contradiction between this verse and verse 22 is only apparent. There the unbelievers are those who have heard the word and rejected it. For them 'tongues' are for a sign of God's judgment on them. Here the thought is of those who have never heard the word. For them 'tongues' are no more than a token of madness. But prophecy leads them to God.

v. The practical outcome (xiv. 26–33). This little paragraph is very important as giving us the most intimate glimpse we have of the early Church at worship. Here we are able to see something of what the first Christians actually did when they assembled to worship God, though we must not think of the description as a complete one.

26. *Come together*, i.e. come together for worship. *Every one* (or 'each', *hekastos*) need not be pressed to indicate that every member of the congregation always had something to contribute. But it does mean that any of them might be expected to take part in the service. It is curious that Paul does not speak of anyone having 'a prophecy', but perhaps *a revelation* means much the same. A *psalm* for us has come to mean a member of the canonical book of Psalms. But the word itself signifies a song sung to the accompaniment of an instrument, and then more generally, a song. Here the meaning is that someone will have a song, presumably of his own composition, to bring before the worshippers (cf. verse 15). A *doctrine* is a piece of Christian teaching (RSV, 'a lesson'). A *revelation* here will be some specific matter that God has revealed to the believer, perhaps something akin to what He reveals to the prophets. An *interpretation* will be the interpretation of a tongue. There are various ingredients in the service. But the guiding rule is *let all things be done unto edifying*.

27, 28. As 'tongues' presented the principal difficulty Paul deals with that subject first. *By two, or at the most by three* will be the number of people exercising the gift who were to be allowed to speak during the one service. *And that by course* means either 'in turn', or 'by shares', i.e. each having a fair share of the time available. It would seem that sometimes those exercising this gift had spoken simultaneously, which must have caused great confusion. Paul forbids this. *Let one interpret* carries on the position Paul has consistently taken up. Edification is the supreme consideration. 'Tongues' must not be used unless there is an *interpreter*. This shows us that we must not think of 'tongues' as being the result of an irresistible impulse of the Spirit, driving the man willy-nilly into ecstatic speech. If he chose he could *keep silence*, and this Paul instructs him to do on occasion.

29–31. Prophecy is likewise subject to regulation. Just as in the case of 'tongues' there should be no more than two or three *prophets* speaking at one service. *The other* is plural. It may refer to all the rest of the prophets, but as in xii. 10 we read of 'discerning of spirits', it is more likely to mean, 'the others, who can discern'. The utterance of a prophet is not to be given uncritical acceptance, but to be tested by those qualified. *Diakrinetōsan, judge,* means 'discriminate', 'discern'. It would seem that certain *prophets* would normally be selected to speak, but the possibility might always arise of a direct revelation being given to *another that sitteth by*. The designated speaker should in this case give way. In the course of time, *all*, which may possibly mean all the congregation, but more likely is all the prophets, will have the opportunity of engaging in prophecy. The purpose of this activity is that *all may learn, and all may be comforted*. This last word is *parakalōntai*, which means more than *be comforted* in our sense of the term. There is the thought of exhortation, and of strengthening.

32, 33. Just as those speaking with 'tongues' had the ability to keep silent when they chose, so is it with prophecy. It is not an irresistible divine compulsion that comes upon a man. All three nouns are without the article in the Greek, which makes it read like a proverb, 'spirits of prophets are subject to prophets'. Prophecy is a means of divine illumination, but a prophet may keep silent. This arises, says Paul, from the fact that *God is not the author of confusion, but of peace*. If *the prophets* had no control over their *spirits*, gone would be any prospect of an orderly assembly. But Paul sees a guarantee against such disorder in the character of God. Such a God will produce *peace*, not *confusion*. Probably we should place a full stop after *peace*, and take what follows with the next verse. There are not wanting those who favour the division of AV, but it is difficult to think that such a high-sounding principle as the one we have been examining should be given simply as the custom of the churches.

vi. Women in church (xiv. 34–36). Paul was concerned with the status of women in xi. 2ff. (where see notes). This is a further application of the principles on which he there acted. Christian women ought not to be 'forward', they should not seek needlessly to flout the accepted ideas of the day. Barclay comments: 'In all likelihood what was uppermost in his mind was the lax moral state of Corinth and the feeling that nothing, absolutely nothing, must be done which would bring upon the infant Church the faintest suspicion of immodesty. It would certainly be very wrong to take these words of Paul out of the context for which they were written.' We must exercise due caution in applying his principle to our own very different situation.

34. If we take *as in all churches of the saints* with this verse Paul is calling on the Corinthians to conform to accepted Christian practice. For women to take on themselves the role of instructors would have been to discredit Christianity in the eyes of most people. Paul calls on them to observe the customs. He does more. He refers to *the law* to remind them of women's proper place. Probably the passage he has particularly in mind is Gn. iii. 16. In view of xi. 5 it is possible that Paul contemplated the possibility that a woman might occasionally prophesy in church. Moffatt takes the view that Paul 'never vetoed a devout woman from exercising, even at public worship, the prophetic gift which so many women in the primitive Church enjoyed'. He understands this prohibition to refer to 'matrons taking part in the discussion or interpretation of what had been said by some prophet or teacher during the service'. Calvin takes Paul to mean that, while the necessity may arise for a woman to speak in public, she must not speak in a regular church service.

35. The prohibition of women speaking in church extends to the asking of questions. This should be done *at home*. It is the speaking in church which is regarded as the shameful thing (*shame* is the same word as in xi. 6), and Paul is anxious to avoid this.

36. This verse indicates that the practice he has been condemning had actually been taking place at Corinth. More than once Paul has had occasion to complain of the pride of the Corinthians. Clearly they felt free to strike out on new lines, justified only by their own understanding of things Christian. It is in the light of such a temper that Paul inquires ironically whether *the word of God* took its earthly origin from the Corinthians, or whether it was to them only that it came. They must not think that they alone know what is Christian. The customs and the thinking 'in all churches of the saints' (verse 33) must be given due force.

vii. Conclusion (xiv. 37–40). Paul sums up the discussion in words reminiscent of the 'Whether they will hear or whether they will forbear' of the prophets. He has given his judgment faithfully on the matters raised, and he is in no doubt that God has guided him in what he has said. He makes the high claim for the things he has written that they are *the commandments of the Lord* (*the Lord* is emphatic). No higher claim could possibly be made. The bearing of this on the question of the way the New Testament writers viewed their inspiration should not be overlooked. Paul maintains not only that he has written the 'commandment' (the word is singular in the better MSS) of the Lord, but that anyone who is *a prophet, or spiritual* should acknowledge this. Some of the Corinthians thought they had spiritual discernment. Let them show it by recognizing inspiration when they saw it!

38. The meaning of AV is that if a man does not recognize this, Paul has done with him. Let him remain in his state of ignorance. This is well attested and may be correct. But for *agnoeitō, let him be ignorant*, some good MSS read *agnoeitai*. This is usually taken to mean 'he is not known', e.g. RSV, 'If any one does not recognize this, he is not recognized' (by the church? by God?). But the verb may be a future, in which case the meaning is as Moffatt, 'Anyone who disregards this will be himself disregarded'. The reference then will be to the day of judgment. It is impossible to be sure which of these is right.

39. In keeping with his attitude all along, Paul enjoins his friends to seek prophecy rather than 'tongues', but not to despise 'tongues'. These, too, are a gift from the Lord, and their use should not be forbidden.

40. The chapter closes with a notable principle. Public worship is very important. Everything in it must be done in as seemly a manner as possible, and with due regard for order. Indecorousness and undue innovation are alike discouraged.

VII. THE RESURRECTION (xv. 1–58)

Paul comes to the last great subject of the Epistle. Some of the Corinthians had denied that the dead will rise (verse 12). He sets out to show that such a denial cannot be countenanced for a moment, for the resurrection of the believer is integral to the faith. Lacking such hope Christians would be 'of all men most miserable' (verse 19). Paul starts from first principles. He shows that Christ's resurrection is fundamental to the gospel, then that the resurrection of the Christ implies the resurrection of the Christian. Next he goes on to deal with objections that were, or might be, raised, and shows how baseless they are. This is the classical Christian discussion of the subject.

a. The resurrection of Christ (xv. 1–11)

1. It is noteworthy that Paul does not speak of reminding his friends of the gospel he had preached, but of making it known to them (*gnōrizō*, rendered *declare*, = 'make known'). The word contains a gentle rebuke. Some were far from appreciating what the gospel meant. But they had *received* it (the verb is aorist, pointing to a single act of reception). They *stand* in it (cf. 2 Cor. i. 24). Clearly it is fundamental.

2. *By which* is 'through which'. The gospel is the means Christ uses to bring about salvation. *Ye are saved* is present continuous, the meaning being, 'you are being saved'. There is a sense in which salvation is once for all (as in the 'which you received' of verse 1), and there is also a sense in which it is progressive (e.g. i. 18; 2 Cor. ii. 15). It is to this progressive character of salvation that Paul directs attention. Salvation is not exhausted by a man's experience when he first believes. It is something that goes on from strength to strength and from glory to glory. *If ye keep in memory* is better, 'if you hold fast' (*ei katechete*). The word-order is 'by what word I preached the gospel to you if you hold fast', and this poses some problems. We may think of the construction as a conditional clause with the 'if' coming late in order to give emphasis to what precedes. This is the sense adopted by av and others. This is not a very natural Greek construction (though it is far from impossible). There is the further difficulty that it would make Paul demand that they hold fast, not only to the gospel, but to the actual words in which he presented it, as Moffatt's translation makes clear, 'provided you adhere to my statement of it'. The other way of understanding the passage is to connect 'by what word I preached the gospel to you' with 'I make known' at the beginning of verse 1, giving the sense, 'I make known to you . . . in what terms I preached the gospel to you'. This would be unhesitatingly accepted were it not for the following 'if you hold fast'. This is a real difficulty, for Paul is not telling them something 'if they hold it fast'. He is telling them whatever

their attitude. But 'if you hold fast' may be a kind of parenthesis, or it may attach to 'you are being saved' (as Goodspeed, RSV, etc.). The construction is difficult, but the
second solution is to be preferred. *Unless ye have believed in
vain* refers to the possibility of belief on an inadequate basis.
If men's grip of the gospel is such that they are not really
trusting Christ, their belief is groundless and empty. They
have not saving faith.

3. The derivative nature of the gospel is stressed. Paul did
not originate the message he passed on to them. It was what he
had himself *received* (for this verb and *delivered* see notes on
xi. 23). *First of all* is probably not concerned with time but
with importance. 'I put in the first place . . .' This introduction
to the summary of the gospel message is important. It shows
that this is a very early summary. Paul is not giving us his
interpretation of what had been told him. He is giving us what
had been told him. This takes us back to the gospel as originally preached, the *kērugma*, to use the expression C. H. Dodd
has made popular. The first point is that *Christ died for our sins.*
The cross is at the heart of the gospel. The death that Christ
died was an atoning death. It was *for our sins. According to the
scriptures* indicates that the gospel was no afterthought. The
saving death of Christ was something foretold long before in
sacred Scripture. Paul does not mention specific passages, but
Is. liii will be particularly in mind.

4. In such a brief statement it is a little surprising to find
this reference to Christ's burial (cf. the Apostles' Creed). The
early Church was in no doubt about the reality of the death of
Christ, and the fact of burial is evidence of this (it is mentioned in all four Gospels). Moreover the burial of a dead
body is the necessary prelude to the empty tomb. Paul's next
point is the resurrection on the third day. *He rose again* is
really 'he has been raised' (*egēgertai*). The passive points to
the activity of the Father in raising the Son (as usually in the
New Testament), and the perfect tense points to the con-

tinuing state. It 'sets forth with the utmost possible emphasis the abiding results of the event'.[1] Christ continues in the character of the risen Lord. The perfect is used in this way six more times in this chapter (verses 12, 13, 14, 16, 17, 20), and twice only in all the rest of the New Testament. It is likely that *according to the scriptures* is to be taken with *rose again*, rather than with *the third day*. There is little Old Testament evidence for a rising on the third day (unless an argument be based on Jon. i. 17), but Is. liii. 10–12 may fairly be held to prophesy Christ's resurrection (cf. also the use of Ps. xvi. 10 in early preaching).

5-7. Paul gives his own list of the resurrection appearances. It is not an exhaustive list, and we may speculate, for example, on the reason for the omission of all appearances to the women. The appearance to *Cephas* is mentioned in Lk. xxiv. 34 (cf. Mk. xvi. 7), and nowhere else. There is no information as to what transpired then, but we may conjecture that the Lord, in His mercy, was concerned to give assurance of forgiveness to that servant of His who had three times denied Him. *The twelve* is clearly a general name for the apostles, for Judas was not there, and, if the reference is to the appearance on the evening of Easter Day (Lk. xxiv. 36ff.; Jn. xx. 19ff.), Thomas was absent also.

The appearance to *above five hundred brethren at once* may be that referred to in Mt. xxviii. 16ff. Otherwise it is mentioned here only. It is obviously of the first importance, for on no other occasion could such a large number of people testify to the fact of the resurrection. Paul's insistence that most of them were still alive shows the confidence with which he can appeal to their testimony. They could be interrogated, and the facts elicited. Notice the beautiful way in which he refers to those who have died. Death, which is an antagonist no man can withstand, has become for the Christian nothing more than sleep (see further the notes on 1 Thes. iv. 13f.[2]).

[1]Moulton, *Prolegomena*, p. 137.   [2]*Op. cit.*, pp. 84ff.

Nothing more is known of the appearance to *James*. Nor is it certain which James is meant. Most think that it is James the Lord's brother, and that it was this appearance which led to his conversion and through him to that of his brothers. This is supported by the fact that they did not believe on Jesus during His ministry (Jn. vii. 5), but as early as Acts i. 14 we see them among the believers. What else accounts for the sudden change? *Then of all the apostles* could possibly refer to such an appearance as that recorded in Jn. xx. 26ff., but more probably it is the appearance at the time of the ascension (Acts i. 1ff.).

This muster of witnesses indicates the importance Paul attaches to the resurrection of the Lord. He is about to show its consequences for Christian faith, and he lays the foundation by showing how well based is belief in it. He does not give a complete list of witnesses, but he gives enough to show that the fact is extremely well attested. So reliable is the evidence that it must be accepted, and Paul can go on from there.

8. Paul puts his vision on the road to Damascus on the same level as the other resurrection appearances. He thinks of himself as the last in the line of those who have seen the Lord. *One born out of due time, tō ektrōmati*, means 'the untimely birth' (of the apostolic family), 'the miscarriage'. The word may point to his violent and unnatural entrance into the band of the apostles. But AG points out that the word was used as a term of abuse. Perhaps it had been hurled at Paul by his opponents. He was not a handsome man (2 Cor. x. 10), and they may have combined an insult to his personal appearance with a criticism of his doctrine of free grace, by saying that, 'so far from being born again, Paul was an abortion' (Barclay). *Of me also* comes last in the Greek with a certain emphasis. Even to Paul, the abortion, Christ appeared.

9. The emphatic personal pronoun *I* again draws attention to the greatness of the condescension of Christ. The risen

Lord appeared even to Paul, *the least of the apostles*. This is not a reference to gradation within the apostolate, for elsewhere he can say, 'I suppose I was not a whit behind the very chiefest apostles' (2 Cor. xi. 5). In this spirit he could resist even Peter (Gal. ii. 11). What Paul means is that his character as persecutor had made him the least of them all. Indeed, he was not worthy to be an apostle at all. Paul holds firmly to two things. The one is the high dignity attaching to his position as an apostle, as we see from several passages in his writings (cf. chapter ix). The apostolate is the highest office in the Church, and Paul is an apostle in the fullest sense. The other is his profound sense of personal unworthiness. He is the chief of sinners (1 Tim. i. 15). He is not worthy to be an apostle, for he has persecuted that Church which is the Church *of God*.

10. Paul freely ascribes all that he has done in Christian work to *the grace of God*. That alone transformed him from a persecutor into a zealous preacher. He would not appear before the Corinthians as an apostle were it not for that *grace*, and what it has done in him. Far from being *in vain* (*kenē*, 'empty', 'without content'), it had caused him to labour *more abundantly than they all*. His word for laboured is *kopiaō*, 'labour to the point of weariness'. Deissmann reminds us that the expression Paul uses 'came originally from the joyful pride of the skilled craftsman' (LAE, p. 313). Paul stresses that he had toiled hard in the discharge of his apostolate. He does not say that he has accomplished more, but that he has worked harder than others. *More abundantly than they all* could mean 'more than all of them put together', or, 'more than any one of them'. As he is magnifying the grace of God it is perhaps more likely that the former is his meaning, and as far as our information goes this was indeed the case. Though his beginnings had been so unpromising, yet *the grace of God* had enabled a marvellous volume of work to be done. This might be interpreted as something reflecting credit on Paul, so he immediately adds, *yet not I*. It was not the man, but *the grace of God* that did the work. He speaks of this grace as *with* him, rather than 'in' him, or the like. This way of putting it almost makes the grace a fellow-labourer working alongside him, and thus emphasizes that the credit does not belong to Paul.

11. The upshot of the preceding is that there is but one gospel, by whomsoever it might be preached. Paul has stressed that he received the gospel, he did not originate it (verse 3). He has listed some of the more important points in the apostolic message, in particular mentioning evidence for the resurrection. Now he is able to say that this is the common message of the preachers (cf. Knox, 'that is our preaching, mine or theirs as you will'). *So we preach* is the present continuous tense. Paul is indicating the way both he and all the other apostles habitually preach. This is the authentic gospel, that which all the apostles make it their practice to proclaim. *So ye believed* reminds the Corinthians that this is the basis of their faith. It was this message, and not another, that they had believed when they became Christians. Anything else is an innovation.

b. The consequences of denying the resurrection of the dead (xv. 12–19)

Having set forth the salient points in the gospel message Paul comes to grips with those who denied that the dead will rise. They probably held the Greek idea of the immortality of the soul, but found it hard to think of the body as rising again. Paul draws the logical conclusion from their position: if 'dead men do not rise', then Christ could not have risen. If He did not rise, then the Christian faith is empty. The objectors are striking at the heart of the faith.

12. Paul has shown that the resurrection of Christ is central to the gospel. In the summary in the foregoing verses it is the resurrection which is stressed. Now he inquires how, in the light of that, it is possible to deny the resurrection. *Resurrection of the dead* is without the article in the Greek, and is perfectly general, 'resurrection of dead men'.

13. Paul begins to show the consequences implied by the erroneous doctrine. If dead men in general are not raised, then it will follow that Christ has not been raised. *Then* is *oude*, 'neither'. If men are not raised, 'neither hath Christ been raised' (RV).

14. The argument is carried remorselessly on. *If Christ be not risen, then is our preaching vain. Then* is *ara*, an inferential particle. It implies that what follows is the necessary logical consequence of the preceding. *Vain* (*kenon*) comes first with emphasis. The word means 'empty'. If there is no resurrection of Christ behind it, the preaching, which he has shown to be not peculiar to himself, but common to all the apostles (verse 11), has no content, no substance. It is the resurrection which shows that God is in it, and if the resurrection did not take place then the whole thing is a sham. *Preaching* is *kērugma* (see note on i. 21). It denotes not the act of preaching, but the content of preaching, the thing preached, the message. The word-order in the latter part of the verse is 'vain also your faith', which again puts the stress on *vain*. The faith of the Corinthians depended on the gospel which had elicited it. If that gospel was a sham, then so was the faith it produced.

15. There is a further consequence. If there is no resurrection, all the apostles are shown to be liars. *We are found*, means 'we are caught out', or, as Moffatt renders it, 'we are detected'. It cannot be said that they are honest men who, in sincerity, have given advice they thought to be good, though it is now shown to be not as good as they had imagined. For Christianity is not a system of good advice, and the preachers had not simply told men of a good way to live. They had testified that God raised up Christ. Christianity is basically a gospel; it is good news of what God has done. The function of preachers is to bear witness to God's saving acts. The apostles had done just that. They had testified that God raised Christ. But if it be granted that the dead do not rise, it is impossible that God should have done this. *Testified of God* is literally 'testified against God'. They said He did something (almost they accused Him of something) that He did not do. *If so be, eiper ara,* is an unusual combination. There is an emphatic 'if' coupled with the implication that what follows is another's opinion.

16. Paul repeats his statement of verse 13, with the change from 'no resurrection' to *rise not* (lit. 'are not raised', i.e. by God). Goodspeed renders, 'if the dead are never raised'. The repetition drives home his point. These men must be made to see the logical consequences of the position they have taken up.

17. As he had repeated the sense of verse 13, so he now repeats that of verse 14. Here, as there, *vain* is in the emphatic position, but he has changed his word to *mataia*, which has about it the air of futility, of fruitlessness. Faith in Christ is an idle thing if its result is *ye are yet in your sins*. To 'be in one's sins' is not a common expression. Paul elsewhere speaks of being 'dead in sins' (Eph. ii. 1, 5; Col. ii. 13), and we are reminded of our Lord's words about dying in sins (Jn. viii. 21, 24). Paul has already pointed out that 'Christ died for our sins according to the scriptures' (verse 3). But if men are still in their sins this death has availed nothing. 'Christ dead without resurrection would be a condemned, not a justified, Christ. How could He justify others?' (Godet). In that case faith is futile. The words can be given a second meaning. If Christ was not raised they would still be living in their sins like any pagans. But they have a new power over sin stemming from faith in a living Christ. Therefore Christ must have been raised.

18. A further consequence concerns the fate of the departed. As I have tried to show in the notes on 1 Thes. iv. 13f.[1] few things are more characteristic of early Christianity than the changed view it gave men of death. For pagans death was the end of all things. It was that adversary that in the end would defeat all men. For Christians it was no more than sleep. Christ had drawn the sting from it (verse 55). Paul could speak of death as 'gain' (Phil. i. 21), and of his desire 'to depart, and to be with Christ' (Phil. i. 23). Thus when believers died they were not mourned as those irretrievably lost. They were with Christ. But only, Paul insists, if there is a resurrection. If Christ did not rise, then neither will they. They *are perished*. Edwards brings out the force of the aorist, ' "perished" in the act of falling asleep, as they thought, in Christ'.

19. The perfect *ēlpikotes esmen*, *we have hope*, carries the idea 'we have set our hope and continue to hope'. *Only* comes at the end in the Greek, and applies to the whole clause: 'if in this life we have set our hope on Christ, and that is all'. In that case *we are of all men most miserable*. The last word is better translated 'pitiable'. It refers not so much to the harshness of the Christians' lot, as to their character as objects of pity. If there is no resurrection they are pitiably deluded men. They have set their hopes on a Lord who is to bring them a richer, fuller life, and all that distinguishes them from others is a special form of hardship (cf. 2 Cor. vi. 4ff., xi. 23ff.). While Paul never minimizes the compensations the Christian has in this life in the way of peace within and the like, yet it is only common sense to see that, if this world is all there is, anybody is better off than the Christian.

c. The consequences of Christ's resurrection (xv. 20–28)

From the consequences of denying the resurrection of the body Paul turns joyfully to the certainty of the resurrection of

[1]*Op. cit.*, pp. 84ff.

Christ, and to its consequences. He shows that it implies the resurrection of believers, and from that goes on to enumerate the due order of events at the last time. All things will then be subdued to Christ; even death itself will be overcome. With a few bold strokes he paints a thrilling picture of God's final, complete supremacy. Paul leaves no doubt as to the importance of his subject. It is full of significance both for the present manner of life of the believer, and also for an understanding of the great events which are to take place at the end of this age.

20. *But* is adversative. Far from Christians being the most pitiable of men, there is a fact which alters the whole situation. *Now* is logical, not temporal; 'now, as things are'. Moffatt renders: 'But it is not so! Christ did rise from the dead.' The fact of the resurrection of Christ is stated with simplicity and assurance. There is no doubt in Paul's mind at all. He uses the perfect tense of the verb to rise (see note on verse 4) with all the fulness of its meaning. Not only did Christ rise on a certain day: He continues permanently in His character as the risen Lord. *And become* should be omitted with the better MSS. *Firstfruits* comprised the first sheaf of the harvest, which was brought to the temple and offered (Lv. xxiii. 10f.). In a sense it consecrated the whole harvest. Moreover, *firstfruits* implies later fruits. Both thoughts are to the point here. Christ was not the first to rise from the dead. Indeed, He had raised some Himself. But they were to die again. His resurrection was to a life which knows no death, and in that sense He was the first, the forerunner of all those that were to be in Him. Hodge sees in the comparison to the *firstfruits* the idea that 'the resurrection of Christ is a pledge and proof of the resurrection of his people'. *Them that slept* is a perfect participle denoting the continuing state of the faithful departed. For the idea of death as sleep see note on verse 18.

21. The thought of Christ as the second Adam is more fully developed in Romans v. *By man came death* refers to the penalty pronounced on the first sin (Gn. ii. 17). This was more than physical death, but it included it. As I have written elsewhere, 'When man sinned he passed into a new state, one dominated by, and at the same time symbolized by death. It is likely that spiritual death and physical death are not being thought of as separate, so that the one involves the other.'[1] Adam's sin brought disaster not only on himself, but also on all his posterity. But if Adam's sin had far-reaching consequences, so had Christ's resurrection. It concerned not Himself only, but also all those who should believe on Him. Just as death came into the world through Adam, so did life come into the world through Christ. Paul's repeated *by man* points to the reality of the incarnation. Christ was as truly man as was Adam. It was fitting that, as it was *by man* that the corruption entered the race, so it should be *by man* that it was overcome.

22. The thought is further brought out. *In Adam all die* points us to the mortality of the race through our kinship with the progenitor of the race. But it points us beyond that to the spiritual evil of which physical death is at once the symbol and the penalty. We are involved with Adam in a solidarity of guilt. There is a sense in which the race is one. But just as Adam's sin brought untold consequences of evil, so Christ's atoning work brought untold consequences of good. *All* in the two halves of this verse probably has different meanings. In the first half it refers to the whole of mankind, for all are *in Adam*. But in the second it is more limited, applying to all those *in Christ*. The verse gives no countenance to universalism. In Adam all that are to die, die; in Christ all that are to live, live. *Be made alive* refers to more than resurrection as such. It includes the thought of the abundant life that Christ brings all who are 'in' Him.

23. The quickening of men does not take place all at once. There is a due *order* which is observed. *Tagma, order,* was

[1] *The Wages of Sin*, London, 1955, p. 12.

originally a military term referring to a detachment of soldiers, but it came to be used more generally. Paul now separates Christ from men, just as in verse 21 he had linked Him with them. The first company is *Christ the firstfruits*, and only after that is the second, *they that are Christ's*. *At his coming* makes it clear that Paul is referring to the second advent. The word he uses is *parousia*, which basically means no more than 'coming' or 'presence' (see, for example, xvi. 17). But it came to be used among the Christians as the technical term for the Lord's return. The examples cited by Deissmann (LAE, pp. 368–73) make it clear that the word was in common use for a royal visit. Christians came to use it for the coming of the supremely royal One.

24. There are some who hold that we now come to a third *tagma* or 'order'. The first order was Christ, the second (at His coming) the redeemed, and now we have a third, the unbelievers. This is not impossible, but it seems unlikely. Throughout this passage Paul has believers in mind, and he does not deal at all with the fate of the wicked. It seems to me more likely that he thinks of two 'orders' only, Christ and believers, and that (whatever be the lot of unbelievers) he then moves on in thought to the final phase. The word *eita*, *then*, does not necessarily mean 'immediately after'. It indicates that what follows takes place at some unspecified time after the preceding. *The end*, *to telos*, has a purposive ring about it. *Telos* means the end or aim, and the thought is thus of the consummation of all things, of that climax to which everything is destined to lead up. *When* is the indefinite *hotan*; the time is not known. There is a dynamic meaning to the Greek *basileia*, which does not so readily attach itself to the English, *kingdom*. Paul's thought is that Christ will at the last have full and complete authority over all things and all men, and that He will then 'deliver up' this authority, this rule, to His Father. When Christ comes back it will be to reign in majesty (cf. 2 Thes. i. 7ff.). All that opposes God will then be subdued. So Paul speaks of Him as bringing to naught *all rule and all authority and power*. These three words are probably not used to define various kinds of authority with precision. But the putting of them together gives emphasis to the thought that in that day there is no governing power of any kind that will not be completely subservient to Him. *Put down* renders the verb *katargeō*, a word of multitudinous translations (see note on i. 28). Its basic significance of 'render null and void', 'make inoperative', is much in point here. Paul does not speak of battles, or of rulers being dethroned. But he does speak of all rule, other than that of Christ, as being rendered completely inoperative. Although this is mentioned after the delivering up of the kingdom it takes place before it (cf. the change from the present, 'delivers up', not *shall have delivered up* as AV, to the aorist, *shall have put down*).

25. There is a compelling divine necessity about Paul's *must*. He is speaking about what God has determined, and therefore there is no uncertainty about it. It is a thought well worth keeping in mind when the powers of earth and hell seem strong. Often to the Christian it seems that the wicked will triumph. But such an appearance can only be temporary and illusory. At the climax of history Christ and none other *must* reign. His reign is thought of as a career of conquest, as He brings the *enemies* into subjection (cf. Ps. cx. 1). These *enemies* are not named, with the exception of 'death' in the next verse. But this one exception perhaps indicates that the *enemies* Paul has in mind are not evil men, but evil forces.

26. *Death* is characterized as *last enemy* (there is no article in the Greek, the force of this being to put the emphasis on the character or quality of death as *enemy*, and *last* enemy at that). *Destroyed* is *katargeō* once more, the same verb as in verse 24 (where see note). It is in the present tense, and the use of this tense for future action strikes a note of vividness and certainty. Death will be robbed of all its power. At present no man can resist the touch of death. Then death will be able to touch no man.

27. *He* is not defined, but it clearly means God the Father. The opening words are very similar to those of Ps. viii. 6. There they refer to the dominion that God has given to man, the summit of creation. Here they apply to Christ only, and they are more far-reaching; for, as the context shows, they include everything except the Father Himself. *All things* is emphatic. There is an interesting change of tense here. *He hath put . . . under* is aorist, pointing us to the single once-for-all act of subjection. *Are put under* is the perfect tense, including the thought of the permanent state of subjection. *Did put all things under* is aorist again, pointing to the same action as the first verb. Paul's point, then, is that God the Father has given to the Son unlimited sovereignty over all creation. That, however does not involve any infringement of the Father's own sovereignty. That Paul takes as obvious (*it is manifest, dēlon*).

28. The connection of thought with the previous verse is somewhat obscured in AV by the use of the translations *shall be subdued* and *be subject* for the same verb as was there three times translated by 'put under' (and is translated again in the same way at the end of this verse). The climax of the process of 'putting under' of which Paul has been speaking comes with the Son's being subject to the Father. This presents a difficulty to some people, who cannot see how to reconcile with a Trinitarian view of the nature of God the fact that one member of the Godhead should be subject to another. But it should be borne in mind that Paul is not speaking of the essential nature of either Christ or the Father. He is speaking of the work that Christ has accomplished, and will accomplish. He has died for men, and He has risen. He will return again. He will subdue all the enemies of God. The climax of His whole work will come when He renders up the kingdom to

Him who is the source of all. In that He became man for the accomplishment of that work, He took upon Him a certain subjection which is necessarily impressed upon that work right up to and including its consummation. The purpose of this (*hina*) is *that God may be all in all*. This is a strong expression for the complete supremacy that will then so obviously be His. Calvin says, 'all things will be brought back to God, as their alone beginning and end, that they may be closely bound to him'.

d. Arguments from Christian experience (xv. 29–34)

At this point there is a very abrupt change. From the Christ Paul turns to the Christian. He mentions certain practices associated with baptism which logically imply resurrection. He points to the dangers that Christian preachers so constantly underwent. If there is no resurrection, the argument runs, it is impossible to see a reason for this constant jeopardizing of one's life.

29. This reference to baptism *for* (*huper*) *the dead* is a notorious difficulty. The most natural meaning of the expression is that some early believers got themselves baptized on behalf of friends of theirs who had died without receiving that sacrament. Thus Parry says: 'The plain and necessary sense of the words implies the existence of a practice of vicarious baptism at Corinth, presumably on behalf of believers who died before they were baptised.' He stigmatizes all other interpretations as 'evasions . . . wholly due to the unwillingness to admit such a practice, and still more to a reference to it by S. Paul without condemnation'. That Paul is quite capable of reasoning from a practice of which he disapproves is shown by viii. 10, where he refers to sitting at meat in an idol's temple without showing it to be wrong in itself, though that he believed this is clear from x. 21ff. It is perhaps significant that, while Paul does not stop to condemn the practice of which he speaks, he dissociates himself from it ('what shall *they* do . . .'; contrast 'why do *we* also stand in jeopardy' in the next verse). He mentions it as taking place, and asks what meaning it can possibly have if the dead do not rise. The practice of vicarious baptism is attested in the second century (though apparently among heretics). If it was known at Corinth it would strongly support Paul's argument for the resurrection. Others suggest that the passage may refer to the symbolism of baptism (cf. Rom. vi. 1ff.), but it is difficult to see the relevance of such an argument to the resurrection of the body. Others think of baptism as being effected by the deaths of people martyred for the faith before they could be baptized ('baptism in blood'), baptized into the Church of the dead. If so, Paul has expressed himself in a very strange way. Again, it is suggested that there is an ellipsis of 'the resurrection' so that the expression means 'with a view to (the resurrection of) the dead'. This involves a very questionable meaning for *huper*, and an inexplicable ellipsis. Others think that relatives of the dead, mindful of the interest of their Christian kinsfolk when they were alive in their conversion, were baptized as a result of their thought for the dead. Between thirty and forty explanations have been suggested, and we cannot traverse them all. It seems to me that the language points to the first suggestion. If that is rejected as not in accordance with what Paul would have done, we are left to conjecture.

30. Paul turns to the experience of all Christians. They were in constant danger, even though there was no official persecution of the faith. Why should men take the trouble to join themselves to such a religion if death is the end of everything?

31. 'Daily I die' comes first in the Greek for emphasis. Paul's danger was very real, and very constant. He was never out of peril. He uses the strong affirmative *nē* (often used in oaths). *Your rejoicing . . . which I have* is not an easy expression.

But *kauchēsis, rejoicing,* may refer to 'boasting' as well as to the expression of joy, while *your* appears to be used in the objective sense (as in Rom. xi. 31). 'Your *kauchēsis*' will accordingly mean 'the pride I have in you'. Moffatt brings out the meaning: 'Not a day but I am at death's door! I swear it by my pride in you, brothers, through Christ Jesus our Lord.' It is interesting to see this expression of Paul's basic satisfaction with his Corinthian converts despite the many things for which he had to rebuke them.

32. It is not easy to be sure of Paul's meaning here. That he had been in some great danger in the province of Asia (in which Ephesus was) is clear from 2 Cor. i. 8, and it could be that he had been compelled to enter the arena with wild animals. It is often said that Paul, since he was a Roman citizen, could not have been compelled to fight wild beasts. This, however, cannot be pressed, for even Roman aristocrats appeared in the arena; for example Acilius Glabrio, an eminent Roman, was compelled by Domitian to fight wild beasts. However, it is not very likely. The word might be used metaphorically, as, for example, by Ignatius in his letter to the Romans, 'From Syria even unto Rome I fight with wild beasts, by land and sea, by night and by day', and he explains this as 'being bound amidst ten leopards, even a company of soldiers'.[1] There is also the point that Paul would hardly have omitted such an incident in 2 Cor. xi. 23ff. On the whole it seems as though we should take the words metaphorically. The aorist tense points to a specific occasion, but we have no means of knowing what it was. The Corinthians knew how the apostle was in constant danger, and could appreciate the force of his reference to this specific peril. If there is no resurrection, his whole life in general, and his conduct in this particular incident, are inexplicable. Lacking belief in the resurrection the logical course would be to follow the easygoing proverb which Paul quotes (cf. Is. xxii. 13). Deissmann

[1] v. 1, Lightfoot's translation.

cites 'the exhortation to drink in anticipation of approaching death' as 'one of the well-known formulae of ancient popular morals' (LAE, p. 295).

33. *Mē planasthe, be not deceived,* has about it the idea not so much of deception as of error (*planaō* in the passive = 'to go astray', 'to wander'; cf. our term 'planet', for the wandering stars). 'Make no mistake' is the sense of it. *Homiliai, communications,* is a word which means 'intercourse', 'fellowship', and then the communications that people make with each other, especially speeches (we get our word 'homily' from it). Here it is perhaps the first meaning, 'bad companionships'. *Manners* translates *ēthē,* which would be better rendered 'habits'. The whole expression is a proverb, found, for example, in Menander, and perhaps as early as Euripides. The point of Paul's citation is that keeping the wrong kind of company (i.e. that of men who deny the resurrection) may well corrupt good Christian habits, and turn men away from the true position.

34. *Eknepsate,* translated *awake,* originally had the sense of becoming sober after drunkenness (cf. Weymouth, 'Wake from this drunken fit'). It is very appropriate to an appeal to 'come to your senses'. Robertson and Plummer suggest that perhaps 'these sceptics claimed to be sober thinkers, and condemned the belief in a resurrection as a wild enthusiasm'. If so, Paul's verb is much in point. *To righteousness* is really an adverb meaning, 'in a righteous manner'. *Sin not* reminds us of the way the whole of life is interwoven. On the face of it Paul is discussing a doctrinal question, and not a moral issue. But throughout his correspondence the apostle insists on right doctrine. Doctrine leads to conduct, and unsound doctrine in the end must lead to sinful behaviour. *For* shows that Paul is linking this failure to live rightly with failure to think rightly. *Have not the knowledge* is 'have *agnōsian*' (i.e. 'hold on to ignorance'), the noun indicating not so much a purely intellectual ignorance, as an ignorance in religious things. AG tell us that it is used in the mystery religions of a 'lack of religious experience or lack of spiritual discernment'. The error with which Paul is concerned in this chapter arises basically (as do so many others) from a lack of real knowledge of God. The seriousness with which Paul regarded it is seen in his avowed intention of writing to shame his friends. In iv. 14, in connection with another matter, he explicitly excluded this from his aim.

e. The resurrection body demonstrated from nature and from scripture (xv. 35-49)

From arguments proving the fact of the resurrection Paul turns his attention to the nature of the resurrection body. Some had evidently ridiculed the idea of a resurrection with questions as to the nature of the body with which men would rise. 'How can men possibly rise when their bodies have disintegrated?' must have been the kind of objection raised, an objection not unfamiliar in modern times. Paul counters by pointing to the miracle of harvest. The seed is buried, but it is raised up with a new and more glorious body. From this he goes on to consider that there are different kinds of body, and different kinds of glory. This leads to the great triumphant fact that, though our bodies are 'sown' in corruption and dishonour and weakness, they will be raised in incorruption and glory and power. God's power is adequate for all this. As He has willed that we should have bodies fitted for our life on earth, so has He willed that we shall have bodies fitted to our heavenly existence. Paul's insistence on bodily life should not be overlooked. Those who thought of the immortality of the soul, but denied the resurrection of the body, usually looked for nothing more than a shadowy, insipid existence in Hades. Fundamental to Paul's thought is the idea that the after-life will be infinitely more glorious than this. This necessitates a suitable 'body' in which the life is to be lived, for without a 'body' of some kind there seems no way of allowing for individuality and self-expression. But Paul does not view this 'body' crudely. He describes it with the adjective 'spiritual' (verse 44), and he expressly differentiates it from 'flesh and blood' (verse 50). His thought is in marked contrast with that of Judaism in general. The Rabbis held that the body to be raised would be identical with the body that died. The writer of the *Apocalypse of Baruch* asks whether there will be any change when men rise, and the answer is 'the earth shall then assuredly restore the dead. . . . It shall make no change in their form, but as it has received, so shall it restore them' (l. 2). Paul will have nothing to do with this view (see verses 42ff., 52, etc.). While there will be identity there will also be difference.

35. *But* is the strong adversative *alla*. Far from conforming to the kind of conduct Paul has just outlined, someone (the word is indefinite) will offer an objection. Paul gives the objection either in quotation, or in the sort of words he would imagine the objector to use. *How are the dead raised up?* queries the mechanics of the process. *With what body do they come?* inquires as to the form they will have. *What is* from *poias,* 'of what kind?' It was obvious to these Greek sceptics that a body quickly decomposes, and they thought to laugh the whole idea of resurrection out of court with their query as to the body. What kind of body would arise from a heap of decomposed rubbish?

36. Paul deals sharply with such objections. *Fool* may not be the most tactful form of address (even if it be softened slightly, as in rv, 'Thou foolish one'), but its bluntness makes clear Paul's view of the worthlessness of such arguments. In *thou sowest,* the word *thou* is strongly emphatic. Paul uses the personal pronoun, which is not strictly necessary (for the verb indicates the subject with sufficient clarity), and he adopts the unusual course of putting it before the relative pronoun *that which.* The effect is to make clear that what Paul has been saying about the resurrection is not without its parallels in activities familiar to, and even engaged upon by, the objectors. If only they would think, they themselves had the answer to their own objection in their own habitual practices. They sow seed, which is destroyed in the form in which it is sown. The act of sowing, taken with this destruction, is so similar to the process of death among mankind that Paul can speak of the grain dying. Carrying on this metaphor the growth that follows is a process of quickening, and the quickening of the grain depends on its having 'died'. The seed must be destroyed if the new life is to appear. Familiarity with the marvel of growth has dulled our sense of wonder. But if we did not know, how would we ever guess that casting a seed into the ground and burying it is the way to produce living plants? Why, then, should we regard as incredible the transformation of a dead body? Notice the passive *is . . . quickened*. The seed does not come to life of itself, but God gives it life. Moffatt's and Goodspeed's 'never comes to life' misses this. Paul is preparing the way for that other statement of God's activity in the resurrection (cf. verse 38).

37. What dies is nothing like what appears. A dead-looking, bare, dry seed is put into the ground, but what comes up is a green plant, vigorous and beautiful. It is not *that body that shall be* that is sown. Paul will presently develop the thought that the body that is raised is incomparably more glorious than the body that is buried. Here he leaves it to be implied. Far from the decomposition of the body presenting an obstacle to the resurrection it merely prepares us for the thought that the body that is to be raised is much more wonderful than the body that was buried. Plant life is always on hand to teach us. We sow nothing more than *bare grain*, grain without the clothing of verdure that characterizes the plant. This is common to all seeds. Paul mentions *wheat* and adds 'or one of the others'. It matters not which plant is sown, the lesson is the same.

38. This is the only place in this particular section where Paul explicitly mentions the divine oversight of the whole process, but what he says here must be held to be determinative for his thought throughout. Plants do not rise (and men do not rise) of their own volition. Nor do they do it by chance. They do so because that is the way God has determined it shall be. There is an interesting change of tense here. God *giveth* is the present tense and it indicates the habitual practice. God is always giving seeds bodies in this way. *As it hath pleased him* is the aorist, signifying a decisive action. God once and for all planned what should be. All things accordingly follow His plan. Though there is regularity, in accordance with this there is no uniformity, for God gives its *own body* to *every seed* (lit. 'to each one of the seeds').

39. From grain and plants Paul turns to *flesh*. *All flesh* is not of the same kind. The flesh of *men, beasts* (the word denotes properly 'beasts of burden', 'cattle', but the point is not important), *birds*, and *fishes*, are all different. Paul is preparing the way for the thought that there can be a difference between the kind of body we have before the resurrection and the kind we shall have after the resurrection.

40. In keeping with this differentiation between various forms of earthly life there is a difference between *celestial bodies* and *bodies terrestrial*. We would, in accordance with our idiom, tend to interpret 'heavenly bodies' of the stars. But, despite the opinions of some eminent commentators, this is probably not Paul's thought (he comes to the stars in the next verse; besides the counterpart to 'heavenly bodies' in our sense of the term is 'the earth', not *bodies terrestrial*). It was an accepted idea that heavenly beings, or at least some of them, had bodies. Paul's point is that their bodies are those proper to heavenly beings, while earthly beings have different bodies, bodies proper to earthly beings. Another stage in the argument is reached with the reference to *glory*. The *glory* of earthly beings may be resplendent, but it is not the *glory* of the heavenly. They are of a different order, and the glory appertaining to them is likewise of a different order.

41. This leads on to a consideration of what we call the heavenly bodies. The sun, the moon, and the stars are all glorious, each in its own way, and each in a way differing from anything on earth. Even the stars differ from each other. One is more glorious than another. Wherever he looks Paul sees evidence of this principle of differentiation. It is a marvellous universe, and in it God has set so many things, so many glorious things, which yet differ markedly from each other.

42. Having made his point that there are different kinds of bodies, and different degrees of glory, Paul now gets to grips with the bearing of this on the resurrection. *So also is the resurrection.* It is along this line of differing bodies and differing glories that the resurrection is to be understood. There is an article with *the dead* (as there is not, for example, in verses 12f.), so that the dead are being regarded as a class. Paul does not give a subject for his following verbs, but the *it* is easy to follow. Paul has used a number of examples in the previous verses, but his choice of verb, *is sown*, indicates that the sowing of seed with the resultant new and vigorous life which he has mentioned in verses 36f. is primarily in his mind. Of the series of antitheses which this thought arouses the apostle begins with that between *corruption* and *incorruption*. While the former word refers primarily to the body's liability to decay, the analogy between physical and moral corruption may not be out of mind. The latter word is one in common use to indicate the quality of life in the hereafter, and it is particularly telling in this connection. The chief objection that the typical Greek had to any doctrine of resurrection was that the body is essentially corruptible. It is, by its nature, subject to decay. He looked accordingly for an existence when the soul would be untrammelled by the corruptible body, when the soul would exist *in incorruption*. Paul associates this very state with the resurrection body. He agrees that *corruption*, liability to decay, is a property of man's earthly body, the body that is to be put in the grave. But the body that is to be taken from the grave at the resurrection will be a transformed body. It will be *raised in incorruption*. That very feature which the average Greek regarded as incompatible with the body (because he thought only of the present body of flesh and blood), Paul sees as characteristic of the resurrection body.

43. Paul continues to pick out those features of bodily life which seemed to the Greeks to demonstrate the folly of the idea of the resurrection, and to show that they have no relevance to the resurrection body. *Dishonour* translates *atimia*, a word sometimes used of loss of the rights of citizenship. A corpse has no rights. Whether Paul has this in mind or not, there is nothing particularly honourable about a decaying body as it is put into a grave. But that has no relevance to the way the body is raised. The resurrection body in Paul's view is a glorious body, just as far surpassing the present body as does the beautiful plant the seed from which it sprung. The Greek's doubts arising from the dishonourable nature of the body that now is are groundless. The body that is to be raised is to be a body in glory. Again, the present body is comparatively powerless. Cultivate it as he would (and the Greek did cultivate bodily prowess) it still remains a weak instrument far outspanned by the mind that is in it. And when it dies (the primary reference is to the dead body) it is the very symbol of powerlessness. But the resurrection body will not be limited as this body is. Just as this body is characterized by *weakness*, so the body that is to be raised will be characterized by *power*.

44. *Natural* translates *psuchikon*, 'pertaining to the soul (or life)'. It has to do with the present life in all its aspects, especially as contrasted with the supernatural life (cf. its use in ii.14 of the merely 'natural' man). There is nothing necessarily sinful or blameworthy about it, unless there is the thought of a man choosing deliberately to live on a lower plane when he could live on a higher. In this place it signifies that the body we now have is a body suited for the present life. It is adapted to the *psuchē*, the rational principle of life. But such a body is ill-adapted for life in the world to come. For that a body is needed which is attuned to the spirit, in fact, *a spiritual body*. This does not necessarily mean 'composed of spirit', but rather 'which expresses spirit', 'which answers to the needs of spirit'. In the latter part of the verse we should read, 'if there is a natural body, there is also a spiritual'. Nobody can deny that a natural body exists, a body related to the *psuchē*. If this is so, reasons the apostle, there must also be a body related to the spirit. The *spiritual body* then is the organ which is intimately related to the spirit of man, just as his present body is intimately related to his earthly life.

45. Characteristically Paul appeals to Scripture to clinch his argument. This is not something he has thought up for himself. Yet we should notice that he does not employ his usual formula of citation, *kathōs gegraptai*, 'as it is written', but *houtōs kai gegraptai, so it is written,* which may indicate something less than strict proof. He quotes from Gn. ii. 7 (inserting *first* before *man*, and *Adam* after it). His point appears to be that the characteristic of man from the very beginning is *psuchē*, *soul*. That was true of Adam, and it is true of all his descendants. The first Adam passed on his nature to those who came after. Scripture does not include the second point that Paul makes. He may have intended to prove only the first point from Scripture, the second being his own supplement. He may mean that Scripture as a whole witnesses to Christ as *a quickening spirit*. Or he may possibly have held it to be implicit in the Scripture. That is to say, Adam was the progenitor of the race, and his characteristics are stamped on the race.

Christ is *the last Adam*, the progenitor of the race of spiritual men. By virtue of His office as *the last Adam* He stamps His characteristics on those who are in Him. The first Adam implies the last Adam, and the first Adam's work implies the last Adam's work. Christ's characteristic in this office is that He is *a quickening* (i.e. 'life-giving') *spirit*. Not only is He the pattern of those who are in Him, but He is the source of that spiritual life which will result in the bodies of which Paul speaks. AV correctly supplies *was made* as the verb with this. Paul implies that it was in His saving work for men that Christ became a life-giving spirit. Some see a reference to the incarnation, others to the resurrection or the second advent. But Paul is not specific.

46. Paul insists on the right order of things. *Howbeit* is the strong adversative *alla*, which is a little perplexing, for what follows is not in strong contrast with the preceding. Perhaps, as Ellicott thinks, it contrasts the following 'broad statement' with the preceding details. Or Paul may mean that though the 'quickening spirit' of whom he has just been speaking is before all time and before all men, yet in the order of creation we see not what is particularly related to Him, the *spiritual*, but what has particular relevance to life in the here and now, the *natural* (*to psuchikon*). In the order of creation we enter into *natural* life first; it is only after that that we may enter into the *spiritual*.

47. *The first man* refers to Adam. *Choikos, earthy,* is from a different root than *gē, earth.* It signifies 'made of dust', and is reminiscent of Gn. ii. 7, 'And the Lord God formed man of the dust of the ground'. *Of* in the expression *of the earth* denotes origin. *The second man* is the Lord Jesus, set over against Adam once more, this time not in terms of work accomplished or of natural constitution, but of origin. Though He appeared on earth, and lived and died and rose again, He is not to be thought of as originating from the earth, as is Adam, but as *from heaven* (the better MSS omit *the Lord*). Some refer these words to the incarnation, and some to the second advent. The point is not clear, but the primary reference is to our Lord's heavenly origin in contrast to that of Adam.

48. *As is the earthy* points us to Adam once more. He is the pattern for all them that come after. As is his nature, so is theirs. This includes the whole race, so that all men are, in this sense, *earthy*. Over against this is set *the heavenly*, which, in accordance with the description in the previous verse, is the Lord who came 'from heaven'. The use of the adjective, rather than the longer expression, stresses His nature as a heavenly Being, and not His origin. The really important point is the conclusion, *such are they also that are heavenly*. There is no question in the minds either of Paul or of the Corinthian converts, or of the Greeks at large, that all men are *earthy*. Our bodies are earthy bodies and they share in the corruption that is part and parcel of earthy things. But Christians are not only *earthy*. They are also *heavenly*, because of their relationship to Christ. For Paul that has far-reaching consequences. It has implications for this present life, but it also has its implications for the time in the world to come. It means that Christ's people will then be like Him. (Cf. 1 Jn. iii. 2, 'it doth not yet appear what we shall be: but we know that, when he shall appear, we shall be like him; for we shall see him as he is.') The resurrection body of Christ shows us something of what life will be like for believers in that new world which their resurrection will usher in. Then He will change their 'vile body' so that it will be 'fashioned like unto his glorious body' (Phil. iii. 21).

49. *We have borne* is from the verb *phoreō*, which is more intensive than the more usual *pherō*. Whereas the latter means simply 'to bear', the former has about it the idea of bearing continually, bearing habitually (it is often used of wearing clothes; cf. verse 53). It is thus a natural word to use here, where Paul wants to convey the thought of our habitual state. The use of the aorist may, as Parry thinks, be inceptive, 'began to wear, put on'. Or it may, from the standpoint of the resurrection, regard our life as a completed whole. The bearing in question is seen in the whole of life, and not simply in some parts. *Eikōn, image*, is used of man being made in 'the image of God' (xi. 7). It can denote simply representation (as in the *eikōn* of the Emperor on a coin), or it can denote something much more exact. Here it will be the image that corresponds to and reproduces the original. The majority of the more ancient MSS read 'let us bear' instead of *we shall bear* in the second part of the verse. If this reading be adopted then Paul is exhorting the Corinthians to put on their heavenly state, progressively to make it their own, 'let us also try to be like the man from heaven' as Goodspeed translates. This sounds as though it were something that men could do by their own efforts. This is so far from Paul's usual approach that we are justified in regarding 'let us bear' as a primitive corruption of the text by scribes interested in ethical exhortation, and not quite clear on the apostle's meaning. The context seems to make it clear that *we shall bear* is the right reading. There are some good authorities for this text, including the Codex Vaticanus. Paul is saying then, that just as throughout this life we have habitually borne the form of Adam, so in the life to come we shall bear that of our Lord. Just as surely as we have done the one, so shall we do the other. This is not a matter for doubt. The considerations he has adduced are in Paul's mind conclusive.

f. Victory over death (xv. 50–58)

The chapter comes to a magnificent climax. Paul makes it clear that those who rise will not be creatures of flesh and blood. They will be 'changed', as will those who are alive when that day comes. They will no longer have bodies liable to decay and death. In a lyrical passage the apostle exults in the triumph won over death itself. This calls forth a thanksgiving to God, the source of victory, and an exhortation in the light of all this to be steadfast.

50. *Now this I say* (or 'assert', *phēmi*) heightens the significance of what follows. It is important. *Flesh and blood* is a not uncommon way of referring to life here and now (e.g. Gal. i. 16; Heb. ii. 14). It directs attention to two of the most important constituents of the physical body, and two which are peculiarly liable to decay. The expression is thus symptomatic of man's mortality and of the weakness of his mortal frame. It does not signify moral frailty. *Flesh* by itself is often used in a moral sense, but the combination *flesh and blood* seems always in the New Testament to have a physical meaning. The blunt statement that flesh and blood *cannot* participate in the kingdom plainly excludes all crude ideas of resurrection. It is not this present physical body that Paul envisages as taking its place in the kingdom. *Inherit* must not be pressed. The word strictly signifies 'receive by inheritance', but in the New Testament the meaning has broadened to include possession, whether brought about by inheritance or in some other way. For *corruption* and *incorruption* see note on verse 42.

51. Paul continues to employ an emphatic style. *Behold* has the effect of focusing attention on the following. For *mystery* see the note on ii. 7. Men could never have worked out for themselves what will happen at the second coming, but God has revealed it. *Sleep* is the same beautiful way of referring to death that we have seen in verse 18. Some have felt that Paul means that the second coming will take place within his own lifetime. But this is to press his words illegitimately. The same process applied to vi. 14 would show that he would then be dead! But Paul often classes himself with those he is describing without any implication that he actually is one of them (e.g. vi. 15, x. 22). The plain fact is that Paul did not know when these events would take place, and nowhere does he claim to know. When he says *we* he means 'believers generally',

'Christians alive at that day'. Some will not die, but whether we are among that number, or whether we die before the day, *we shall all be changed*. Earthly bodies will not serve in the kingdom that will then be set up. Notice that the difficulty is the opposite of that in 1 Thes. iv. 13ff. There Paul assured his readers that those who die before the Parousia will be at no disadvantage. They will rise first. Here the difficulty is with the living, for Paul has just said that 'flesh and blood cannot inherit the kingdom of God'. How then can the living enter that kingdom? The answer is *we shall all be changed*. Early scribes found some difficulty with the text, and there are variant readings. One of them is important, for it found its way into the Vulgate, and so represents the way Roman Catholics have usually understood the verse. In Knox's rendering it runs, 'we shall all rise again, but not all of us will undergo the change I speak of' (the second clause referring to the unsaved, who, though raised, will not undergo the glorious transformation). However, the text behind AV is to be preferred, as Knox concedes in a footnote.

52. The change will not be a long-drawn-out affair. The resurrection of the dead might be likened to the slow growth of a seed, but the change in the living will take place with startling suddenness. *Moment* is *atomos* ('that which cannot be cut, or divided', i.e. the smallest possible; we get our word 'atom' from it). It signifies the shortest possible moment of time. *Twinkling (rhipē)* is connected with the idea of throwing. *The twinkling of an eye* is the time it takes to cast a glance, or perhaps to flutter an eyelid. Paul mentions *the trumpet* also in 1 Thes. iv. 16. In the note on that passage[1] I have drawn attention to evidence in the Old Testament, in the teaching of our Lord, and in contemporary Judaism, associating the trumpet with the events in the end-time. The trumpet was frequently in use in connection with festivity and triumph. Both ideas are in place here. The sounding of the trumpet

[1] *Op. cit.*, pp. 87f.

seems to be the signal for the dead to rise. *Last* refers not to the last in a series of trumpet blasts (as in Rabbinic speculation), but last among events on earth. It marks the end of things as we know them. The dead will be raised *incorruptible*, which prepares the way for Paul to repeat his statement that *we shall be changed*. He is making it very clear that he does not envisage a return to the sort of life we live now.

53. Something of the nature of the change is brought out. The two points singled out are men's present corruption (liability to bodily decay) and mortality. These things are totally incompatible with life in the hereafter. *Put on* is the usual word for putting on clothing. The body now is but the garb of the real man. In the life to come the real man will put on another suit, so to speak.

54. It is characteristic of Paul to see in all this a fulfilment of Scripture. He remembers that it is written in Is. xxv. 8, 'He will swallow up death in victory'. What God had planned long since, and had revealed to His servant the prophet, He will fulfil in the way Paul has outlined. The expression points to the complete destruction of death.

55. In language reminiscent of Ho. xiii. 14 Paul sings of the triumph that will be wrought. Probably we should follow those MSS which reverse the order of the questions as given in AV, that referring to *victory* coming first. Then the question about the *sting* is taken up immediately by the statement in the following verse. The word *kentron* refers primarily to the sting of bees, serpents, and the like. This metaphorical use pictures the harmfulness of death. It is a malignant adversary. Perhaps we should notice that in the best Greek MSS both questions are asked of *death*, and not one of *grave* (lit. *Hades*) as AV.

56. We are brought face to face with the seriousness of moral issues. It is not *death* in itself that is the harmful thing.

It is *death* that is 'the wages of sin' (Rom. vi. 23) that matters. For death, considered simply as the passing out of this life into the immediate presence of the Lord, is a gain, not a loss (Phil. i. 21, 23). Where sin is pardoned, death has no sting. But where sin has not been dealt with, there death is a virulent antagonist. The *sting* is not in *death*, but in *sin*. By *the strength of sin is the law* Paul turns us to such thoughts as those expounded in Rom. v. 12ff., vii. 7ff. *The law*, though it is divine in origin, and Paul can speak of the commandment as 'holy, and just, and good' (Rom. vii. 12), is quite unable to bring men to a state of salvation. Indeed, by setting before men the standard that they ought to reach and never do, it becomes sin's stronghold. It makes sinners of us all. It condemns us all.

57. But the work of Christ has been to satisfy the law's claims (He has 'redeemed us from the curse of the law, being made a curse for us', Gal. iii. 13). He has dealt thoroughly with the problem of sin. The believer accordingly has nothing to fear from death. Its sting has been drawn. Paul exults in a paean of praise to God who *giveth us the victory*. The use of the present participle may convey the thought that it is God's characteristic to give victory. There is also the implication that we participate in that victory now, and that we participate in it daily. The Christian life is characteristically a life of victory. The use of the full title *our Lord Jesus Christ* heightens the sense of the majesty of His Person. There is victory for the Christian, but it is only through what Christ has done for him.

58. Arising out of this comes the exhortation to Christian stability. *Hedraioi, stedfast*, was used in vii. 37 of him that 'standeth stedfast in his heart', and this gives us the sense of it. There is the thought of stable purpose, something that will not easily be disturbed, for the man's whole bent is behind it. There is an underlining of this thought (not the addition of a new one) in the following *unmoveable*. The Corinthians were prone to fickleness, shifting without reason from one position to another. Let them get a firm grip on the truth of the resurrection, of God's final plan for all men and all things, and they will not be so readily shaken. *Ginesthe, be*, might be rendered 'become'. Paul sets before them a state from which they were as yet all too far. Their rightful condition is described as *always abounding in the work of the Lord*. This thought of the abundant life should not be passed over. There is nothing cramped or narrow about the genuine Christian experience. Edwards speaks of faith in the resurrection as producing 'a consciousness of boundless and endless power for work', and adds, 'In the case of a believer, youth's large dreams never contract into commonplace achievement'. *Forasmuch as ye know* should probably be rendered 'knowing'. The construction is exactly the same as the previous *abounding*, and there seems no real reason for a different way of translating the participle. What follows is not the reason for the foregoing (the reason is rather the resurrection truth that Paul has been expounding), but its accompaniment. Because of the resurrection with all that it implies of God's final triumph, and of the survival of the believer through death, Christian *labour* (*kopos*, giving prominence to the thought of the fatigue involved in hard work) is *not in vain* (*kenos*, 'empty'; Moffatt, 'never thrown away'). Deissmann sees in these words 'a trembling echo of the discouragement resulting from a piece of work being rejected for alleged bad finish and therefore not paid for' (LAE, p. 314). The Christian fears no such discouragement. His labour is *in the Lord*. All that he does is in Christ's strength and for Christ's glory.

VIII. CONCLUSION (xvi. 1–24)

The great themes of the Epistle have been dealt with. But there are still some matters requiring attention, and Paul turns to them. In a little 'chatty' section he gives directions for the collection for the poor, outlines his projected movements, speaks briefly about mutual friends, Timothy, Apollos, and others, and brings his letter to a close.

a. The collection (xvi. 1-4)

1. *Now concerning* is the formula used to introduce topics mentioned in the letter from the Corinthians (see note on verse 12). *The collection* (the word is in common use, more especially for a collection for religious purposes) meant much to Paul. This is the first mention of it in his extant writings, but we read of it also in Rom. xv. 26; 2 Cor. viii 1ff., ix, 1ff.; Acts xxiv. 17. Here he speaks of the collection simply as *for the saints*, but from other references (e.g. verse 3) it is clear that it is for the poor at Jerusalem. Paul was very anxious for the collection to be a success. He was no doubt deeply concerned about the need of the Jerusalem church. We do not know why this church was so poor, evidently poorer by far than other churches. But Jerusalem as a whole was not rich, being largely dependent on the generosity of Jews from outside Palestine. Christians would not receive such bounty. On the contrary, they would be the objects of special hostility and persecution (1 Thes. ii. 14f.), and might well be in special straits. It is also probable that they suffered from the after effects of the community of goods practised in the first days (Acts iv. 34f.). A second motive for Paul would arise from the fact that, just as the Jews helped their poorer brethren, so did the Greek religious brotherhoods (the *eranoi*). It would never do for the Christians to lag behind the Jewish and pagan world in their care for the poor brethren. There is also the fact that the apostle himself and the whole Gentile mission were held in suspicion by some of the more conservative elements in the Jerusalem church. Paul doubtless felt that a generous response to the need of the poor in that church would strikingly demonstrate the solidarity of the Gentile churches with the mother church, and do much to promote unity. The collection was being made throughout the Gentile churches, at least of Paul's foundation, as we see from the references to *the churches of Galatia* and to those of Macedonia (2 Cor. viii. 1ff., ix. 2ff.).

2. *The first day of the week* signifies 'on every first day of the week'. This is the first piece of evidence to show that the Christians habitually observed that day, though there is no reason to doubt that it was their custom from the very first (cf. Jn. xx. 19, 26; Acts xx. 7; Rev. i. 10). As distinct from the Jewish sabbath the first day was a weekly commemoration of the resurrection of the Lord, which indicates something of the importance the Christians attached to that event. *Every one of you* indicates that each, no matter how poor, would make a contribution. The most natural meaning of *lay by him in store* is, as many commentators from Chrysostom down have maintained, that each is to keep the money in store at home. But as Paul expressly deprecates the collecting of the money when he arrives (which would be necessary if they all had it laid by at home) it is perhaps better to think of it as being stored in the church treasury. Paul indicates no definite amount, no exact proportion of one's income, to be contributed, but leaves it to the conscience of each. He gives guidance only in the expression *as God hath prospered him*. The subject of the verb is not expressed (the word *God* is supplied by AV; there is nothing corresponding to it in the Greek), and it may be 'he' or 'his business'. The verb is passive, and the tense either present or perfect. The forms are the same, the only difference being in the accent, and, as there are no accents in the older MSS, only the context tells us which it is. Either gives a good sense, and both yield the thought of a continuing state. The meaning then is that a man's giving should be in direct proportion to the way he is prospering. *Gatherings* is 'gatherings of money'. It is the same word as that rendered 'collection' in the previous verse. Paul desires the collection to be made before he comes. Incidentally he uses the indefinite *hotan* for *when*. The time of his visit is uncertain.

3. *Come* is a different word, with the meaning 'arrive'. There is nothing in the Greek corresponding to *your*, and we should probably place our comma after *approve* (for this verb see notes on x. 9, xi. 28; it means first 'prove', and arising from this 'approve'). Paul is not suggesting that the Corinthians should write to him or to anyone else about the brethren they approve, but rather that they should choose out men whom he would send with letters (i.e. of commendation). The Corinthians would choose them, and Paul would commend them. Such letters of commendation were common, and Deissmann cites one dated 19th September, A.D. 50 (LAE, pp. 170f.). Notice Paul's scrupulous care in the handling of this money. He was arranging the collection, but he did not plan to touch the money in person at any time. The Corinthians would raise it, keep it till Paul came, and send it by messengers of their own choosing to its destination.

4. Paul's plans were uncertain. He did not know whether he would be going to Jerusalem or not. If it seemed right that he should, then he says they will accompany him. We should probably understand this to mean that if the collection amounted to a worthy sum he would go with it himself (it would not be seemly for an apostle to supervise in person the delivery of a niggardly amount). Moffatt renders, 'if the sum makes it worth my while to go too, they shall accompany me'.

b. Paul's plans (xvi. 5-9)

Paul's movements are tentative. But he wants his friends to know that he plans to stay with them, perhaps even spend a whole winter with them. But he cannot allow his projected visit to take him away from Ephesus until his work there is finished.

5. In iv. 19 Paul has foreshadowed a visit to Corinth, and has intimated that there were some at Corinth who thought that he would not come (see note on iv. 18). So now the apostle lays it down with certainty that he will come to them. He puts the time of his visit as *when I shall pass through Macedonia*. *When* is the indefinite *hotan* once more. Paul does not know when this is to be. *Pass through* points to a systematic tour of the various Macedonian churches. The addition, *for I do pass through Macedonia*, seems to show that this part of the plan was new to the Corinthians. They evidently knew that Paul was planning a visit to them (even if some of them denied that he would ever make it), but they had not known of the Macedonian plans. Now Paul tells them what he hopes to do, and they can see just where his visit to their own city comes in. This use of the present for future action is not uncommon. It lends an air of greater definiteness to the plan.

6. *It may be, tuchon*, reminds us of the uncertainty of the rest of the apostle's movements. Paul is not committing himself. But he would like his visit to Corinth to be more than the passing visit that is all the Macedonian churches can expect (that is the force of his verb 'pass through'). *You* is emphatic. It contrasts the Corinthians with the Macedonians. But at Corinth Paul may well *abide* (*katamenō*) and even pass the whole of the winter (when travelling was normally suspended in the ancient world). This would give the Corinthians the opportunity of 'bringing him on his journey', i.e. providing such things as he had need of for the way. Once again *you* is emphatic: 'that *you* may be the ones to bring me . . .' *Whithersoever I go* reflects Paul's uncertainty as to destination. He was clear on his plan to visit Macedonia, and then to go to Corinth; but from that point he had no intentions. In passing it is worth pointing out that, while Paul evidently had to change his plans more than once, and was accused of fickleness in the process (2 Cor. i. 15ff.), the plan outlined here was the one eventually adopted. From Acts xx. 1–3 we learn that he went from Ephesus to Macedonia, then to Greece, where he stayed three months.

7. *I will* is not the simple future, but the verb *thelō*, 'I wish', 'I set my will upon'. It is not Paul's will at all simply to pay a visit to Corinth in passing. For the third time he employs an emphatic *you*. His desire is to spend some time among them. Notice his qualification *if the Lord permit*. He is the servant of the Lord. He must go where the Lord wills. Therefore all his plans must be subject to the proviso (expressed or not) that the Lord may intervene and direct him elsewhere.

8, 9. However, his hopes of seeing his friends in the various Grecian churches must be deferred for a time. Paul's immediate task is at Ephesus, and it will not be finished before *Pentecost*. *Energōs*, translated *effectual*, is an unusual adjective to qualify a noun like *door*. It means 'active', 'effective', and is here used by a figure of the kind of activity open to Paul as a result of the open *door* of which he speaks. *Is opened* is the perfect tense, yielding the meaning that the door 'stands open'. There is the thought of the continuing opportunity. We do not expect to find a reference to *many adversaries* in this connection. Paul's abrupt reference to them reminds us that the Christian is not usually left to pursue his task unmolested. It is part of the conditions under which we serve God that when we have great opportunities of service there are also great difficulties in our way. Acts xix shows how great were Paul's adversaries at Ephesus.

c. Timothy and Apollos (xvi. 10–12)

10. In iv. 17 Paul has spoken of sending Timothy to Corinth. From Acts xix. 22 it would seem that Timothy was accompanied by Erastus, and that they went to Macedonia first. It is possible that Paul doubted whether Timothy would reach Corinth, but his use of *if* need not imply uncertainty. It may be like the 'if' in 'If winter comes, can spring be far behind?' Moffatt and RSV both translate 'when'. Paul's injunction that they look to it that he be *without fear* among them points to Timothy's rather timid disposition and to his youth (his youth could still be referred to years later when 1 Tim. iv. 12 was written). From the contents of this letter we may infer that there were among the Corinthian believers some who were confident and self-willed. Paul evidently feared that Timothy might not be adequate for the task of dealing with the difficulties raised by such men, a fear that subsequent events were to show was well founded. But Paul puts in a word for his young assistant. He calls on the Corinthians to do nothing to frighten him, and he reminds them that he and Timothy are engaged on the same work, *the work of the Lord.*

11. In the spirit of 1 Thes. v. 13 Paul urges that the work Timothy does is the reason he should not be despised. *Despise* is a strong term, meaning 'make absolutely nothing of' (see note on i. 28). It indicates something of what Paul feared for Timothy. *Conduct him forth* employs the same verb that we have seen used in verse 6 of setting Paul on his way. He asks that they should do the same for Timothy as for him. The fact that he looks for Timothy to return to him shows that Paul had sent him for specific tasks. He was not on a roving commission. The reference to *the brethren* is not clear. Acts xix. 22 mentions only Erastus as being with him, though, of course, there may have been others. Paul may mean that he looks to Timothy to come back to him with certain brethren from Corinth. But it is just possible that he means that he, and the brethren with him, look for Timothy's return.

12. We come in this verse to the last occurrence of the formula *peri de* introducing topics mentioned in the letter from Corinth. Previously it has been rendered 'now concerning' (vii. 1, 25, xii. 1, xvi. 1), and 'now as touching' (viii. 1). Here it is *as touching.* Apollos clearly stood in high esteem at Corinth, and in their letter the Corinthians had evidently expressed the desire that he should pay them another visit. In this Paul concurred, and he had 'besought him much' to come *with the brethren.* Clearly Paul and Apollos were in no sense rivals. The repetition of the phrase *with the brethren* (used in the last verse in connection with Timothy) may not be accidental. It may be that Timothy had travelled with others, and Paul had wished Apollos to join the party. Or it may be that on Timothy's return certain *brethren* would go to Corinth and Paul had tried to persuade Apollos to be of their number. However the Alexandrian's will was *not at all* (i.e. 'altogether not') to come just then. This did not mean that he would not come. But he awaited the *convenient time*. This may mean no more than that Apollos was too busy, and would come when he had more leisure, or it may signify that he did not think the time was yet ripe for him to pay the visit in question.

d. Exhortation (xvi. 13, 14)

Paul interjects a brief, sharp exhortation. The Corinthians had shown a distressing immaturity in some things, and the apostle in a series of compelling imperatives points them to a better way.

13. *Watch, grēgoreite*, like all the imperatives in these two verses is a present imperative. Paul is not treating of momentary attitudes, but of continuing states. The word denotes more than the mere absence of sleep. It implies a determined effort at wakefulness: 'Be on the alert' as Barclay renders it. It is often used of watching for the second coming (Mt. xxiv. 42f., xxv. 13; Mk. xiii. 34ff.). *Stand fast in the faith* points to the stability of the Christian firmly grounded in Christ, a stability distressingly absent from the Corinthians. *Quit you like men* may point to the immaturity shown by some of the things the Corinthians had been doing. They must be like responsible adults. Moreover, they are engaged in a desperate strife with the forces of evil, and it is therefore imperative that they play the part of men. *Be strong* may be passive, 'be made strong'. The strength of the Christian is not something native, inherent; he derives it from God.

14. *En agapē, with charity*, is better rendered 'in love'. We are reminded of chapter xiii, with its emphasis on the all-pervading nature of Christian love. Nothing we do is outside its scope. The significance of 'in' rather than *with* of AV should not be overlooked. Love is more than an accompaniment of Christian actions. It is the very atmosphere in which the Christian lives and moves and has his being.

e. Have a due regard for men like Stephanas (xvi. 15-18)

15. It is always good to have an example before us that we may follow. Paul has had much to say by way of blame, but he now selects certain people among the Corinthians and holds them up for imitation, namely *the house* (i.e. 'household') *of Stephanas*. Paul has already mentioned baptizing this household (i. 16). Now we have the additional information that they were the *firstfruits* of this province. As the province included Athens, where Paul had some converts before preaching in Corinth, this raises a minor problem. It may be that the household of Stephanas was in some way converted before Paul preached at Athens. It may be that while there were earlier conversions of individuals this was the first household to be won. Or, it may be that *firstfruits* indicates those fruits which gave promise of the harvest to come. 'To the Apostle's mind the pledge of a future Church came not in Athens, but in Corinth' (Edwards). They were shining examples of what Christians should be for *they have addicted themselves to the ministry of the saints*. Moffatt speaks of the verb rendered *addicted* as a 'trade metaphor' used, for example, by Plato of certain people who 'set themselves to the business of serving the public' by retailing farm produce. Stephanas and his family have taken as their particular responsibility, their piece of Christian service, this task of *ministry*. This is a general word, and is not to be understood of clergy as against lay people. It is service of the church. The house of Stephanas did not appoint them-

selves to any place of leadership or prominence, but to one of
lowly service.

16. That is the Christian way, and Paul commends this
example to the church at large. They should *submit* to such
people. Paul speaks a good deal about Christians submitting
themselves to one another, which is very necessary, for man's
natural tendency is the reverse. It may not be an accident that
the verb he uses, *hupotassō*, is a compound of the verb he has
used of the household of Stephanas addicting themselves to
lowly service. Not only should they submit to Stephanas, but
also to others who help and labour. There is no *us* in the
Greek. The expression is general. They should submit to all
helpful Christian souls (and so should we). On the word
laboureth ('labours to the point of weariness') Edwards has the
succinct comment, 'Many work, a few toil'.

17. Stephanas and two other Corinthians (Fortunatus and
Achaicus are otherwise quite unknown) had recently reached
Paul, and he lets us see some of his pleasure at the meeting.
He does not specify the meaning of *that which was lacking on
your part*, but we may conjecture that Paul was feeling the
absence of the Corinthians. 'My lack of you' is the sense of
it. He had missed his Corinthian friends, and this trio had
renewed his acquaintance with the city. In their persons they
had brought him 'a little bit of Corinth'. *Aneplērōsan, supplied*,
has the meaning 'filled up'. The three had left no lack.

18. They had *refreshed* Paul's spirit. The verb is that used
in Mt. xi. 28 of our Lord's giving rest to them 'that labour and
are heavy laden'. It may indicate that Paul had been restless
without news from Corinth. But the coming of the three had
been a real refreshment to his spirit. *And your's* is an interesting
addition. Not only was it good for Paul to receive news from
Corinth; it was good for the Corinthians to send the messages
to Paul that they had done through these three men. The

believers should *acknowledge* people like this, i.e. know them for what they are, and ascribe to them their true worth.

f. Final greetings (xvi. 19–24)

19. *Asia* is, of course, the Roman province of Asia. Roughly it is the western part of what we now call Asia Minor. Paul sends greetings from the churches of this region (*salute* = 'greet'). *Aquila and Priscilla* (the better MSS have the shorter form of this latter name, 'Prisca') were a devoted couple. Aquila was a Jew originally from Pontus (on the southern shores of the Black Sea), but he had evidently settled in Rome. When the Emperor Claudius expelled all Jews from Rome he and his wife Prisca went to Corinth, and then when Paul first came to that city he lodged and worked with them (Acts xviii. 1–3). They were evidently a couple who placed their home at the service of the Lord. Not only did they receive Paul, but we read of a church being in their house in Rom. xvi. 5 as well as here. They were courageous, for they risked their lives for Paul, though we know no details (Rom. xvi. 4). They were able, for they instructed no less a personage than Apollos in the correct understanding of the faith (Acts xviii. 26). An interesting point is that, of the six times when this couple is mentioned, Prisca's name comes first four times. Evidently she was an outstanding person in her own right. *Salute you much in the Lord* goes beyond a normal polite greeting, and indicates a warm Christian affection.

20. It is not clear who *all the brethren* are, but the description is comprehensive. The custom of kissing was rather more widespread in the ancient world than in the modern West. Paul suggests it as a proper mode of greeting for the Corinthians. Such a warm greeting would itself be a rebuke to all cliquishness. There are references to such a *holy kiss* in Rom. xvi. 16; 2 Cor. xiii. 12; 1 Thes. v. 26 (where see the note[1]), and to a 'kiss of love' in 1 Pet. v. 14. These early passages refer to a

[1] *Op. cit.*, p. 109.

greeting, and not to the liturgical 'kiss of peace' (a kiss exchanged during worship), though doubtless passages like the present one in due time led to the later practice.

21. It was Paul's custom to dictate his letters to an amanuensis, who wrote them down. But as the letter drew to its close the apostle would take the pen and write a few words himself. His handwriting was the mark of genuineness. In 2 Thes. iii. 17 (where see note[1]) he says that this is 'the token in every epistle: so I write', i.e. it is his usual custom to authenticate his letters in this way. Sometimes he draws attention to this (e.g. Col. iv. 18), and sometimes he does not. But as he says it was his custom, we must believe that he did it in the case of other letters also. In the note on 2 Thes. iii. 17 I have drawn attention to a letter cited by Deissmann (LAE, pp. 170ff.) in which the writing is in one hand and the final greeting and date in another, clearly that of the author, though there is no mention of his taking the pen. As this letter is dated A.D. 50 it affords contemporary evidence of Paul's practice.

22. Paul calls down a solemn curse on any who does not love the Lord. For *Anathema* see note on 'accursed' in xii. 3. The strong expression is indicative of the depth of Paul's feelings on the importance of a right attitude to the Lord. If a man's heart is not aflame with love for the Lord the root of the matter is not in him. He is a traitor to the cause of right. Paul cannot contemplate such a man calmly.

Maran-atha is an expression of great importance. It is not a Greek word, as is *Anathema*, but a transliteration from the Aramaic. Being Aramaic it cannot have originated among the Greeks, but must go back to the early days of the Church in Palestine. Moreover it must have expressed a sentiment that the early Church regarded as supremely important, else it would never have been taken over in this way by the Greek-speaking Christians. The first part is the word *Mar* which

[1]*Op. cit.*, pp. 151f.

means 'Lord'. The significance of the ascription of this title to Jesus in the early days of the Palestinian Church should not be overlooked. 'Our' is denoted in Aramaic by the addition of the suffix *an* or *ana*. The latter part of the expression is from the verb *'atha*, 'to come'. *Atha* might mean 'has come', in which case the reference would be to the incarnation (Chrysostom understood it this way). Or it could mean 'cometh', which might refer to the truth of Mt. xviii. 20, or might be meant as a future, 'Our Lord will come'. Probably the most likely of all is to understand the verb as imperative (possibly dividing the word differently, *Marana tha*), 'Our Lord, come'. This is a prayer like that in Rev. xxii. 20, 'Even so, come, Lord Jesus'. In this case it expresses the eager longing felt by the Church in those early days for the speedy return of the Lord. Others have suggested that the words might be interpreted to mean, 'the Lord art thou', or, 'Our Lord is a sign', but both seem improbable.

23. Paul moves on to a prayer for *grace* for his readers, which is his invariable conclusion to a letter. Sometimes he expands it, as in the well-known formula of 2 Cor. xiii. 14, while the shortest form is that in Col. iv. 18, 'Grace be with you'. But a prayer for grace is always there.

24. This is an especially tender note on which to close. Despite everything there is not the slightest doubt that Paul held the Corinthians in high esteem, and that he regarded them with tender affection. So he ends his letter by sending his love to them. Notice the *all*. He had some doughty opponents at Corinth. But he sends his love to them all. *Amēn* is absent from the best MSS, and should be omitted. It is the kind of scribal addition that naturally tends to creep into a text. Paul's last word to the Corinthians is *Jesus*.

The subscription is no part of the original letter. The oldest manuscripts have no such addition at all. Some of those that have it read 'from Ephesus', and some 'from Asia'. All are nothing better than early estimates of the probabilities. That which has crept into the text of AV seems to be based on a misunderstanding of xvi. 5. This was held to mean that Paul was actually at the time of writing passing through Macedonia. We have seen good reason for thinking that the letter was written from Ephesus. The names of the bearers of the letter are simply an inference from the mention of these people in the letter.